Go Together

Go Together

Adhyathma Ramayanam

Swamiji Sri Iraianban

GenNext Publication

Published, 2020

Published by

GenNext Publication
5, Ansari Road
Daryaganj, New Delhi-110002
Phone: 9811692060
E-mail: gennextpublication@hotmail.com

Printed at: G. Print Process, Delhi.

Cataloging in Publication Data—DK
Courtesy: D.K. Agencies (P) Ltd. <docinfo@dkagencies.com>

Puranas. Brahmandapurana. Adhyatmaramayana. English.
Go together : Adhyathma Ramayanam / edited by Mr. Swamiji Iraianban.
pages cm
Translated from Sanskrit.
ISBN 9789353241865 (PB)

1. Rama (Hindu deity) I. Iraianban, Swami, editor. II. Title.
LCC BL1140.4.B7342A34 2020 | DDC 294.5925 23

Contents

PART IV
KISHKINDHA KANDHAM

PART V
SUNDHARA KANDHAM

PART VI
YUTHA KANDHAM

PART - VII
UTHARA KANDHAM

Introducation

Yes! Go together…! For what? With whom? Why? To get her, i.e., Go to Get her. 'Her' means victory both mundanely and as well as spiritually, the sole motto of human life is nothing but to realize the inner self, that is Paramathma, which is shielded by the fleshy body and thus it underestimates itself as the body itself and it wastes its whole life in earning everything to attain mental contentment and lastly it comes to realize that nothing can be had full-fledged through the processes of all the passages of this life. So, Lord Rama Himself, incarnates as a human being and thus he leads a simple (Soulapya bava), orthodox life by which he exemplifies Himself as the life's motto, to be attained. He shows the pathways thoroughly to adhere to the principles and regulations to attain ecstasy. In Ramayana, (the pathway which was shown by (the Lord) Ram Himself feels everything and shows the depth of nothing in this world and He, as a son, shows His eminence and teaches us now to behave the livelihood of son and parent; He shows the inner eminence prophecy as a master with Gughan and Hanuman and thus He reveals the best relationship between both the planes of mundane life. As a warrior, he shows bravery and valour and How we should be ready to forgive anyone, if he surrenders wholeheartedly, and even Lord Ram was ready to give Ayodhya to Ravanan and thus the Golden sentence is in upto date life i.e., whoever rules, Rama or Ravana everybody is quite suitable to rule and give a balanced government. As a husband, he lived along with His wife Sita and children Lava and Kusa – without any narrow-mindedness and he shows his vast love, and delivered all of his duties to the entire satisfaction of all, even today also. Rama's life, whenever we go through it with a divine taste, giving so many experiences and we can taste the inner ambrosia of Rama nama's excellence. As a king, he ruled over the country very well and he established `Rama Rajya'. As a Guru, he preached `Rama Gita' through which he insists on the holiness of Dharma and ceremonies. As a brother, he mounts himself as everest in all of his six brothers (Lakshman, Bharathan, Sathrughna, Gugha, Sugrivan and Vibishana) through a faithful approach not only by word, only through Rama's deeds. Rama is everliving as a word, holy manthra and an Epic and that is why so many saints and Rishies, chanting this manthra, dhraga divine word attain the Eternal Bliss. This can be experienced through our own livelihood only; it can be written inwards but it is to be realized only by our self; this is the motto of our life; and that is why we are having this unequivalent and unfparallaled most enriched valuable life. Through Ramayana, we can know easily the synopsis, i.e. if a man lives with ahimsa and sathya, all human beings, Rakshasas, even birds and everything will assist and help us to attain success in our worthful succeeding without any failure., at all.

"Go together – Go to get her", it emphasises unity of all and through this book we expect the whole universe should be bound with universal love, as Lord Rama teaches over all.

Mr. Swamiji Iraianban

Preface

'Adhyathma Ramayana' is the soul stirring epic of the sublime human being, Raman, an incarnation of Lord Vishnu. While it is sheer human nature, which tends to deify men of heroic qualities, in this scriptural epic it is God enfleshed, God who humanizes as Raman. the hero, epitomizing a person who should elevate himself to a perfect state through his efforts, thus serving as a role model for mankind.

Our deep sense of spiritual values have been deluged by a new sense of misapprehended or misinterpreted secularism, rapidly weakening our hold on the basic truths of spiritualism and religion. This breathtaking new sense has inevitably led to the present tempo of materialistic modes of thought and life, which pose as a serious distortion to morals, philosophy, religion and God. Hence there is an urgent and great need for a reinterpretation and a redefinition of the role of religion and spirituality in human life.

At this stage it has become necessary to fall back on our great epic "The Adhyathma Ramayanam to delve deeper into the realms of spiritual knowledge for a mobilization of our spiritual resources and for an insurgence of spiritual values into the tenor of our life, to mould the thought and moral life of mankind, as the 'Adhyathma Ramayanam' is the fountain head of our spiritual heritage, with an elaboration of even the minutest details relating to several miniscule facets of life.

There happens to be scores of Ramayanam. Yet, the 'Adhyathama Ramayanam' is a lofty work presented in the form of an interlocution between God Shivan and Devi Parvathi in the Padma Puranam. It is taken for granted that the great Sage Yagnavalkya reproduced it in the form of Adhyathama Ramayanam. However, as the name indicates, the 'Adhyathama Ramayanam' is a hypostatic union of the 'Word made Flesh', a living embodiment of words presented out of divine will.

The original Sankrit text is classified into Seven Kandhams (Parts) with sixty-four chapters (Sargas) comprising four thousand and hundred slokas together with hundreds of Sruthis with analysis of the Tattvas. The

'Adhyathama Ramayanam' conveys the story in brief but touches all the themes, yet its contents are quite summarized and briefly dealt with. It too has the sixth kandham as the Yudha Kandham whereas Tulasidas has given the name Lanka Kandham.

The descriptions here are given in slightly different styles. The Bala Kandham commences with Sage Naradhar's invocation to Lord Brahman to suggest an easy way out for the atonement of one's sins. Brahman propagates that there is no greater spiritual exercise benefiting mankind than the reverential study of the 'Adhyathama Ramayanam', the most efficacious act of expiation, which is par excellence.

Then unfolds the interlocution between Devi Parvathi and God Shivan, the latter revealing to the former the hidden mysteries of Sri Raman's life history, which liberates human beings from the seemingly unbreakable link of bondage with transmigration in this secular world. Then ensue the episodes or Raman's birth, His departure to the forest, the annihilation of the demons, Raman's marriage to Sita and the encounter with Parasuraman. The episodes of the ensuing Kandhams unravel naturally and fluently.

The salient characteristic feature of the 'Adhyathama Ramayanam' is that every verse is drenched with philosophical and spiritual wisdom, throughout, right from the start with 'Ramahrdaya', meaning Sri Raman's heart, which is the most sacred of all scriptures, of the meeting of Naradhar with Raman in Ayodhya. The 'Adhyathama Ramayanam' does not digress from its profoundly sagacious path in delineating the scintillating forms of Sri Raman, unfolding the mysteries of his various manifestations, incarnations and the purpose behind them and projecting His innate trait of easy accessibility. It contains the core of the message of the Vedas, which are the primary scriptures, eulogized as the breath of the eternal, as seen, when Naradhar says that it is due to Sri Raman's desire that Brahman etc., are created by His illusion, that Maya sparkles impregnated with the three attributes (gunas) of Sathwic, Rajas and Thamas, talking of its very foundation on Him.

The Vedas describe the nature of the ultimate reality (Brahman). They are divided into two major sections, the Karma Kandham and the Jnana Kandham. In the contemporary world the 'Adhyathama Ramayanam' is celebrated, significantly, because of the explicit elucidation of Kriyayoga (Yoga of actions) in the chapter 'Sri Rama Githai', wherein Sri Raman instructs his younger brother Lakshman in the ways of Karma yoga while Karma yoga deals with rituals and sacrifices that are to be performed according to one's station in life, the latter comprises the Upanishads which is philosophical in nature. Hence the preoccupation here is totally with the goal of liberation from worldly bondage, which is the ultimate goal of human life.

Likewise Lord Raman illustrates Maya form (illusive form) which is Athma Buddhi that abides in the Anathma entities of the body. The concept of Athman and Brahman is intrinsically woven into the collective thought and life of the people of this land. Athman and Brahman are the same entity. So it is only one supreme Athma. Here Lord Sri Raman is the Supreme Athman, the real self, Vishnu, in human garb on earth, to vanquish the forces of evil and uphold the laws of Virtue. Despite facing severe jolts, Raman, a disciplinarian and leader, never failed to remain steadfast in the law of Righteousness. The Lord does not descend without his divine consort Sita, His divine energy, without whom he is bereft of the potential to act. This is evident when Sita unravels to Hanuman the hidden truth, saying that she abides in the Supreme Self Raman and is even jealously engrossed in her activities of Creation, Preservation and Annihilation conjointly with Him.

Besides the transcendental philosophy that the 'Adhyathama Ramayanam' is packed with, the charm lies in the divine characters who manifest every feature of human life such as duty, love, truthfulness, friendship, humility, compassion and integrity. It highlights the true relationship and bond between brothers.

Above all, the ideals projected have sublime appeal as the Adhyathama Ramayanam details with the upliftment of an individual. He, Raman, the replica of Dharma, remains the eternal ideal for mankind to aspire and grow to higher proportions and standard of perfection. For this the mere chanting of Raman's name, incessantly, and praising his glory with deep faith and an inner craving to reach the Supreme, the aspirant will stand to benefit. The Rama Manthra proves to be an ever new Channel of Turth that can free us from the chains of contemporary secular thinking. so when too. In short, the 'Adhyathama Ramayanam' is regarded as God and hence mere possession of this compendium will ward of evil forces.

Mr. Swamiji Iraianban

The Holy Intellectual Path of Lord Sri Rama

Part - I
Bala Kandam

Chapter - I

Rama Hrdaya

Chanting of and meditation on the holiest mantra 'Rama', on whom the scriptural epic 'Ramayanam' pivots, purifies the heart and mind, scorches all worldly sorrows and afflictions and sanctifies the soul dispensing the chanter with freedom from bondage, bestowing complete liberation.

The 'Ramayanam' is the real essence of spotless Raman and everything that is conceivable and inconceivable of Him. Salutations to this Lord whose attractive beautiful form is immaculate without any stain of sin. He is the sea of ravishing bliss, the universal consciousness, the only cognizer of His own self. Prostrate before the Lord of Sita, she is the sole cause of creation, sustenance and annihilation of the universal universe. Though, He is the mere immutable conscious reality and the supreme resort of that mysteriously deceptive Maya, He remains unchangeable and unimaginable in His true essence.

It is the time, when the heavenly beings filled with fear and horror approach the Lord of Janahar and most solemnly supplicate Him to redeem the world from the evil clutches of maleficent spirited beings. The conscious reality incarnates as a manifest human being with preternatural and unlimited potentialities called Maya. He accomplishes the tremendous feat of complete extermination of the entire devilish clan and returns to His own again – the Transcendental Everlasting Entity. And yet, His glorious name and eternal fame, vibrantly alive, echoes in all the three worlds.

It is mandatory that the spiritual scripture 'Ramayanam' which is in accordance with all Puranas, the epical histories of Gods, should be piously read by everyone to be purged of all sins and to ward off recurrent births, and begin to live and have their beings in Lord Hari Himself. The exalted beings who have set their heart on being rid of births on earth and be filled full of God's love, should devoutly read the Ramayanam daily, and even those who listen to it with religious fervor reap as much holiness as they would if they freely gifted hundreds of thousands of cows daily.

The 'Ramayanam' is a divine force that emanates from the lips of Lord Shiva, and flows like a sacrosanct river which merges into Raman, the perennial blissful Ocean, sanctifying the three worlds. The abode of the God of Gods, Lord Shiva, is atop the Himalayan mount Kailash. It is there in the interior of this gorgeous mansion that radiates as it does like a hundred suns, that Lord Shivan sits on a luminous throne in parley with his divine consort, Devi Parvathi, on his left, with gods and seers and sages dancing attendance on them. In course of their interlocution the Devi extols her three-eyed doughty and beatific beloved as the flood of sweet ambrosia, who dwells in the heart of every creature and is the silent spectator abiding in the nucleus of the soul of every being. She makes known to him her desire to know about the awe-inspiring incarnation of the Eternal Lord Raman. She most deferentially and most modestly solicits her Lord, who propitiates the sinners, who is the niche of the Universe, to acquaint her with the eternal truths about the infinite Lord Raman who is the only one, who permanently fills the whole universe.

This ostensible world is a turbulent sea which has to be crossed inorder to reach the Eternal shore and be free of births. Devotion and Renunciation are the compulsory qualities which are the means for crossing this chaotic path very successfully, but not very easily. Devi Parvathi postulates that there is no greater instrument other than devotion to eliminate egoism, leave this maya world and get lost in Him. Her mind is clogged with perplexing doubts; she pleads to Lord Shiva to dispel them and at the same time enlighten her with spiritual knowledge, both practical and theoretical, together with other aspects like true devotion, detachment and divine help that are necessary for all women, as well as others, to cross the illusive world.

Annihilation of ego and enrichment of mind with spiritual knowledge, lead the yogis and saints to experiment with truth and realize that Sri Raman is the Infinite Soul, the seed from whom evolves all creation and creatures. The natural flow of love and devotion from the heart to Raman, the Ideal being, makes them easily attain their highest goal. But witless people argue that Raman, the Supreme Brahman, Paramathmam in human form, is wrapped up in illusion and unlike an omniscient being, He has to learn the transcendental truths from His preceptor Vasisthar; He has to look up to him for enlightenment and spiritual knowledge. They also contend that He, like any ordinary human creature, bemoans His separation from Sita.

Parvathi Devi enquires of her Lord as to why Raman, the Manifest Being, if He were really ignorant should command eternal devotion, respect and love. She requests him to clear such doubts that are ingrained on her mind.

Her requisition is complied with by the Lord and at the very outset he commends her as a true devotee of the supreme conscious being, Sri Raman. There has been on one in heaven or on this earth so extensively curious to know the truth about Sri Raman. Lord Shiva is highly pleased with her avidity and dedication to know, and his opportunity to reveal these hidden truths about Sri Raman. Initially, he pays obeisance to the Greatest Soul, Raman of the Raghu race. Then, he proceeds to enunciate the authentic nature of Sri Raman's incarnation Lord Sri Raman is not a mediocre mortal; He is god in human form, who is immanently hidden in the nucleus of every soul. He is Brahman itself, and has created the Universe and all the worlds by His illusory quality. He is the self-created being who has no beginning or end. He is omnipresent and permanently fills both heaven and earth like ether. He is purer than the white snow; flowless, without any stain of sin. He is the immutable self-enlightened Supreme Soul. A fact that stands towering above all others is that the Universe, in toto, is captivated and drawn towards Raman in the same fashion as iron is attracted to magnet. Base individuals are beset with ignorance; they cherish false beliefs and hazy notions. Hence, they cannot cognize Raman to be as He is and what He is, but unfortunately drag him down to their plane of nescience and only know him as but a man of just flesh and blood and, therefore, attribute all mundane elations and ties and ordinary human traits to the Absolutely Spotless, Perfect Immortal Being. As a result, these ignorant people wallow indefinitely in the cycles of birth and death. Lord Raman is 'The Self' and at the same time, the self in all beings, creatures and everything, dwelling within the core of their heart. Just as people are oblivious of the presence of the necklace hanging around their own necks, so too, people who are tied down to the worldly pleasures, sense objects and congeneric ties, do not visualize or even sense the presence of him seated in their hearts.

Raman is God of all Gods. He is absolutely pure. He is knowledge itself and the source of all knowledge, both practical and theoretical, he is the science of all knowledge and is the only perennially abiding entity.

That the whole universe and its objects are created by God is a misconstrued assumption by an individual, but, in fact, they are the operations of 'Maya'. This is just like a man who, possessed with defective eyes and deranged mind, thinks the earth to be rotating because he is moving them around sharply due to his dizziness.

Light and darkness cannot exist simultaneously; in the same way knowledge cannot synchronize with ignorance. Darkness flees before the light of the mighty sun; so Raman the glorious light of all knowledge scorches away the darkness of ignorance. He holds the reins of illusive Maya, it has its abode in Him; but cannot victimize Him. therefore, in reality, Raman as the brilliant sun has no paradoxical traits of day or night, good or bad, ignorance and its antonym. He transcends them all.

Having said so much, Lord Shivan discloses the actual disquisition that takes place among Sri Raman, Sita and Hanuman, in which the unique, yet, secret path to salvation is divulged. The occasion is the grand coronation of Sri Raman on his return to Ayodhya, when after He has destroyed the heinous Ravanan and his tribe. Lord Sri Raman and His divine spouse Sri Sita Devi are seated on a Magnificent throne. The ceremony is attended by His kith and kin including Sugrivan, Vibhishanan, Lakshman, Vasisthar and Viswamithrar. At the request Raman, and for the advantages of the duty conscious Hanuman who has performed his mission to the letter, Devi Sita relates the real truth about Isvara, for in the eyes of Sri Raman, Hanuman is an eminent intellectual enthusiast worthy of liberation.

The divinely ascertained transcendental truth is delineated to Hanuman by Sita. Raman is existence, the source of all, and the First One who surpasses everything else. He is unparalleled, next to none in the Universe. He is the Almighty, the omnipotent Supreme Authority. He is Peace, Bliss, the All-pervading Force, formless, yet with form, unchangeable, imperceivable, yet perceivable, and immutable in all the worlds and its objects.

The inherent nature of Sita Devi is made clear at this juncture. Her main quality is Sakthi, who is the creator, the sustainer and the destroyer of the Universe. It is the nescient and ignoble people who presume that Raman alone is the director, actor and creator of the Universe which in truth is only her play of creation. She coexists with Raman, has her existence in Him and in unison with him, the Supreme Soul, Raman, She is ever sedulous in her activities.

Devi Sita makes it explicit that Raman is beyond the range of all knowledge and sight. He neither acts, nor moves, nor stands, nor walks, nor does he feel pleasure or pain, heat or cold, sorrow or joy. He is the Divine Effulgence which knows not any contraction; He is the elegant symbol of eternal bliss. None can know His greatness, none can measure His length and breath; he is limitless, all-pervading and is beyond and above nature. His beginnings are unknown, but is the only reality, the Supreme Soul.

All these events-the birth of Sri Raman into the sacred Raghu race in Ayodhya, His assisting Vishwamithrar in performing his yagnas without hindrance by killing Tadaka, exterminating Subahu, Mareeson and other iniquitous demons, absolving Ahilya of the consequence of her past sin, Raman's Marriage to Sita, then, humiliation of egoistic Parasuraman, His residing at Ayodhya with Sita Devi for twelve years, His abdication of the throne, His venturing to and sojourn at the forest Dandakaranya, the slaying of Viradhan and Mareeson, the episode of the deer in disguise, Sabri's worship of Lord Raman and the friendly acquaintance of Sugrivan, then, Jatayu and Kabandha's attainment of absolution, the infliction of the death punishment upon Vali, the vigorous quest for Sita, the construction of the bridge over the sea, entering and surrounding the city of Lanka, Rama's valiant feat of vanquishing and killing Ravanan and his sons and the subsequent enthronement of Vibhishnan, finally, Raman's return to Ayodhya with Sita by the Pusphak Plane-that occur from His birth right up to the present day are the actions ascribed to be performed by Raman alone. Raman is immutable, the One and the All. As it is, Sita merges in Raman but remains as a separate entity. Yet, all the same she is closely united with Raman. She is Sakthi the Kinetic and He is the potential aspect of God.

Now Raman Himself elucidates to Hanuman the secret of the Supreme philosophy-the difference between the Supreme Brahmam, the Soul and the Spirit, the Paramthman, Athman and Anathman respectively. Brahman, the first cause, is omnipresent, pervading the whole universe like the infinite sky. The soul is but the actual essence of Paramathman, the Luminant irradiation of the intellect of an individual, quite similar to the fashion of the boundless sky being limited to the surface of the pond. Anathman or spirit, that is Jiva, is the simulacrum of Brahman or Paramathman, the Supreme Soul, reflecting upon the intellect which is the creation of nature, much in the same way similar to the reflecting of the sky upon the pond. These three entities though real in existence are inseparably united in Shri Raman who is the Paramathman, the Absolute Reality.

The Athman or Soul is all pervading, eternal and a conscious agent capable of enjoyment. The confinement and limitation of the soul of the body and the sense organs makes the Jiva forgetful of his natural glory and power. The soul becomes fettered and bound to the world by the invisible thread of ignorance. The Jiva or Anathman, the spirit of an individual only is the creation of nature and ignorance. This fettered individual soul, Jiva or Anathman, is the doer. He thinks himself as a distinct entity; due to superfluous egoism he feels pleasure and pain, suffers because he mistakes himself to be finite, limited in thought, will and action Strongly overshadowed by ignorance, the Jiva, thinks that the doer is the Soul (Athma) which, infact, does nothing but illumines the Jiva and stands as only a silent witness and is perpetually fixed and inert. Hence all the reflections which are the origins of individual spirits of Jiva (Anathma) are the aftermath of ignorance and as such they are evidences of ignorance.

Here, Raman categorically declares that the Jiva, the creations of ignorance or the reflection of the Soul (Athma) imprinted on the intellect is not false, but he is reality, the same as Paramthman or Brahman because his soul is an inseparable entity of the same Paramathman or Brahman. It is erroneous on the part of the Jiva to think that he is a separate individual different from God. The Jiva's ignorance, separateness of individuality or egoism will be naturally effaced and the manacles of worldliness sundered at the very moment he realises that he is the same reality, 'Tattwam Asi', It is to be understood that he is the sum and substance of all transcendental knowledge and spiritual philosophy, as He is God.

It should be borne in mind that superior knowledge or liberation cannot be ferreted out of religious scriptures or philosophical books. Unalloyed love and single-minded devotion and faith in Lord Raman alone can bring about salvation. Those who do not love the Lord and are indifferent to Him indulge in all manner of actions acquiring merits and demerits entangling themselves into a maze of unending cycles of births and death and falling into the pits of diversity of knowledge, although they may learn and read in many births to follow.

Undoubtedly because it is the divine assurance of Lord Raman Himself, it is only by self-realization the heinous sins committed and accumulated in many births, such as murder of saints and sages, be totally uprooted and destroyed.

The Lord, in addition, proclaims that the most virulent and sinful person, though possessed of spiritual knowledge, but has been constantly addicted to pernicious crimes of coveting another man's wife and stealing another's wealth and property or guilty of patricide, matricide or killing of Brahmins, shall be warranted the very highest and holiest abode, revered and envied by all the Gods, which is rare even to the highly enlightened ascetics, if, only he reads the Holy Rama Hrdaya with profound devotion, unalloyed love and one-pointed worship.

These lofty, yet confidential spiritual truths are disclosed by the Supreme Lord Raman to his most beloved and celebrated devotee Hanuman. In the same breath, Hanuman has been cautioned against revealing these transcendental facts to those wretched persons who are devoid of love and faith in the most exalted soul, Sri Raman, though they may be as great as Indhran, the king of Gods. Thus, Lord Shivan concludes the most significant philosophical concept which the Supreme Consciousness, Lord Sri Raman had personally interpreted to Hanuman. For certain, this pansophy is the heart of Raman and is therefore called Rama Hrdaya, meaning Raman's heart, the very heartbeat of all creatures, which is the holiest of all holy scriptures.

Accordingly, in the distant face of time, in this context, the divine saga Naradhar is perplexed by the anomalies in the worldly affairs. Nurturing some sobering reflections of redeeming the world which is sinking into the quicksand of immorality and sin, he approaches Lord Brahman, the Creator. He spells out his anxiety and concern for the people in Kaliyuga, who have turned the world topsy-turvy by their sinful ways. They are vulnerable and easily susceptible to, and have a penchant for perpetrating vicious acts. In order to fend for themselves a hand-to-mouth existence, they barter and sell even the Vedas. The sage goes on to enumerate the ignoble sins they commit. It has become their way of life to disrespect and disregard their elders, deceive and disobey their parents and in-laws and remark on their intolerance and distrust in religions which are some of the innumerable deeds they soon fall a prey to. Over laden with great distress for the lot of the people of Kaliyuga, he pleads with Brahman for a way out to make the people atone for their sins and bounce back to the path of virtue.

Lord Brahman very assuredly states that the easiest, the most accessible and the most enduring course for the reparation of their sins is to read the "Adhyathma Ramayanam" and imbibe the great teachings found therein.

All these trails and tribulations lurking in the world of Kaliyuga are bound to persist so long as the "Adhyathma Ramayanam" does not come under the purview of the people, and so long as they do not go in quest of it inorder to make amends and turn-over a new leaf. It is a moral obligation that a person should, even in a small way, have recourse to the "Ramayanam", as it annunciates the absolution of all sins, however grave they may be. The stubborn fact that is very perspicuous is, the soul of the reader is made holy even if half a slogha of each verse of the 'Ramayanam' is recited with the odour to sanctity. Doubtlessly, to go a step further, multifold benefits accrue when a devotee accepts and acts according to the great doctrines enshrined in the Ramayanam; he inherits the priceless gift of piety and peace which can hardly be obtained even after his interminable, long-winding, laborious penances he undertakes, which includes the holy yagnas he performs. Positively, one can reap a harvest of desired boons the heart has been hankering after, when he sits in the presence of the deity Hanuman and recites the 'Rama Hrdaya' in the quietude of his heart.

The study of the paeans of Sri Raman and the eloquent outcome of this study is indescribable. It is beyond the ken of even Brahman to know it in full; but he can comprehend only half of what the Goddess Parvathi knows and she, on the other hand, has gleaned only half of what Shivan discerns, for Shivan is the only Lord and master who is able to cognize it totally.

When Parasuraman heard the story of Raman being narrated by Parvathi Devi, he instantaneously procured the gift of the Supreme divine culture 'Narayana Kala'. So it is an empirical declaration that there is no sin that cannot be washed away by the reading of the apologue of Lord Sri Raman.

Eventually, in other words, the 'Adhyathma Ramayanam' itself is a hypostatic union of the 'Word Made Flesh', nay, vice versa, spirit becoming word – God incarnate in speech. Though Goddess Lakshmi abides in the inner most recesses of Lord Vishnu's bosom, yet, she regards with envious eyes the 'Tulsi' flower offered at the altar of His holy feet, as if it were his wife. The Lord Himself in all, suffuses the whole world with love beyond measure and His love for His devotees and aspirants whose lives are dedicated to mindful practices and right effort, is greater than his love for his consort Devi Lakshmi, because His single minded devotees and aspirants possess a higher nature and are unselfish and truthful, wanting nothing more in this world than only offering their unflinching devotion to His lotus feet, ceaselessly.

So Lord Brahman follows suit and craves for the affection of Lord Vishnu only because it is the per-se the panacea for all the ills and desires of this mundane world.

Lord Vishnu discerns that the visit of Brahman has got a purpose to serve and so asks him outright what He could do for him.

Brahman narrates that Ravanan, the son of Vishravan, who is at present the king of demons is tormenting the righteous and the innocent people.

Because of his obliquity he has obtained boons from Lord Brahman and has, by and large, turned out to be heinous, cruel and self-conceited. He has let blossom a myth that he is invincible. He reigns over the people with an iron heel and tyrannizes all the creatures of the three worlds Heaven, Earth and Netherland. He is an abominable threat to the whole creation of Brahman.

Therefore, Brahman's obsecration to Lord Vishnu is to kill Ravanan by incarnating himself in the form of a man, for he, Brahman, has sealed his doom at the hands of an all powerful man.

Lord Vishnu readily complies with the request as he has, at sometime, been pleased by the austere penances of sage kashyap to whom he had granted a boon; He, Vishnu promised him to be born as his son at his request. The sage is now born as Dasarathar and is the king of Ayodhya, and he, therefore shall incarnate himself into four forms. Lord Vishnu chooses to be the son of Kausalya and the others the sons from other Queens. His divine consort and yoga Maya Lakshmi Devi shall appear in the form of Janahari and shall live in the house of king Janahar. Rest assured, Lord Vishnu is to accomplish his mission by taking her with Him.

Chapter - II

Lord Brahman's invocation to Sri Vishnu

Lord Shiva's brief narration of the reasons behind Sri Raman's incarnation has dissipated Devi Parvathi's doubts, fears and ignorance. She pays her eternal respects and gratitude for having inspired her. Though virtually impressed, her mind is still not set to rest for she relapses into avidity, and implores her Lord of the Universe, Shivan, to tell her more about Raman's nectar-like, soul-stirring story very comprehensively.

And rightly enough, Lord Shivan unveils to her the hidden and impenetrable mysteries of the holiest life of Lord Sri Raman, which, he, Sri Raman, was very gracious to reveal to him in the fullness of time. Again, he reassuringly expounds the fact that any individual who listens to the life history of Sri Raman will be positively saved from the three fold miseries (egoistic, divine and natural) of human life. The earth has fallen on evil days and she is in mortal danger. She morphs into a cow. This metamorphosis takes place for the sole reason that she is extremely afflicted and overburdened by the incompassionate persecution and mordacities of Ravanan and his innumerable forces of savage demons. So in the guise of a cow and accompanied by her tutelage of Gods and saints, she converges upon the abode of Brahman the creator, who, by his acumen can divine the ways to redress her woes. Brahman, then with his retinue of the cow, the Gods and the saints wends his way to the seashore to have access to the Omnipotent, Omniscient and Omnipresent God, Lord Vishnu, who is evergreen and Juvenile. He puts forth their desire for an audience with him.

Being corroborated philosophically, and mythologically, Brahman's prayer is very noteworthy and solemn. And Lord Vishnu out of His inherent benignity to conciliate them, emerges from the eastern side of the ocean. This spectacle is so wonderful that the brightness of the sun which rises from the east is put in the shade the by the glittering splendor of Lord

Vishnu, who surpasses the radiance of a thousands suns, for, He it is who illumines the sun itself; and when He motions out of the eastern horizon of the Ocean, He irradiates every nook and corner completely dispelling every trace of obscurity, so much so, that even Brahman is momentarily dazzled at Lord Vishnu's radiant form, who, infact, can never be seen by the ubiquitous and worldly people.

The intrinsic beauty, nature, and appearance of Lord Vishnu beggars description. Yet, His appearance is so arresting! His countenance dulcifies and coruscates like blue gems. His smiles are enchanting and extraordinarily delectable and His benign eyes are as lovely as lotuses. Bedecked with the brilliant crown, ear-rings, divine necklaces, jewels precious gems like 'Shri Batsa' and 'Kausturbha' He looks glorious. Saints like Sanaka ete., and the celestial retinues attend on Him singing prayers. Adorned with his garland, conch, chakra, mace and lotuses in each of His lovely hands, His ethereal beauty is all the more pronounced. He is dighted with the sacred gold thread around His neck, is mounted on Garudha, is clad in yellow satin and is accompanied by His divine consort Lakshmi Devi and the Goddess of Earth.

Lord Brahman is exceedingly happy and charmed at having set eyes on such a venerable personality. He invokes Him most fervently and very deferentially bows to his lotus feet. He highlights the greatness of Lord Vishnu's pair of holy feet as one which disciples, throughout their whole life time, constantly seek and worship with their intellect and senses inorder to attain liberation. Lord Brahman lauds Him as the creator of the universe merely by His threefold powers of Maya. He clearly articulates that Lord Vishnu is the source of all things; his attachment to the creations is superficial and in reality it is non existent, as He is the one who sunders all the three fundamental ties of attachments, and is self-enlightened and self-blissful and self-existent. An individual whose sensitivity is benumbed, whose mind is unclean and unholy cannot conceptualize him; nor can he establish piety by learning and sacrifices or by his enunciations. But it is only those who step out of their narrow individuality and love His holy name shall they be able to envision Him.

Lord Vishnu's holy feet are the center of attraction for all saints and aspirants, for they are the main objects of constant contemplation. As it is, Lord Brahman's mind is wholly sanctified to the inner core, at they very sight of His holy lotus feet. Many a time, even in the past, Brahman and the Gods seek the Holy one's feet and claim sanctuary there only to feather their nest, whereas, saints, sages and devotees love the Lord solely for enlightenment with divine knowledge and salvation.

So promising, he makes his disappearance from the scene and Lord Brahman assures the Gods of Lord Vishnu incarnating Himself in the dynasty of King Raghu, during the same time all the Gods are to descend on the earth to play their part as monkeys and their race to help Lord Vishnu. With his heart at ease, Brahman retreats to his abode. He assures the Earth who is happy in the form of a cow of peace that is soon to return and apprises and instructs the Lords. The gods thenceforth, are to take birth in the form of monkeys at different places for the assigned task. Armed with patience they wait to meet their enfleshed Lord and prepare themselves to fight even by means of hillocks and trees. So the stage for the concurrence of the divine regiment of monkeys and the divine play to be enacted is all set.

Chapter - III

Nativity of Raman and His Brothers

Dasarathar the crowned head of Ayodhya is an inspiring example of truthfulness, integrity, bravery and might. The renown of such a man of distinction has spread to even far-flung countries the world over. Yet, this potential king is in the doldrums. The lugubrious king, time and again, relapses into distress and delusion over the one irreconcilable, cardinal issue that he is heirless. It is difficult for him to quaff the bitter cup of being issueless as he experiences mind-smattering agony day in and day out. He has become vulnerable; yearning makes him cudgel his brain as to what could be done. Rightly enough, he opts to seek out his preceptor Vashisthar who is a power of strength to him, and be enlightened on this matter, to beget sons endowed with all virtuous qualities.

Vashisthar, the friend at court, readily assures Dasarthar of the explicit outcomes if he performs the ritual sacrifice (Yagna) particularly stamped to begetting offsprings. He further avows that he shall have four illustrious sons as puissant as the savior of the three worlds, if, he brings Rishi Shringa, the husband of Shantha, the greatest yogi, to speedily perform the ceremony in his own presence. Of all benefits one can acquire, begetting good children with all virtues is the greatest one.

As instructed, Dasarthar with inveterate faith and great enthusiasm gets ready the ritual sacrifice under the aegis of holy preceptors and pious sages.

When the oblation is ready and the sacrificial fire is ablaze, an extra-ordinary being, the god of fire, of matchless splendour appears in all glamour, shining like heated gold, from within the fire with a gold bowl replete with celestial food-milk mixed food prepared by the gods and offers it to king Dasarthar, promising that his visit heralds the descent of the supreme Lord Vishnu into the world. The god of fire disappears as he hands over the divine food to the king. With a heightened sense of joy and great satisfaction the king pays his salutations to his preceptor Vasisthar and sage Rishi Shringa, and with their consent makes both the queens, Kausalya and Kaikeyi, to partake of the divine food, and eventually, completes the yajna paying due obeisance to the sages.

Queen Sumitra too is offered a share of the celestial food by her two sisters, Queen Kausalya and Queen Kaikeyi. Now, there is nothing to fracture their happiness and hopes and their sanguine dignity sprouts up. Thus all the three Queens conceive after partaking the food and the palace awakens to a mood of joyful celebrations.

In due time, when the star is on the ascendant, on the ninth lunar day, when five favourable stars and planets are in the month of March, (Chithirai) at its zenith and the sun stands in the zodiac sign of Aeries (Mesha rasi) the Lord and Savior Vishnu is born of queen kausalya. On this auspicious day, at this glorious occasion, the heavens open up and the gods rain flowers on the Paramathman, the universal soul, who has incarnated as flesh. The palace is supercharged with powerful emotional contentment-a great desire to be fraught with children has materialized and the queens' gait and carriage are so graceful that they go about glowing like goddesses.

Even great sages who have achieved absolute mastery over the senses by rigorous penance are fascinated by the beauty of Lord Vishnu's form and features. Dressed in gold yellow satins, his super eminent form is as blue as lotus. He has four arms and in each He is holding a divine chakra, a mace, a disc and a lotus respectively.

The loveliness of His lotus-like eyes captivates, so much so, that the pupil of His eyes glitter and sparkle like red petals of the lotus, expressing affection and grace. His ears are studded with glittering ear-rings. His visage is more brilliant than a thousand suns and He sports a gorgeous crown with curly locks of hair flowing down His fore-head. His tranquility and beauty of the moon are featured in His smiles which exude joy and blessings from His ever-blissful and moon-like heart. Divine ornaments like shreebasta, keyur, katak, kaustuva adorning His handsome body, enhance and accentuate the rich beauty of the ornaments. Queen Kausalya's eyes are drenched in tears of joy at the sight of Lord Vishnu. Flabbergasted at his glorious vision, she luxuriates in soulful gladness and begins to humbly pray to Him.

She hails him as the Lord holding conch, mace, disc and lotus in each hand and pays her respectful and sanctified homage to him, the God of gods. Lord Vishnu is the Absolute Being, perpetual and omnipresent. He is infinite, imperceivable and even the realm of imagination cannot express

His state of being. He is inexpressible, above the mental senses. There is none like him because of the unquestioned and undoubted superiority of the Lord, He knows all in an everlasting present. The volitional individuality of the Supreme Being is self-determined and self-regulated. He is a plenum of infinite excellences. He has also created the three violent and indolent 'gunas' which are saintly, materialistic and predatory and yet, He is indifferent from and untouched by them and lives always in the Turiya state-the state of highest consciousness which is truth, reality and bliss, that it does not divide itself into walking, dreaming and sleeping.

He is the whole self, integral and therefore complete in reality. He is the uncaused cause of all and uncreated creator of all. He is the absolute self who creates the entire Universe, who animates, actuates and moves the entire cosmos and all it stands for created and uncreated.

The Vedas declare that He is the cause of the projection, the continuance and the dissolution of the Universe. He is pure, holy and free, who takes everyone's qualities and characteristics into his self and yet shines as the Lord of All creatures, and to say more, He is not the doer; he appears to be doing everything. Both motor and sensory functions do not have their sway over him. He blossoms out as the lives and yet parts from them and stands out as the distinct one dwelling in the minds of all individuals. But his Maya, which generates ignorance, creating the illusions of birth body, mind, senses of active action etc., is a great bouldering obstacle to know Him.

None can judge Him correctly. On the other hand, he springs up and swells with great rank and authority within the hearts of saints, wisemen and holy persons, who with their five good senses brought under control are concentrated on Him alone. This is the pure reason why they envision him dwelling in their hearts.

A special touch of the divine inspiration makes noble lady; Kausalya to wonder how she has been bearing the Lord, in flesh and blood, in her womb, who in turn has innumerable universes contained in the form of atoms in His own stomach. Thus the Lord, Sri Vishnu, obligates himself of favouring His devotees and aspirants who are intoxicated with dedication to him alone and becomes an example par excellence of abiding by his word.

The regal lady ponders on a central issue which is self-assessment. She bewails to the Lord that she has been all along bewitched by illusion and has been boisterously loitering in the regal fantasies of worldliness, progeny, material comforts and prosperity, which have so thwarted her thought and mind from gravitation towards him who is the supreme wealth. And eventually, the hardest part is that, this has set in train a kaleidoscopic pattern of uneventful happenings like being absorbed in the so-called love ties of husband, parents and kith and kin and the like. Realization of her waywardness now makes her surrender to the anklet feet of Sri Vishnu. She pleads to him to make her ignorance, which overcomes her, be scorched forever and adds that his august form be engraved in her heart.

The holy lady coaxes the Almighty to transform himself into a lovely babe so that she may shower all her affection to the fullest satisfaction of her heart, bathing him with embraces, kisses and endearing baby talk. She hopes that this will enable her to cross the turbulent sea of bulging egoism.

The Universal Soul, Lord Vishnu, complies with the plea of Queen Kausalya. At first, he acquaints her of Brahman's request to him to descend to the earth in human form for uprooting evil, sin and impiety. At this point, he also unfolds the hidden mystery of his nativity into this world. It is because He is highly pleased with her qualitative and quantitative penances that she had subjected herself to in her previous births. King Dasarathar's and lady Kausalya's robust faith and earnest prayer to him to be born as their son, had formed the bedrock of their lives. And in the plenitude of power his greatest boon granted to them has come to pass and now, she has the fortunate privilege of envisaging the Lord in Vishnu form, which is the result of holy deeds performed in former births. The flowing of soul and the feasting of reason that she is now experiencing with him face to face, have obtained salvation for her, that which is ever unobtainable by the accursed and unholy.

At this moment, Sri Vishnu stipulates that whoever reads or listens to this verbal intercourse shall obtain His form and be saturated with him, be endowed with the boon that even at the moment of death their heart, mind and tongue shall never refrain from repeating his holy name.

Now this Lord cradled as an infant, his form so lusciously beautiful and dainty, His appearance unparalleled, beings to cry as do babes. His hue is that of the sapphire 'Indrakama' and his eyes shaped like the lotus flower has blossomed out of light which is pure. King Dasarathar's joy knows no bounds when he hears of the birth of his son. Thus, by His birth He has delighted also all the sentinels of heaven and earth. Soon after, Queen Kaikeyi is delivered of a child and Queen Sumithra gives birth to twins. These new born cherubs are as lustrous as the full moon.

King Dasarathar calls upon his preceptor Vashishtar to administer and consecrate the baptismal ceremony. The largesse of the king, who enjoys the luxury of doing charity, finds expression now as he distributes varieties of precious gems, ornaments, robes, dresses, huge quantitites of gold and favourably disposed cows and at the same time bestows thousands of villages on the Brahmans, authors of the ceremony.

Vashishthar christens the son of Kausalya as Raman who is the niche and inspiration to all the professed saints and sages, making them delve deeper into the realms of spiritual knowledge inorder to extirpate their ignorance totally. Bharathan, which means the sustainer of all beings is the name given to Kaikeyi's son. Then he proposes names to Sumithra's duo-Lakshman and Sathrughnan, the former meaning one who is the epitome of all virtues and the latter indicating the destroyer of enemies.

The divine-portion given by Kausalya and Kaikeyi to Sumithra makes way for fraterrity, joy, cheer, unity, affection and warmth run like invisible threads among the siblings, and Lakshman naturally aligns himself with Raman and Sathrughnan with Bharathan. It is a period of jubilation in the royal palace to see the little lads frisking about like lambs, playing childish pranks and making merry. Yet, their composure, conduct, bearing and comportment are all conspicuous, well defined and at its best. This is clearly visible by their obedience and respect to parents, Gurus, elders and others.

In particular, Raman stands distinguished as He is the cynosure of all eyes. He drowns His parents, king Dasarathar and Queen Kausalya in the ocean of pleasure and happiness by His frivolities and his pack of childish stuff and nonsense. None but Himself can be His own parallel. His warmth, bustle, brilliance and animation shed luster on His personality. Attired in silks and yellow satins so profusely pranked with pipal leaf shaped gold arnaments, decorated with rare varieties of pearls and gems upon His forehead and with necklaces of gems around His graceful neck, studded with ear-rings of gold like the fruit of Arjuna tree and with gold anklets on His feet and armlet on arms, He looks a picture of wonder taken out from the world of fantasy. He looks as lustrous and blue as sapphire. His frolicking and running after the calves is a feast for their eyes.

Raman engages Himself in a wide spectrum of innocent fun and frolic and childhood triviality. He quibbles and twaddles sending everyone into roars of laughter. When inviting Him to partake food, He would frisk away to play. At times He is fed a morsel and then instantly He would romp about. The royalty would get into a mood of endearment trying to feed Him mouthfuls of food, and He protesting and she cajoling Him, they keep trying to run after Him inorder to feed Him, but He would elude their grasp as his exuberance and buoyancy cannot match their desire to scoop Him up in their arms. Running behind Him, time and again, proves to be a tiresome task. Queen Kausalya has a bent in duly celebrating his birth anniversaries with great pomp and show, preparing niceties and dainties and distributing them to Brahmins and children. Ceremonies in honour of the child is performed regularly, dressing Raman very fashionably and richly and distributing sweet meats to everyone on such occasions.

Raman's puerile tricks, gambols, escapades and naughtiness have no end; on account of His frivolities His mother has to punctuate her household activities and duties. At times, in a fit of anger, when food is not served when He wants it He goes about breaking earthen utensils and pots, throws away butter that is garnered, takes milk, curds and other sweet meats eats them and also distributes to His siblings and friends. On hearing complaints from the cooks, lady Kausalya tries to scold the kids, but Raman, the head of His peer group just guffaws, mimes and the rest follow suit, capering away from the place after their stint is over. She slips and falls at every step, trying to run after Raman to get hold of Him but, has no heart to chide Him and when He whines, whimpers or cries in a childlike fashion, she takes Him on to her lap caresses, cajoles and kisses Him and showers great affection on Him and other sons too.

Nothing is more beauteous and more entertaining for the royal couple than savouring and basking in the childish sports of Raman. Though He is God incarnate, the Supreme Savior and bestower of happiness and prosperity, He now pleases His parents by His play of being born as their son, unfolding and exposing a fact of childhood traits of parents, fun and frivolity, His multi sided personalities, so that they may in this birth satiate their long desire for begetting children and thereby fondling, caressing, fostering and osculating them. Because, when accessing all the benefits of prosperity and success one can achieve, begetting such good, worthy children stands out as the greatest wealth of all. The investiture ceremony and the adornment of the sacred thread are performed by the preceptor Vasishthar as the boys grow older.

In this global theatre, these celestials who are masters of the universe, taking the form of human beings, go about performing their worldly routine affairs as would ordinary beings such as mastering the Vedas and religious scriptures and at a very early age, zealously acquiring skills in the most skillful tactics like archery and military and shaping themselves as erudite scholars in the arts and literature.

Lakshman is naturally drawn to Raman accompanying Him everywhere, even to the forests to hunt on horseback fully equipped with bow and arrows.

Raman gains distinction and prominence in the courses of His hunting spree, killing tigers and lions that stand testimony to the skills he has acquired, of which his father is highly proud.

Raman, an early bird, finishing all His morning chores and ablutions, first prostrates before His parents, as respect to parents is an unwritten code of conduct, and then humbly attends to His civil duties. He holds the centre stage, as there is a sweet display of his routine, yet rare activities. He dines with his brothers, and occasionally holds discussions with courtiers and officers. He deliberates on religious scriptures by sages to take decisions on important issues and takes animated part in discussions too.

One is inclined to argue that Raman, the Supreme Lord, has deigned to do even such household activities and perform such mundane chores as any ordinary creature. Though, if it be contemplated deeply, it can be concluded that He, in fact, does nothing as an agent in the three worlds, and is inactive, immanent and always unchangeable in himself and no one can equate him but Himself.

Chapter - IV

Vishwamithrar's Arrival in Ayodhya

The divine sage Vishwamithrar, supercharged with the fire of wisdom, and percipient that Sri Raman has condescended to be on earth with His Maya, hastens to visit Ayodhya to behold him in human form. King Dasarathar, in company with Vasisthar, greets him paying obeisance and pronouncing that he is much appreciative of and, at the same time, honoured by his visit which has in its train brought prosperity to his land, assures him to do the needful for him.

The sage is querulous. He reprobates the evil designs of Mareeson and Subahu, who with their followers thwart and fracture the yajna ceremonies that he performs to propitiate The Gods, his ancestors and departed souls as well. He beseeches the king, in consultation with his preceptor to empower Sri Raman and Lakshman to go with him and extirpate the demons outright.

In a tete-a-tete with sage Vashisthar, the emperor, Dasarathar, spells out his apprehensions about sending his godlike sons whom he has obtained as a boon in his declining years after going through such onerous tasks as performing penances, yajnas, sacrifices etc; he is desperate for a way out to retain Raman, his highly prized possession. Whom he holds dearest to his heart amongst all his other sons and without whom he cannot life.

The thin thread of restraint on the part of the king is snapped by his preceptor Vashisthar, who unravels the secret of Raman being God incarnate and not just an ordinary being of flesh and blood. He imparts the mystery of Lord Raman's birth saying, once, the denizens of heaven and the creator Brahman had importuned Lord Vishnu to assume human form and redeem the earth from the evil influence and sinful deeds of fiendish spirits. And, therefore, Raman has been born in his home,. He continues to inform the king that, in his former birth he was born as Kasyapa, Prajapathi's son and Kausalya was God's mother, Aditi. His long-drawn-out penances and sacrifices have gratified Lord Vishnu and He willed Himself to be born as his son, a blessing as desired by him. Consequently, Raman is Lord Vishnu, Lakshman is 'Sesh Nag' the serpent God, Bharathan the incarnation of his mighty weapon the 'disc' and Sathrugunan is his divine conch. Infusion of celestial knowledge, the most hidden truths never to be disclosed, on the part of Sage Vishwamithrar continues and the emperor learns that Goddess Lakshmi has incarnated Herself as Sita in the house of King Janahar and that he, the sage, has come to take Raman to conjoin Him, in marriage to Sita. He is therefore instructed to send Raman and Lakshman with the pansophist Vishwamithrar with great respect, pleasure and fanfare. The Royalty's fears are neutralized as he comprehends the extraordinary truths.

Elated at this divine dispensation his highness basks in the sunshine of felicity and joy. Thinking that the turn of events is providential, he toes the line and immediately summons Raman and Lakshman. He hugs them both to his heart, embraces them and anoints their head with blessings and sweet kisses; he entrusts them with the illustrious Vishwamithrar, whose principal duty it is to see that Sri Vishnu and Sri Lakshmi, in their manifest forms, are united as Sri Raman and Sri Sita without delay.

Happily the lads with their weapons fully equipped, along with their teacher Vishwamithrar make their journey towards his hermitage. Midway as they travel, the stalwart sage bestows upon them divine knowledge called 'Bala' and 'Attibala' by which hunger thirst and exhaustion can be subjugated.

They traverse the river Ganges and peregrinate deep into the forests where Tadaka the demoness lives. The sage briefs them about Tadaka's invidious nature and her witchery to assume any form at her own will and fancy. Nevertheless, he requests intrepid Raman to kill her instantly to which Raman most obediently strings His bow and shoots his arrow.

When Raman fires the arrow a thunderous din is produced which reverberates throughout the forest. This sound unbearable to the demoness, makes her to dash out helter-skelter in indescribable appearance to kill the author of this pandemonium Soon Valiant Raman's sharp shaft pierces her heart shuffling off her mortal coil.

Instantaneously she is transmuted into a beautiful, well attired, bejeweled girl. This is so because Lord Sri Raman has absolved her of her past sins and has emancipated her from demon form assumed as the consequence of an imprecation long ago. Immediately she falls on her knees and deferentially worships the Holy Feet of Lord Raman. By His orders, in His bountiful mercy, she is welcomed into heaven.

The sage's appreciation and acknowledgment of Raman's glorious deeds take the form of a number of bows and divine arrows and other arms, supercharged by divine mantras, being presented to Him as a gesture of his blessings. And yet again, he anoints His head and tenderly embraces Raman, the eternally poised perennial spirit.

Chapter - V

Raman's Sojourn at Sage Gauthama's Hermitage

The Lord of Sages, Vishwamithrar, together with Raman and Lakshman, temporarily suspends his journey to sojourn for the night at the kama-Ashramam where a congregation of sages and aspirants live together.

Eventually, the trio reach their destination and arrive at the 'Siddha-Ashram' to a rousing welcome and adoration by the sages and innumerable disciples inhabiting the hermitage under the punctilious care and leadership of sage Vishwamithrar.

Raman appeals to His master Sage Vishwamithrar to conduct the proposed ritual ceremony as scheduled so to enable Him to see the demons who hamper, fulminate and disturb the solemnization.

Once the platform is set for the ceremony to be performed by Vishwamithrar with the help of other sages, the diabolical demons, Mareeson and Sabahu, make their weird presence hovering over the hermitage, and are the prestidigitators of blood and bones all over the place.

Taking note of this ridiculous sorcery, Raman strings his bow with divine arrows and fires at each of the demons, a shaft hurling Mareeson some thousands of miles away into the depths of the deeps and in a flash cauterizing Subahu to ashes. No sooner Lakshman makes short work of the rest of the demons' followers.

The sinister atmosphere is cleansed; happiness and joy and jubilation prevail everywhere. Besides the sages and disciples who rejoice, the delightful deities sound trumpets and drums and rain flowers upon them in joy and admiration.

The Master Vishwamithrar is spell bound at this spectacular feat of the young lads whose courage galvanizes the whole community. In his exaltation, he worships them with tears of joy brimming his eyes, settles them on his lap and proffers delicious fruits to them in all simplicity. And thus, in the ensuing days Raman and Lakshman pass their time cheerfully and fruitfully in the company of the sage, who amusingly regales them with prolific stories from sacred texts.

Later, after spending about three days in this manner. Sage Vishwamithrar suggests to Raman that they attend the great sacrificial ceremony called the 'Dhanush Yajna' to be carried out by King Janahar. At the palace, the king himself would be enchanted to welcome Him, where he is to peremptorily, see the mighty and magnificent bow of Lord Shiva displayed on the occasion.

In the company of sage Vishwamithrar and other saints, Raman and Lakshman set out for the imperial kingdom of Janahar. During the peregrination they come upon the consecrated hermitage of sage Gauthama, situated near the banks of the river Ganges, laden with fruitful trees all around. And, therein, Ahalihai perforce is absorbed in austere penance.

The striking feature such as calm of the hermitage fascinates Raman. He reflects on why the place wears a very deserted and forlorn look, and the vicinity in and around is completely free of ferocious beasts. So His tempered spirit of enquiry requests sage Vishwamithrar to furnish Him with details of the strange happenings in the hermitage, the ownership, etc.

The stately Vishwamithrar recounts that Gauthaman, a sage of long ago used to reside at the hermitage. The selfsame horrific Gauthaman inorder to assuage and propitiate Lord Hari had undertaken stringent mortifcations. His renown redounded that even Lord Brahman was satiated his purely ascetic life and favoured him entrusting his most comely and docile daughter with him. Very significantly, as Gauthaman had avowed celibacy in life he was gratified at the divine favour and, therefore, resigned to admit her into his hermitage as a mere attendant.

The beautiful Ahalihai meets with an accursed life at the hands of sage Gauthaman. Basically, Indhran from the state of divinity degenerates into a vile mood when he is ciliated with infatuation for the pulchritudinous Ahlihai, assumes the form of Gautaman and surreptitiously conjugates with her in his absence. This clandestine affair triggers off suspicion in the mind of Gauthaman, when he sees Indhran with unfeigned pleasure, in his own form and trappings, coming out from the threshold of his hermitage shedding furtive glances in all directions.

At his injunction, the weak-kneed Indhran reveals his identity; he meekly confesses that as he was devoured by salacity he had committed such a nefarious crime and begs pardon. The sage lashes himself into a fury and imprecates Indhran that his face be stained with a thousand marks of the vagina for his fornication, so that everyone may come to know he is such a libidinous person.

In an equally characteristic impetuous vein, Gauthaman on entering his hermitage sees Ahalihai who stands trembling with fear suffering from compunction. He anathematizes that she be turned into stone, starved without food and water, weather beaten, experiencing the rigours of heat and cold in the same place. The malediction holds well till Raman reaches the same abode after thousands of years and until such time she is to constantly contemplate on Lord Raman in her heart. He further vituperates that, henceforth, the place would be isolated and remain free from all kinds of human as well as animal habitation. On the day the venerable Raman sets His holy feet upon the stone slab she, Ahalihai form, would be relieved of her pile of past infraction, regain her original from completely chastened by Raman and return to Gautaman's residence and be in his service as in the past. Since then, the Himalayas have become the abode of the sage.

Having replenished Raman with these details, Vishwamithrar impetrates the all-merciful Raman, the greatest of the clan of Raghus, to liberate Brahman's daughter from her past execration by the dust of his holy feet, which trace the opening up of a transcendental possibility of being emancipated, since she has been waiting with abundant patience and appetence. Vishwamithrar leads Raman to the spot where she lies in form of stone. Raman places his foot on it and lo and be hold, instantly, the stone flowers into a beautiful girl. Efficaciously Raman reveals his true self and identity.

Ahalihai sees Raman's esoteric form of Vishnu, attired in a flourish of yellow satin and silk robes, with His four arms bracing the conch, disc, mace and lotus. She is flooded with joy and is dumbfounded at his divine spectacle. She sees the bow and the quiver hanging over his broad shoulders with Lakshman standing at his side. Sage Gauthaman's words ring like a bell; cognizing Raman to be the Almighty, she worships him with the fire of piety suffusing her whole being. The tender smile dancing on his fine lips, wearing Shri Bastsa gems on his bosom, His brilliant eyes luminous as lotuses in the sun and his radiant face emanating the luster of blue gems illuminates the entire place. In her humble way she makes an offering of sweets and water to him.

Experience of a heady rush of devotion, an all pervading sense of holiness, with joyful tears cascading down her eyes Ahalihai hails Raman as the abode of the universe. A resurgence of gratitude of obtaining the dust of His holy feet wells up from the depths of her mortal frame Rich plaudits are paid to his anointed feet which sanctify the Ganges, the creator Brahman, Lord Shivan and other Gods, and which the self same beings and other deities clamour to see, and which she is now destined to behold. He is the consummate soul and also a cabalistic actor, whose actions and plays sometimes enthrall and at times baffle the creatures of the three worlds. Though he possesses no mortal coil, He is very illusory, yet very blissful, and meanders everywhere, moves everywhere and moves everything to His own choice and fancy. Her age-old pious deeds accumulated over in her previous births, has resulted in coming face to face with Raman, the Supreme God. Of all human incarnations of Lord Vishnu, Raman with his splendid bow is the noblest piece of art whom she unfailingly prays to.

Raman is the personification of righteousness and all virtues a human being should possess. Heavenly Sage Naradhar and other celestials invariably sing the peerless essence of his life in the domain of the creator Brahman, who is born from his navel. Even he and his divine consort Saraswathi are beside themselves with ecstasy, and her pair of soft eyes do not stop to shed an endless stream of joyful tears on listening to the mellifluous songs. Not ruling out the Vedas, even they are continuously in search of the inviolable dust of His flower-like feet. His nectarine name 'Raman' is not just the name of the Lord, as the manifest son of King Dasarathar on earth, but the name of the Almighty Himself; Lord Shivan himself stands testimony as knower, endorser and admirer who dotes and chants His holy name, proclaiming its invaluable merit to humanity. Prayer is an arbitrary frill to Ahalihai; so she focuses her mind on Raman's auspicious qualities and evidently, she repairs to His own pair of Rapture-Feet as her place of shelter.

An endless string of praises on Raman, bearing the luster of pearls is strung by Ahalihai He is the self born, self enlightened, Infinite Soul; hence he is not created, but is the source of the universe and its creations; he creates the creator of all things too. Notwithstanding His formless entity, He is an illusive being, who, from time to time and age to age, has changed forms and has taken up different moulage, a constellation of characters and qualities. Into this oft changing world he comes camouflaging himself in heterogeneous forms and shapes that excite and enthuse every living being in it. It is corollary that Raman is the only perfect and absolute supreme God, who is most adored and most respected. He is unknowable and inexpressible, for no one can judge him correctly as he is the mysterious and finely sensitive power of immediate understanding without reasoning and, yet dwells as the subject of understanding. It is solely people who are plunged in ignorance overshadowed by his illusion, that cognize him to be a mediocre mortal being. But he is the Supreme Soul, Paramathman, above and beyond the ken of all souls. In this wide universe He is the subject, the meaning and the object too.

Lord Raman, the Supreme Infinity, who is the first one, the first and the only one without a second is omnipresent as the pervading air, the unseeable ether and the peerless sky, is the cause as well as the effect, the doer and the deed, is the whole and undivided, is mutable, motionless and self conscious. He is the creator and the created which are the various agents mechanized by his thaumaturgically illusory force. He is too far away in space and time that he cannot be grasped or even be understood by the mind.

Ahalihai crowns Lord Raman as the invariable glory of the universe. She chides only her grave ignorance which veils her mind from apperceiving the Lord wholly. In blind faith she descends to the depths of servitude, earnestly pleading for such favours that she may with indivisible mind, be ever mindful and implicitly devoted to his Lotus Feet, day in and day out, wherever she may be.

She approaches him as the sympathizer of all aspirants, as king who lords over all souls and senses and as 'Rishiksh' the haven of every living being after his quietus. She professes her innermost yearning and sentiments, praying for inspired faith; she honours him as the supreme Effulgence, more luminescent than a hundred thousand suns, robed in golden outfit, the head crowned with precious gems, holding bows and arrows and his looks so dignified, benign and magnificent that Lakshman always attends on him, and as the only one who alleviates the miseries of egocentrism.

After the panegyrial outpouring of her soul on Lord Raman who is a visible, tangible apparition before her eyes, Ahalihai with his acquiescence traces her way to the Himalayas, after duly and most subserviently bidding adieu to meet her husband sage Gauthaman.

Recitation of this invocation, which Ahalihai has offered to Sri Raman, by anyone, with sincerity and devotion, shall be purged of all sins and also shall conceputalize the Supreme Brahman at the time of attaining salvation.

It is observed that anyone can accomplish his wishes and desires by Sri Raman's grace; even the most sinful sinner whether he be a prosecutor of Brahmins or has coveted his own preceptor's wife or has committed matricides, slain his father or brother or is ever libidinous, a thief or a drunkard, if he with single minded devotion to Sri Raman has recourse to this prayer and atones for his sins shall be saved from perdition. A woman especially, though a barren, in whose hands this invocation is a coup de maiter, if she with robust faith in Raman recites it with the intention of begetting a son, shall verily have a worthy son. It is emphatically enunciated that the study of this compendium of Sri Raman's inimitable qualities will proffer inspiration and courage to stand up against wrong or evil, to brave the worst afflictions and attain everlasting peace.

Chapter - VI

Raman's Marriage to Sita
or
The Matrimony of Raman and Sita

Responding to the cue of their master Vishwamithrar to resume their journey, Raman and Lakshman under his tutelage proceed toward Mithila. They reach the banks of the Ganges where to their amazement the boatman begs to wash the dust of Raman's feet before entering the boat, lest the dust of his feet should change his boat into a lovely lady. The boatman has had prior knowledge of the glaring example with a visible outcome, when Raman placed His foot on the stone, it had instantly changed into Ahalihai. Hence, his apprehension surfaces now, as for him, Raman, there is no difference between stone and wood and if his wooden boat, by the supernatural power of the dust particles of His sacred feet, is transfigured into a beautiful person then, his profession would suffer a great set back, thereby throwing him out of gear, unable to fend for a livelihood to support his family resulting in utter starvation. So he pleads with Raman to allow him to carefully clean and wash his feet, after which he shall ferry them across the river.

On this pretext the humble, yet all too clever boatman, has the occasion to lovingly touch, caress and wash the twin feet of Lord Raman and thereafter, he conducts them to the other side of the river.

The next morning Vishwamithrar with Raman and Lakshman land in the city of Mithilai and reach a hermitage where they intend to halt.

Perhaps, the scent of Raman's arrival in Mithilai is in their air; a flurry of excitement prevails everywhere. More significantly perhaps, king Janahar has got wind of Vishwamithrar's presence. On learning of his arrival, the king prepares for a dramatic welcome with assorted gifts to be presented to the sage. Obviously, with an elated heart and enlivened spirit, King Janahar accompanied by his advisor and priest hasten to the hermitage the next morning to greet the sage. He translates his obeisance to the sage in the manner of worshipping and gifting the many articles to him. The dazzling brightness in all directions, by which the king is flabbergasted, draws his attention and summarily, his eyes alight on Raman and Lakshman, iridescent as the sun and the moon, the cause for the brilliance.

His mind queries as to who these two alluring young lads are. He conceptualizes these stalwart heroes, majestic and powerful as lions, to be divine beings. King Janahar, whose mind is strongly drawn towards these supernatural beings, opines that they seem to be no other than the incarnations of Nara and Narayanan.

The valiant lads are introduced as King Dasaratha's sons by sage Vishwamithrar who proceeds to brief king Janahar of the natural sequence of happenings and their explicit outcomes, his invitation to Raman and Lakshman, their effectual presence at his hermitage to protect the yojna ceremony, the Mighty Raman's Killing of Thadahar by a single shot of his arrow, the burning of Subahu in a trice, the pitching of Mareeson a thousands miles away to the sea, then Lakshman slaying the remaining wicked demons defiling the yajna and their visit to Gauthaman's holy hermitage, Wherefore, the sages wife, Ahalikhai, is emancipated by Raman, their present visit to his palace is Raman's wish to lay His eyes on Lord Shiva's divine bow.

Sage Vishwamithrar greatly commends the established sovereignty of the invincible Bow, revered and honoured by king Janahar and many a prince, and impresses upon the king for a display of his mighty bow to Raman and Lakshman, who will then return to Ayodhya after paying their respects to it, as is the custom. King Janahar after reverentially welcoming Raman and Lakshman to his court, worships and entertains them as rightly deserved, and in the same breath puts forth a huge proposition that if Raman can elevate the bow and string an arrow to it, he would offer his only daughter Sita to him in marriage. He quickly commands his wise ministers to have the bow displayed immediately before the beatific and valiant Raman. Humility lends grandeur to Raman's prowess, and it is only at Sage Vishwamithrar's bidding-an affable smile of endorsement directed towards Raman, that he, Raman, ventures to have a look at the formidable bow of Sri Shiva. In his characteristic modesty, Raman, pronounces that he will make an endeavor to lift and string it. At the behest of the Chief Minister, and as it is an onerous task, it needs around five thousand rock-ribbed soldiers to carry the ornamental bow exquisitely studded with precious gems glittering with a muti-faceted sheen and hundreds of tiny tinkling bells hanging upon it. As is his wont, Lord Sri Raman, with the Sage's blessings lifts the bow as if it were a garland of flowers with perfect facility and dexterity, bends it to fix the string to the dismay of the princes and the kings of other territories and countries present at this pageantry.

Lord Raman, the Universal Soul, the heart beat of every heart, having strung it with unrelenting perfection pulls the bow string back with his right hand and breaks the bow in a way legitimate to His phenomenal and prodigious valour and with it draws the heart of Devi Sita towards Him. The mystical sound caused at the breaking of the bow creates a cosmic oneness as the sound suffuses and reverberates throughout the universe, in the three worlds, the heavens, the earth and the netherlands. To celebrate this remarkable feat the deities and celestials in the heavens dance in ecstasy and shower flowers on Raman.

The queen mothers who are watching this extraordinary feat are filled with consternation and happiness. At the moment the bow is snapped, King Janahar's fear that he might not be able to find a suitable bridegroom of prowess to marry Sita is dispelled. And, with a joy that is unconfined, Janahar enfolds Raman in his arms in an affectionate embrace. Propriety and Modesty, The inborn and binding virtues make chaste Sita, bejeweled with priceless ornaments, gorgeously dressed, walk gracefully with bowed head, blushing, turning touchingly pink, towards Raman. Yet, stealing furtive glances at her handsome Lord and smiling radiantly, eyes locked together, reconnecting with each other, Sita joyfully garlands Raman with a garland of Gold.

It is a time for great powerful intellectual and emotional satisfaction. The congregation of the royal guests of kings, Queens and Princes and others at king Janahar's court are overjoyed to see the ravishing Sita garlanding Raman in the most befitting fashion. The ladies and maidens having a peep from the interior rooms of the palace are as gay as ever. In consultation with Sage Vishwamithrar, the erudite King Janahar sends out a royal invitation to the aristocracy in Ayodhya – King Dasarathar, his Queens, sons and ministers to attend the matrimony on good time and the subsequent ceremonies thereafter.

On learning the good tidings of Sri Raman's marvelous deeds and his imminent marriage to Sita, King Dasarathar explodes with great exaltation, riding the crest of good fortune that is incident on the Raghu race. Immediately, a detailed itinerary and preliminary arrangements are extensively drawn out by the ministers at his bidding. The imperatorial company of king Dasarathar, the Queen mothers, Bharathan, Satrughan together with Guru Vasisthar and his wife, all set out on their journey to Mithilai in a splendid chariot, followed by the four components of the army in proud array. They take with them the ritual fire which is on the front line escort.

A red carpet welcome with due formalities, honour and cordiality is served by King Janahar and his preceptor Sadanadhan to the monarchic retinue which arrives at Mithilai. Initially, the pair Raman and Lakshamn offer their dutiful respects to king Dasarathar who envisions them as golden lotuses, and in honeyed words sings their praise, eulogizing their exploits and gallantry which are a glory to him. He anoints their head with a consecrated touch and hugs them repeatedly to his heart's content, in equal measure he offers encomiums to Sage Vishwamithrar who has dispensed him with such favours galore. Later, the nobles retire to luxurious, comfortable chambers well equipped and well furnished in the sprawling mansion. Exquisite artistic decorations set the tone for the marriage celebrations. The entire palace is embellished with filigrees of gold and silver, variegated coloured flags, banners, ribbons, streamers, brocades and laces designed beautifully, precious ornaments and enchanting melodious symphonies from propitious musical instruments such as bheri, dandube, horus, flutes, trumpets etc., fill the air. Especially, the marriage hall, with prominent personalities such as scholarly Brahmins, savants, priests, exhibiting the same pomp, creating an aura of aristocracy and splendour looks picturesque and ethereal. Likewise, ladies exotically attired, decked with invaluable jewels, flaunting ostentation and flamboyance grace the occasion.

The ceremonial rites of the marriage commence. A regal invitation by the devout king Janahar is extended to Raman and his brothers to which they reciprocate, being led by the elders in a gracious gait and made to sit on magnificently embellished thrones on the elevated pavilion in the marriage hall. Janahar's philosopher and guide, priest Sathanantha, attends on the sages Vishwamithrar and Vahsisthar, offering them seats, one on each side of Raman's throne.

Lighting of the auspicious and sacred fire according to the norms prescribed in the Vedas begins, when Sita is guided by King Janahar and his queen to the throne next to Raman. The holy water of the feet of Sri Vishnu, which the sages, saints and even Brahma and Shivan carry on their heads, is sprinkled on the heads of the couples. The act of offering Sita's hand to Sri Raman by king Janahar is crowned with glory, together with a hamper full of rice and a pot full of water, as is the custom, bears testimony to the matrimonial bond that has been established. The king is highly pleased and delighted to hand over the Self of Sita to Sri Raman in this traditional and expedient manner.

Of course, King Janahar is visibly ecstatic, just as the God of Ocean, in offering Devi Lakshmi to Lord Vishnu. He gives his daughter Urmila in marriage to Lakshman, his brother's daughters Mandavi and Srutikirthi to Bharathar and Sathrughan respectively. It is no wonder the four brothers looking blithesome and luminous should be mistaken for sentinels of heaven.

King Janahar goes back little in time to reminisce about sage Narathar's prognostications. Before reading into the connotations of the sage's predictions, King Janahar relates to Vishwamithrar and Vashisthar about his fortuitous discovery in the earth, the promising treasure a female babe, Sita, with a fascinating moon-like countenance, while ploughing a piece of land inorder to collect earth needed for performing the yajna ceremony. He had scooped the infant in his arms, fondled her and entrusted her to his wife. Together they cherished, nurtured and tendered Sita with love and affection as if she were their own daughter.

Even more arresting is Janahar's recollection of Sage Narathar's prophecies which he now narrates to them. After a lengthy stretch of time, the Sage playing on his divine veena called 'Mahathi' meets king Janahar, whom Janahar greets with much cordiality, in which situation, the sage apprises him of the pressing cause and specific sequels of his luck and prosperity. The fortunate and mystical find, child Sita, is the incarnation of Devi Lakshmi whom he should unite in holy matrimony with Raman, the manifestation of Lord Vishnu, in a four-fold way for the well being of mankind on the earth to erase the turpitude and to slay the accursed Ravanan.

In as much, king Janahar broods over his future course of action, for it would entail risk factors of trying to descry the infallible and immaculate spouse to marry away Sita. Nevertheless, incredibly, divine inspiration dawns on the King. The mighty bow, now in his custody, was first committed by Shiva himself to his forefathers after striking dead Tripurshura the titanic demon. Just as the solutions to a jigsaw puzzle fall into place, conceivably, Janahar reflects that the celestial bow is the obvious and the best ithuriel to his apprehensions. Lord Shiva's bow is used as the touchstone to best the power and strength of human beings. Because none other than Vishnu's incarnation, Sri Raman, can be accredited with the potential for bending the bow.

The prophecies of the sage materialize. The king is finally crowned with an off-beat success in his mission, as it is with Sri Raman's grace, he has fulfilled his pledge. He avows that his life has been fruitful because he sees Raman seated on the same throne with Sita.

King Janahar surrenders to the feet of Lord Raman, as he is aware that it is the dust of the self same feet which redeemed Ahalihai from her husband's curse; it is the same which bestows Brahman with the power and fortitude to create the universe and that, which conferred on Bail the seat of Indhran. He accepts Raman, the Divine Self, as his own savior, since sages and celestials who are the cognizers of His divine charm and lulling fragrances of His lotus-flower feet, have mastered time and destiny. By ceaselessly chanting His sacred names, they are able to surmount mountain high obstructions, become totally disencumbered from mundane fears and rid of all woes and afflictions.

Preparations are made to send Sita to her father-in-law's in Ayodhya. King Janahar and his Queens bequeath to Sita a dowry with enormous riches and luxuries in the form of jewellry and ornaments, a complete wardrobe, hundreds of servant maids, elephants, horses, chariots and the like. The same he gives away to his other daughters married to Lakshman, Bharathan and Sathrughan. As a token of his gratitude and reverence to the sages Vishwamithrar and Vashithar and king Dasarathar, he presents them with sterling gift articles.

Sita is affectionately embraced by the Queen Mothers who bless her with a happy life. Their eyes brim with tears of joy while they pronounce that she should be a chaste, ideal wife devoted to Raman while performing her dutiful services to all her in-laws. This moment is lightly marred by displeasure as Sita and Raman are all set to depart. Janahar and his Queen with mixed feelings of happiness and sadness, pleasure and sorrow, and great affection bid farewell to Sita along with Raman in the chariot that carries them away.

This happy occasion is marked by music and dance in the heavens above, and on the earth this farewell marriage ceremony is viewed as an occasion to celebrate and all beings are deliriously delighted.

Chapter - VII

Parasuraman Confronts Raman

An aura of aristocracy, splendor and ecstasy is distinctly visible as king Dasarathar and his cortege proceed on their onward journey to Ayodhya. But, unfortunately, their travel is soured when they have traversed twenty-five miles away from Mithilai. King Dasarathar indulges in misgivings, the result of his having espied star-crossed omens along the way, when voicing his premonitions to Vashisthar that something disastrous is going to befall them. The sagacious preceptor quells his qualms, saying, that his trepidations will come to pass but all will soon melt like mist and come to nothing. He spices up the kings hopes with signs of seeing deer running on his right that spells good omen.

Sooner said, when a hurricane blows violently across sweeping dust helter skelter and blinding the eyes of the travellers. In this great flurry, suddenly, they behold an extremely luminous apparition. The effulgent Parasuraman, more resplendent than a hundred suns, with a shimmering blue appearance as the azure sky, with a tuft of curly locks on his forehead and an axe in one hand and a bow in the other, portraying the picture of the God of death, advances towards Raman meaning to kill him as it were and put an end to the others straightaway. In his present state of phobia the king, forgetting the codes of propriety of paying homage to the sage, instead, very sequaciously falls on his feet and pleads for the protection of his son, Raman's life, owing to the fact that Parasuraman is know to have destroyed countless kings and princes in the past. For this reason an explicable and sustained fear currently clouds them all.

Brushing aside the king's plea, Parasuraman brazenly surges towards Raman in extreme anger. He vocalizes explosively; the earth-quakes and a sudden darkness and gloom envelops the place. Addressing Raman as an ignoble kshatriyan he deprecates and nullifies his action of breaking the bow, which according to him has been corroded and ravaged by time, and accuses him of gloating over with self-conceit, the accomplishment of such a boastful feat. He challenges Raman, if being born into the dynasty of the Raghu race, to prove his might by fixing the string to his Vaishnava bow, failing which he would engage them in a combat and kill all of them thus, fulfilling his life's mission of obliteration of the Kshatriyar race.

Taking hold of the bow from Parasuraman's hand, invincible Raman very easily strings an arrow as if it were a child's play. He requests him to tell him further what else he ought to do for him. then, Raman ordains that Parasuraman, a Brahmin, should become oblivious of all the worlds (Lokas) he has conquered, and so saying, he strikes his feet with his indefectible arrow which drains out all his energy for scampering about, back and forth, from one world to the other.

This special touch of the divine has transformed Bhrigu's son Parasuraman, and he is enlightened on the history of his previous birth. He immediately conceptualizes Raman as the Ominfic God Vishnu. Also, he meekly prays to the Eternal Supreme Being, the Creator, Sustainer and Destrover of the Universe. He pours forth the reminiscences of his past birth. When, as a youth he had performed austere penances in the holy 'chakra' pilgrimage, thereby, pleasing Lord Vishnu who appeared before him with his favourite armour in hand, and in his mercy rewarded him with the harvest, His own powers that make Parasuraman invincible to conquer the earth, for his penances which satiated him thoroughly. Later on, by eliminating Kartabriya who was guilty of patricide, he was to bequeath the earth to Kashyapa. Then, when he has consummated his mission by killing all the vicious kings wandering on the earth, Lord Vishnu would resorb all his powers and dynamism from him, after which, he would still inhabit this earth till he is aware of its delusion, exercising salubrious penances and austerities. And now, face to face, he sees Lord Vishnu on earth in human form, as the son of Dasarathar and married to Sita who is the divine derivation of perennial energy and power. Raman, by being born in this Tretha epoch at the behest of Brahma, the creator, has this day, absorbed into himself his power from Parasuraman. With this, realization dawns on him and he realizes Raman as the real self and power which is beyond even nature and which is impenetrable and inconceivable to the other deities as well as Brahman. His ulterior purpose is achieved as he has cognized Raman wholly.

Parasuraman garlands Sri Raman with accolades and plaudits, describing him as the truth that dwells within each body, and as the inactive and immutable power which is free from the six-fold imperfections of ignorance and egocentrism. He gives natural expression to the illusive quality 'Maya' which intermingles with him like bubbles in water and smoke in fire, further it depends solely on him and acts as really the causes of what appears as the cause, creation.

His stupefaction propels him to exclaim at the trajectories of Maya's strange manipulation, driving men into labyrinths of egotistic advantages and mundane objectives. He is fully aware of the hard boiled sceptics, who so long as they are caught in the web of this illusive Maya and have the veil of ignorance drawn upon them, cannot cognize even a wee bit of Raman. Delusion, in anyway cannot contemprorize with truth or divine knowledge. He is aware of the truth, that it is only the impression of Raman's Supereme Soul alone upon the subtle intellect, which, constitutes even the Jiva or spirit of every individual. Parasuraman professes that the deficiency of true knowledge of his immaculate self is the explicit repercussion merely brought into existence by nescience. The ego is parasitic, drawing its sustaining life force from the image of God, and at the same time, holding sway over the senses which are superimposed on the subtle entities of intellect and mind; here individuality which is mere husk is rendered null and void. But the individual soul which is not matter, fine or super fine, is birthless and deathless, is God Himself, and mere mind or even intellect, overpowered with ignorance, is devoid of this knowledge supreme. Owing to the non-existence of right knowledge of discrimination and prudence, soul and matter seem conflated, and cut figures as separate individual beings similar to hot water which is a compound of heat and water; so to say the soul manifests the ego, intellect, mind, senses and the external instruments.

Soul which is all pervading, free, divine, immanent, pure conscious, immutable, impenetrable, self-enlightened, self-existent, inscrutable and eternal is neither an agent, nor does it experience the dynamic operations of the world of phenomena-bondage, suffering, happiness, sorrow, pain, joy, pleasure, misery, heat and cold, that fall within the boundless realm of Maya; but is the ego commingling with the intellect and sense organs that is the individual, or the doer who feels and experiences these illusive qualities and manifold operations.

The individual in his onward march of spiritual progress cannot makes a headway in realizing, cognizing and visualizing the Supreme being, Raman, until or unless, he comes under the tutelage of a Spiritual Preceptor or Guru. It is only his single minded devotion and undiluted love for the lord that makes him, the aspirant, associate with the spiritual Preceptor, for it is He who in his infinite wisdom chooses to bring two persons together as Teacher and Pupil. In this context, the aspirant is absolved of all sins, exculpated of all worldly ties; and the veil of ignorance rent asunder, has no more its sway over him, and disappears altogether.

Long-aeons and epochs are of little importance and cannot help in knowing the Supreme Soul, Raman, as it is impossible for an aspirant to obtain liberation and sanctity if the heart is arid, devoid of love, sincerity and devotion to Him alone. Saying this much, Parasuraman prays to Sri Raman, the Universal Consciousness to bless him with profound aspiration to His hallowed feet, and perpetual devotion to Him throughout this life and even in the next, if there be any such. He prays for intimate affiliation with his aspirants and devotees because they are God-drunk and embrace others showering the nectar of love on them, easily purifying not only their disciples, their kith and kin and others, but the world at large.

Parasuraman requests that whatever he has done for the sake of the world may be virtually linked with the great bow of his Supreme Self. He repeatedly bows to him, eloquently hailing Raman as the Absolute Soul, the Graceful Eternal Controller of the Universe and the embodiment of love.

Parasuraman being delighted that Sri Raman has favoured him, again pleads to grant him his love and the association with all his devotees forever. Finally, he appends yet another request to bestow knowledge, to perpetuate the memory with his gracious and benignant self and to grant emancipation at last to any person, though he may not be fully devoted to him, when this invocation is solemnly recited by him. Sri Raman being highly pleased concedes all his requests, and Parasuraman with his approval respectfully takes leave of him to settle on the Mandarachal mountain.

Dasarathar's nagging fear about Raman's safety ends in smoke. He gives a great sigh of relief. He joyfully and tenderly embraces Sri Raman as if he has been rescued from the jaws of death, and they proceed on their journey and reach Ayodhya in good time.

Just as Vishnu lives with his consort Lakshmi in paradise, so does Raman live with Sita. All the brothers live happily with their wives to the great satisfaction of their parents. Bharathan and Sathrughnan are sent by king Dasarathar along with their maternal uncle Yuddhajit who comes to take them to his state.

Similar to Aditi who lives with his son Indhran and daughter-in-law Sachi, the daughter of Paulami, here, Kausalya also is very contented and happy with Raman and Sita.

Nothing can be far from the truth to say that Sri Raman's excellence is well known and He is well known to the goodness of all the worlds. He is the Supreme God, the Purushothaman who is ever blissful, at once here and beyond, immutable and mutable, finite and infinite, one and the many, and reconciles and unifies in himself all the multiform diversities of his self-manifestation. He is the highest beatitude, the sole bliss of human beings yet, transcending all parameters of illusion. He is divinely prosperous and lives with Sita in Ayodhya. He is the creator of the universe taking the role of an ordinary human being and moving without any reservation with all around him. Sri Raman expounds, prescribes and Himself follows virtue. Sri Sita is the personification of chastity. She loves, adores and serves her lord with cheerfulness, sincerity, undivided loyalty and total dedication to all her in laws. Indeed Raman, the Supreme Lord of the Universe is.

Part - II
Ayodhya Kandam

Chapter - I

Manthra envenoms Kaikeyi

King Dasarathar, in the bosom of his heart, cherishes the delicious desire of crowning Raman as his heir apparent. The pleasure derived by indulging in such sweet thoughts makes him open up the secret chambers of his heart and express his yearning sentiment to crown Raman as the prince regent, the next day, to his preceptor, Sage Vashishtar. The approval is unanimously given by an assembly of citizens and elders in this matter, convened by king Dasarathar, since Raman is the cynosure of all eyes and the most beloved of all. The King is overwhelmed with joy that Raman, has endeared himself to one and all by his exemplary conduct and comportment. He requests the sage to convey the glad tidings to Raman and to make elaborate preparations for the coronation ceremony. He dictates to his Prime Minster Sumanthan to execute the judicious instructions of Vashisthar in making preparations for the solemnization of the enthronement.

At the behest of Vashisthar, Sumunthran gets ready all the necessary paraphernalia, and invites Sages, Saints Brahmins, Kings and Princes, nobleman, feudatory and chiefs. Ramarkably important things, besides other regalia items, are pots of gold filled with holy water, the royal ensign of gold studded with precious stones, hides of tiger decorated with tinsels of gold and gems and other sundries. The intensive task of offering special worship and offerings to all Gods and deities presiding at the temples throughout the city is initiated immediately. The highly decorated parasol and the scepter are got ready. Beautiful maidens numbering sixteen, flanked with gold ornaments, erudite scholars, musicians, the infantry, the cavalry, elephants of war together with sixteen specimens of four tusked elephants of the Airavatha breed, decorated ornaments of gold are requisites directed to be present at the royal ritual.

Categorically, Sage Vasishthar speeds away in a chariot, crossing the three pathways to Sri Raman's palace where he is welcomed by Raman and

Janaki; as a mark of high respect Raman prostrates reverentially at his feet. He then washes the sage's feet with great deference and sprinkles the water collected from washing Vashisthar's feet on his head and humbly tells the sage that he has been blessed with holy water. Promptly the sage articulates noble sentiments about divine Lord Shiva who has been blessed with the sacred water of his feet, and also Brahman by touching his feet-a confluence of all pilgrimage centers- could make reparation for his sins. He also postulates that such modesty on the part of Raman is exemplary for all to emulate. Also, he says that he has full knowledge of his incarnations and designs to liberate the earth from the atrocities unleashed inordinately by the evil spirits, culminating the mission for the welfare and well being of the Gods and denizens of the world.

The sage is happy that he is Raman's preceptor only on this earth, but lauds Raman as the Preceptor of all preceptors, the Father of fathers because He is the mysterious understanding, and there can be no one who possesses a finer more mysterious and more delicate and subtler understanding than Raman. He is unthinkable, inexpressible as human description of him escapes the limits of language and representation. Dynamic Maya concomitant with Raman is unfathomable and inseparable from Him. He has by His own will along with his Maya, manifested as a human being on this earth. The sage expresses his unbounded joy as his desire has been fulfilled in this birth, for he holds a kinship with Raman by being his preceptor, despite the fact that priesthood is an unbefitting standing in life. He divulges that he had accepted to take on the status of priesthood only after learning from Brahman that he, Raman, would be born into the Ikshwaku's family. He petitions Raman, the sea of compassion, to dissipate his nescience and never allow his illusion to perpetuate and have influence on him, as it behoves him to carry out his obligations and services towards Him as His teacher and priest even as ordained by Raman Himself.

At this opportune moment, the sage spells out king Dasarathar's whole souled desire to enthrone Raman the next day and instructs Him and Sita to groom themselves for the red letter day, conforming to puritanical conventions. He also points out that the mission of His divine birth has been revealed to him under the seal of secrecy. Back at Dasarathar's palace, the sage well informs the king of his conversation with Raman.

After Vasisthar takes leave there is a sharing of consanguineous sentiments between Raman and Lakshman; Raman opines that Lakshman is part and parcel of His self. He jocularly comments that Lakshman is fortunate in enjoying leisure, whereas, He, Raman, would remain only an inert perpetrator if He is coronated. But Raman is tight-lipped about His secret mission on this earth, as advised by the Sage.

The news of Raman's coronation spreads like wild fire. Someone of unknown identity very sportively and delightfully acquaints Kausalya and Sumithra with the news and is amply rewarded by them for such a costly exercise. Kausalya has had previous knowledge of Dasarathar's irresolute and untruthful mind; she floats in a sea of doubt as to whether he would unrelentingly abide by his conception of crowning her son Raman as the regal heir for at present, the intrigue and the affair de coeur of Kaikey's influence might prevail upon him. Yet, she prays and worships Goddess Durga and Goddess Lakshmi as well, for the éclat of the Coronation ceremony.

In paradise, Brahman and other gods intend to obstruct the proceedings of the rites, and at their suggestion the Goddess of learning and speech, Devi Saraswathi, holds sway over the minds of Kaikeyi and Manthra. The hag Manthra, a hunch with three knots, flounces into Kaikey's apartment in a state of dark anxiety and utter confusion; she poisons Kaikey's ears by outrageously telling her about the king's flirtatious idea to delegate none other than Raman to ascend the throne as Prince of State. At the outset, the naive Kaikeyi welcomes the news of the King's decision with unfeigned joy, but, soon to be a transitory delight, is overjoyed that Raman is to be crowned king the next day. Presently she gives away her necklace to Manthra as a token of gratitude for the good tidings she has brought. She authorizes Raman's filial love for her as genuine and that the, who is so genial, complaisant, gracious and loving, loves her more than Bharathan does and that he always looks upon her as his own mother. She asserts that it would be only foolish to fear Raman. And contrary to Kaikey's expectations, Manthra does not second her, but flays her instead for her laxity and insouciance, and obsession with her own vain personal beauty alone. Also, she accuses Kaushalya of lulling the king into complacency so as to install Raman on the throne, By such a step she petrifies Kaikeyi that catastrophe and humiliation would knock at her doors. But, correspondingly kausalya rails at Manthra for insinuating that misfortune would befall her, if Raman succeeds to the throne. Because, she happily basks in the reflection that Raman loves her in good faith as he loves his mother kausalya.

Invariably, the vicious Manthra inoculates Kaikeyi with the poison of jealousy. She plays her cards well and delineates the more conundrumatic details by denigrating his character. She distorts her mind into believing that the king is loveless towards her, his amorous talk, voluptuous desire and erotic passion are all lustful in nature, and incriminates him working as a beneficiary to Kausalya. She cites an example in point of the King sending Bharathan away along with Shathrughnan to the home of their maternal uncle inorder to bequeath the throne to Raman. She incites Kaikeyi all the more by adding that Bharathan will be banished from the kingdom; going a step further she says he will be even put to death. Talking about Lakshman, she says he would definitely enjoy and avail every advantage of Raman's rule, as he, Raman, loves him very much, and this would please Sumithra subsequently. Manthra uses the trump card, which is most effective, to transform Kaikey's mind completely. She asserts that Kaikey would have to for certain be tied to Kausalyas's apron strings, who would have the upperhand, and she, Kaikeys serve serves her as would a slave. She accelerates her indignity saying death would be far better than this sort of submission and subservience.

Manthra does not want to give up. It's her chance to play her last trump card to persuade Kaikeyi to change her mind and gear herself into action. She walks back in time, pulls out a memory from the pages of yester years, and reminds Kaikeyi of the King's commitment to grant her two boons for having saved his life by holding fast to the axle of the chariot, the screw of which had broken in the battlefield. She pressurizes her not to let this chance pass by, but to snatch this opportune moment when the king arrives and have access to the two promised boons. Further, she instigates Kaikeyi to send Raman into exile to the forests for fourteen years and to enthrone Bharathan as the crowned head of the state. By doing so, she will be right royally acknowledged as the Queen mother. The Knavish Manthra spurs Kaikeyi on to use the dark room, utilized by anyone who wants to give vent to his or her anger and grievances in any form, so that the king would read her mind.

Now, a streak of bleak hopelessness creeps into Kaikeyi. Her protean characteristics of naivety, candour and artlessness make a U-turn. However, she is extensively grateful to Manthra for the enlightenment, deemed to be advantageous to her, and finds in her a confidant and well wisher. She makes up her mind to act accordingly and promises to reward her profusely after Bharathan's ascension to the throne.

Manthra puffed up with imperious air of vanity and self-praise leaves Kaikeyi to herself. Mean-while, Queen Kaikeyi goaded by Manthra's instigation and provocation, discarding her rich attire, ornaments and jewels goes straight away to the dark room. She lies in wait on the floor in sullen mood for the king's arrival. Just previously, during their tete a tete Kaikeyi had told Manthra she would even end her life, so long as Raman is not banished from the country, and would fight tooth and nail to install Bharathan on the throne. This is what happens if you take to bad courses with bad companions; it leads to an irregular life that will end in utter ruin.

Needless to say, though not surprisingly, confabulation between Manthra and Queen Kaikeyi is a glaring example of evil begetting evil. An ounce of didacticism is extracted from it to ameliorate and permeate the entire tenor of our life. Nothing is more strongly influential than vile company, spreading its tentacles and closing in on even the people who are ethical, religious, spiritual, scholarly, good natured and deligent. Hence affiliation with such malefic and pernicious forces shatters the mental equipoise of the associates resulting in dire consequences. Evidently, it is imperative that we should shun evil in any form; associate and cultivate the company of good people, so as to ennoble the thoughts and lift the mind from the morass of worldly behaviour, raising it to dizzy heights of righteous endeavor and achievement.

Descending from the heavens, the celestial being, Sage Narathar, looking gloriously luminous, visits the divine couple, Sri Raman and Sri Sita, in a clandestine manner. Sri Raman cheerfully welcomes the sage and in the most human way thanks his stars for having set eyes on him a sage, whom men on earth seldom have the fortune of availing themselves of their auspicious visits, since their presence augurs peace, prosperity and happiness and their instructions edify, enlighten, guide and ameliorate their hopeless condition, paving the way for the development and progress of a perfectly moral as well as worldly life. Raman, appreciative of his visit, humbly waits on him requesting to be permitted to serve him.

On the other hand, Sage Narathar more subserviently and magnanimously exalts Raman as the glory of heaven. He is aware that Raman is befooling him by posing as a worldly mortal being. His perspicacity inspires him to promptly acclaim Sri Raman as the savior sustaining the three worlds heaven, earth and Netherland and Sri Sita, His better half, as Supreme Maya, the prime energy which creates even the creator Brahman himself and all other creatures. She evinces the three principle attributes (three gunas) such as inertness, materialism and predatoriness; She wears the three forms of whiteness, redness and blackness. Maya, Sri Sita, or delusion is all inclusive and indivisible in creating the universe and all its creatures. He announces though, Sri Raman is in the guise of a householder, He is infallibly the manifestation of Lord Vishnu and Sita is Devi Lakshmi. Sri Raman projects Himself in an array of kaleidoscopic forms as the creator Brahman, the God of heaven; Indhran,

God of Fire, Yaman, the god of death other deities and all male Gods, and Sita Devi as Saraswathi, Paulami, Swaha and Samymini and a manifold forms of all Goddesses.

The soul is invisible clouded by Maya named 'Abykrit' which is ignorance; no amount of perceptivity can divine and discriminate the soul from this subtle Abyakrit. Nature and other entities are creations of Maya. The ego, the gross, the subtle and the causal bodies or forms of all individuals are also matter that has been produced by the God of Nature. Contrary to this truth Reality, Immortality and Immutability lie imbedded in the human body in the form of soul or self in every creature. The individual self is yoked to mundane attachments and sensual pleasures; but the Supreme Self is devoid of these qualities. The supreme soul exists as the real perceiver or knower and witness. This seer is the real manifester and the real enjoyer abiding in all the three stages of human life, such as, waking, dreaming and sleep.

It is a foregone conclusion that Raman is the First Cause of creation, the Infinite Soul which is behind the universe guiding, ruling and governing it. He is omnipresent and omnipotent, punctuating life of all beings with nascency, growth, mutation, putrefaction, dissolution happiness and anguish as everything originates from Him. Raman is the same Nucleus Soul residing as spectator within every life animating consciousness just as a lamp lights up a room.

The journey of life, through aeons and aeons, after innumerable cycles of birth and death, should decisively and ultimately end in salvation, the aspiration and goal of all life. None other than the individual himself is responsible for his own salvation. Hence it is mandatory that every individual should strive to attain liberation, since he is the architect of his own destiny. However, the moment the discerning aspirant realizes that he is no more distinct from God, he gets finally emancipated from smug delusions and enchanting snares of short-sighted materialistic living. This is because, the accomplished spiritualist realizes the soul in him as only the Supreme Reality, is God, and God forms the soul of his. Man overshadowed by dark ignorance mistakes a rope for a snake. Similarly, he is misguided by the misconception that he is an alien entity, separate from the Supreme Soul, and that is why he is steeped in delusions and is an ignorant self. Once when he is able to disassociate himself from this distinction, as the rope is recognized in the case of rope-snake as snake, he is a realized soul, a part and parcel of the Universal Consciousness, the total whole, the Universal All.

Sage Naradhar blandishes Sri Raman to be very kind to him as He is his grandson, since His father got his birth from his navel, and not to further depreciate him, but to allow him to be a humble slave to his devotees, as it is only they who are privileged beings having a continuous, unceasing flow of God-consciousness to attain salvation. The sage buoyed up by elation discloses to Sri Raman the intentions of king Dasarathar to crown him as Prince of State, the apparent heir to the throne the next day. He informs Raman that he has been sent by Brahman to remind Him of His secret mission on earth, lest, He should accept the throne and may not fulfill the same.

Omniscient Raman assures Narathar that there is nothing beyond His ken and that He will carry out his task to the letter. He smilingly intimates Narathar that He is ready to leave Ayodhya to retire to the forest and dauntlessly kill Ravanan after he has abducted Sita. Narathar content and happy ascends to his abode.

It is enunciated that this sacred discourse between Sri Raman and Sage Narathar offers dignified hope and confidence for the amelioration of one's hopeless condition and for the development of a perfectly moral life in course of time, and confers salvation at the appropriate time as it is considered to be a soul-stirring doctrine to those who read it fervently and prayerfully.

Chapter - II

Kaikeyi's Anger

King Dasarathar, in a deliriously happy mood, announces himself into Queen Kaikeyi's apartment only to be crestfallen at her absence. It is incomprehensible to him as to why she should languish in the dark room for no reason unknown to him; he is much anguished on finding her unglamorously sprawling on the floor, disarrayed and discomposed. He pleads with her to speak out her mind; and is willing to do the impossible to put her heart at ease. He is virtually ready to give up his spirit and is disposed to take punitive action by taking away life or granting life to anyone, or even make a mendicant a prince and vice verse, if she so wishes. He swears by Raman, more precious to him than his life, to translate her heart's desires into action.

Floating on a cloud of expectation, Queen Kaikeyi is toeing the line, acting her part out as if tailored for it. She sulks, frets and fumes. She takes advantage of the opportunity, with effrontery and insolence she puts forth her cause, a demand for the two boons made as a long ago pledge. The first should be in the form of conceding the throne of Ayodhya to her son Bharathan and the grisly form of the second boon is to deport Raman to the forest for a period of fourteen long years. She stoops to the extent of designing his trappings-dresses of leaves and barks of trees, and defining what he should consume – wild fruits, during the decisive phase of living in the forests. She points out that truthfulness has always been his forte, well known by all throughout the country and if he belies this trait of not complying with her postulations, she threatens to knock at death's door to do away with her life.

Kaikeyi's speech coming as it does so startlingly, unexpectedly with such rancor, excites in Dasarathar a strong disagreement, disapproval and dismay. Greatly alarmed, his world comes crashing down leaving him rudderless. He goes into a swoon falling to the floor at once, like a tree that dashes to the ground by the stroke of a thunderbolt.

However, he recovers from the fainting fit and returns to thoughts of mundane practical considerations. He is unable to discern the hidden significance in her outburst, for she has never betrayed any sinister or ill feelings towards Raman. She has always adopted gentle and loving methods in dealing with Raman for whom she has the highest regard and loves from the very bottom of her heart even more than Bharathan her own son.

Dasarathar braces himself, plucks up courage and pledges his option of bestowing the throne to Bharathan but, condescends to fall at her feet, supplicating her most humbly to be generous to Raman and not make him so vulnerable in himself pronouncing the degree of Raman's exile to the forest, unmindful of Raman being a paragon and the source of all virtues.

The issue of Raman's banishment has become a bone of contention. Undeterred by the Kings pleadings, Queen Kaikeyi adopts an unyielding attitude. All his orchestrated supplications prove null and void, but they only provoke her to an explosion of heightened anger. She takes a decisive and irrevocable step exhibiting magnified hastiness and rigidity. She rants on at length, sneering at his boastful nature of truthfulness which he cannot uphold, and searing that he would certainly fall into hell as he cannot fulfill his promises even after taking an oath on Raman's name, and in the same breath surfaces her suicidal tendencies at this moment. King Dasarathar is cut to the quick for Kaikeyi's illusory beauty and attraction has turned out to be a hollow and bitter disappointment. It is only cold comfort that he experiences all through the night. He spends the night miserably relapsing into repeated swoons. King Dasarathar has run the gamut of his emotions from joy to utter despair in just a single night's time.

Next morning, the city of Ayodhya awakens to a mood of joy; festivity, jubilation and celebrations are rampant throughout the royal palace and its adjoining vicinities. Hectic preparations in full swing for the eventful ceremonial coronation are near completion; everything is in apple pie order, punctually ready for the commencement of the momentous occasion. Soul-stirring music wafts across the entire palace lulling the people into tranquility and ecstasy; but, alas, to Kaikeyi it is revolting; enraged, she brings her foot down heavily on the musicians.

People from all walks of life converge on the precincts of the palace. Functionaries like priests, erudite Brahmins well versed in the scriptures, scholars, saints and sages together with courtiers and other dignitaries wait outside the royal court yard. Citizens of all ages-boys youths, children, men, women and the aged all congregate on the pavements and parks, eagerly awaiting a glimpse of their beloved Raman to be led with his consort Sita in royal procession, in great sublimity, hallowed serenity and mystical magnificence by the royal entourage of functionaries, dignitaries, followers and guards to the place of ceremonies.

Meanwhile, the Chief Minister, Sumanthran, who has yet not seen the king even after very late hours, missing his presence, becomes timorously anxious and enters his apartment only to be unpleasantly surprised at finding King Dasarathar dispirited, downcast and in the depths overwhelmed by heavy grief. On humbly enquiring about his health from the Queen, she retorts that he is in a fragile condition, extremely sick a sequel to the sleepless night experienced by him, owing to his own deeds that have brought in its trail a series of repercussions.

King Dasarathar feebly requests for his principal steadying support, Raman, to be brought in. The Queen also orders the same demand.

Raman is peremptorily brought to the King's apartment with a sweet display of hushed panic and unruffled solicitude. He sees the King on the bed engulfed in deep despair. Too frail to envelop Raman in an embrace, the king attempts but fails. Filial affection, reverence and duty towards parents is exemplified, when he raises the king from the bed and takes him on to his own lap, throwing himself over him in delicate embrace. Vasishthar comes there anon. Attendants, assistants and servants shed copious tears on seeing the deplorable condition of their king and master.

Raman learns about the King's woebegone and infelicitous state of mind from Queen Kaikeyi as she throws light on the long forgotten favours promised by the king in the distant past and her demand for the fulfillment of the two benefactions gifting the throne of Ayodhya to her son Bharathan, to which the king has concurred, and the other, a matter of sharp contention and division between them, the cause for his present crisis, his own banishment from the country for fourteen years. She explicitly expresses also the King's reluctance and scruples about ventilating the fact to Him, Raman. She impinges upon Raman, and in the same breath, imposes on him the decree of exile, further adding that she looks forward to Him proving Himself a worthy son by making good his father's unexpressed command.

Needless to say, Raman is impervious to the treatment meted out by Queen Kaikeyi. In the interest of the King's uninterrupted happiness, peace of mind. He acquiesces even to desert Sita, forsake Mother Kausalya and also consume poison. He is even ready to go to the ends of the world out of consideration for the king's honour and equipoise which are at stake.

King Dasarathar is deeply anguished as he is knowledgeable about Raman, who so young, gentle tender and human, born in affluent circumstances and brought up in the lap of luxury, cannot cope with life and its perils that lurk in the forests. He is laboring under an overpowering feeling of injustice and grieves that he has brought discredit, humiliation and loss of prestige upon his kingship by his unjust gesture of banishing Raman, which has shaken the very base of regal justice. He is fully cognizant that it is a flagrant violation of the principal of natural justice. He cries his heart out, uttering he cannot live without Raman away in exile.

Raman's determined and unflagging high spirits help to keep the King's remorse at bay. He injects solace by assuring the king that He has to fulfill God's mission. Moreover, He stoutly advocates impressing upon the king, Bharathan's validity and genuiness, who is in no way inferior to ascend the throne and predicates that no line of distinction can be drawn between Bharathan and Himself, as they both are the one and the same self. Infallibly taking a resolute and irrevocable decision, He implores His father to emanate from the cloud of hesitation, and benevolently bless and grant Him permission to accomplish the haunting task He has undertaken to return peace to the Gods and the Humans alike.

Thus, promisingly consoling his father, Raman leaves him and presently reaches Queen Mother Kausalya's apartment only to find her absorbed in profound meditation. She is internally communing with God Vishnu, the effulgent consciousness and eternal dispenser, offering him worship and prayers in the temple of her heart for the welfare of her dearly beloved Raman. She is brought down from the ethereal plane to the plane of consciousness by Sumithra who intimates her of Raman's advent. A mother's solicitude throbs deep inside her; dotingly she takes Raman on to her lap and lovingly offers him a variety of delicacies for which he has not time to dally about.

Presently Raman apprises her of Kaikeyi's two stout arrogations made to King Darsarathar, one demanding that the throne be gifted to Bharathan and the other banishing Him to the forest for fourteen years. He persuades Mother Kausalya to concur, without disquietude, with his acceptance to venture into the forests, precisely, to lead a hermits life, luxuriating in the tranquillity that solitude offers and then return safely after the period of deportment has lapsed.

On hearing the painful, non-negotiable statements, the vulnerable Lady Kausalya in a whirl of disbelief, fades into a senseless state for a while. Distraught with a mind-numbing despair, her heartening conclusion is to accompany Raman and so pleads that she cannot, in his absence, live a life fraught with loneliness similar to the cow without her calf. She makes no point of claiming neither the King's throne nor his abundant wealth for the sake of Raman, but points out the King's overpowering strategy of injustice to banish impeccable Raman. Not for the world would she allow him on such a risky venture into the forests.

In the capacity and authority of her maternal kinship with Raman, Queen Kausalya extols the status of mother to be greater than father and even preceptor; and so Raman is commandingly forbidden from going to the forest, and if he happens to transgress her loving ordinance, she threatens to take to an irredeemable course of action-suicidal death.

In an equally characteristically impetuous manner, Lakshman who makes his presence felt, flares up giving vent to his simmering wrath, declaring that he would even enslave the king who is recklessly enamoured of Kaikeyi, and defies to kill Bharathan and his relatives on his mother's side. He seduces Raman to take the throne by force. He displays his mighty bow, the pride of his potency, which is to defend Raman against his enemies and by which he is to exhibit to the world his tremendous intrepidity capable of incineration of the whole globe to ashes. In this disturbed state of affairs, Raman, the quintessence of peace, a silent spectator to the violent outbursts, wraps his arms around Lakshman tenderly, acknowledging him as his immediate well-wisher, and a valiant one at that too, but cautions him that the present occasion now does not call for an ostentation of his valour and courage.

At this juncture Raman brings appeasement with his audiology, a simple out pouring of the soul, didactically, enunciating lofty, idealistic, visionary reflections.

At the outset, the grave message about the evanescent nature of man's life span which is very short lived is brought home with a striking instance of a drop of water vanishing no sooner than it drops on heated iron.

Even so, all variegated mundane pleasures, opulence, prosperity, kingdoms, and our perishable bodies too, are as short lived as lightning that flashes and dies out as quickly as it appears in the sky. Again, in conformity with a frog preying upon a fly, though, in turn, itself being caught by a snake in its mouth, man is ever in hot pursuit purist of materialistic objects and worldly pleasures which are transient, unmindful of the grim reality of death treading ever closely on his heels, waiting every moment to ensnare him in its tenacious clutches.

It is no exaggeration that the individual is puffed up to the maximum with pride and egoism at his unseemingly flimsy life, his insubstantial achievements, feats and successes, which fleeting, replete with incertitude, obscurities, virulent coincidences, difficulties and asymmetrical eventuations, sinking into vapidity, and made unbearably miserable by epidemics, diseases and poverty. As time rolls on with each passing day life ebbs away, the short span shrinking with every breath that is respired analogous to the dripping of water, drop by drop, when stored in an unbaked earthen pot.

Surprisingly, just as the moments of life trickle through the fingers like sand, man, impelled by the insatiable acquisitive thirst, spends all his energies, time and knowledge in entangling himself in materialistic pleasures and speculative businesses accumulating more and more of such evanescent objects. It should be understood that there is a subtle line of clarity distinguishing, separating the immortal self from its temporal gross body. All degrees of familial consanguinity such as father, mother, husband, wife, son, daughter etc., pertain to only the body and not to the soul. These pseudo-relations pseduorelations are as transitory as the sands accumulating on either side of the river bed and being washed away by every ebb and flow of the river water each moment. The soul is not affected by these relations; it is the only Reality, and is the Master of the body. Affluence is likened to water bubbles and carnal pleasures to a dream. Nescience makes a person falsely deduce that his material body, a composition of only flesh, bones, blood, skin, urine and other such stuff, which is doomed to perish and turned to ashes is his factual and perpetual form. He identifies himself as a doctor, engineer, king, teacher, clerk etc., only because his ignorance and conceit constitutes such a mockery.

The sole cause for man to take root in worldliness, spreading tentacles of bondage and attachment on ephemeral pleasures and objects, is his sheer fatuity to presume that he is only the body. Therefore the individual, discerning that knowledge of the soul is the only reality and the only edium for attaining salvation should seek it continuously.

Raman dissuades Lakshman from entertaining desires and nurturing anger as they pervert the mind from acquiring true knowledge. It behoves the individual to steer clear of anger, for a spark fo it is quite enough to trigger of a conflagration making the mind unstrung, robbning it of peace, and the choleric person does not hesitate to put an end to een persons he holds dear to his heart. Also, it stimulates the ego, disintegrates morality and conscience and enoneshes the individual in worldliness keeping his fettered to the earth, earth bound.

Lakshman is, therefore, exhorted to relinquish anger which is man's greatest adversary. The other undesired twin of anger is desire. Just as it is an uphill task to cross the infernal Baitarnni river, so too, it is an upstream stint to cross the ocean of desire. On the plane where mind is equally poised there contentment and peace reigns. Peace is collateral to the divine cow "Kamadhenu" that gratifies the petitions of men who are devoted and pious. Likewise, contentment is only a supplement like the garden of paradise filled with delicious fruits. If a person abides on the plane of placidity and tranquillity, he faces no affront or assault from any quarter of the world, much to say, he will possess no foes. Mind is overpowered by matter but cannot go beyond the limits of the body, and so is clearly distinct from the body; the material intellect and sense organs, seemingly superior, also fall apart as the soul, immanent, spotless, self illuminated, eternal, unchangeable and unformed is transparently individualistic. The miserable state that befalls man is due to his ignorance of the soul as Supreme Knowledge cannot be grasped to figure on the intellect's screen, nor can it be inspirational in nature. A concatenation of desires, which are a nagging aggravation and a disturbance, evolved from worldly bondage can be over mastered if the individual cognizes the reality. Consequently, peace will sink into their being, elevating them to the plane of desirelessness, maintaining an equable state and unexcitability towards happiness or misery, the effect of their past and present deeds. A steadfast sense of perceptivity disassociating the soul from the material body should be cherished. Sri Raman instructs Lakshman to channel his life into the Supreme abode of peaceful living disregardful of prosperity or indigence. He admonishes that it is depreciable and unmerited to flaunter his valour for instant gratification of selfish desire that causes him to crave for sensual satisfaction, possession and control, and therefore, to renounce the mean idea of capturing the kingdom by force.

Thus after the exposition of such deep pansophy, Raman prostrates at the feet of Mother Kausalya and prays to her to suffer his departure to the forests. Furthermore, he requests that these reflections be impressed upon her mind. Also, to anticipate his return with forbearance for a period of fourteen years that would pass away in a trice; such an attitude would not only please Him but dulicify His restive mind of anxiety about her. At last, Queen Kausalya relents and becomes pliant She dismantles her fears, indignation and foolishness. She picks up the loose threads of recipience, reconciliation, love, hope, cheerfulness and assurance with which she fabricates a cloak of benediction, enfolding Raman with it in her arms, with an invocation that all Gods Brahman, Vishnu and Shivan be with him, favour him, sustain him and take care of him in all his actions and in all places in the forests, and bids him adieu very affectionately.

Lakshman's dark ignorance has been dissipated by Raman; prudence dawns on him. He comprehends that rage makes one impotent often impeding future course of actions; he changes his former stand to use violence ignited by anger. And, extensively, inspired by Raman's ounce of down to earth philosophy his course of action is irrevocably taken, to follow Raman to the forests, and swears self-immolation if he declines to accede to his decision. It is fortunate for Lakshman to receive Raman's answer in the affirmative, instructing him to get ready at once, if he has set his heart upon it.

Eventually when Raman meets Sita in her apartment, She is unpleasantly surprised to find that matters are different from what she confidently imagined or expected. She is now in a state of painful suspense and impatient uncertainity waiting to learn what has gone awry with the uncertainty preparations for the scheduled coronation ceremony. Greatly alarmed, she shoots out a number of queries as to why He has not yet adorned himself with the royal ensign, royal robes, the scepter and the crown. She sees no procession of royal guests, nobles, feudal chiefs, ministers and attending officers and attendants waiting on him, all to accompany them to the place of ceremonies; she inquires about them all.

Resolutely calm, unruffled and unexcited, and, perhaps, with a tinge of humour, Raman acquaints her with his father's decree of crowning Him king of the forests and bestowing it as his kingdom. Consequently, he is to leave Ayodhya shortly and retire to the forest. In the meanwhile, until His return, He requests her to minister to and wait on her mother-in-law.

Unable to discern the hidden significance that is not outwardly obvious, Sita solicitously yet, apprehensively, questions why His father is so magnanimous in sending Him to the jungle. Raman recounts the chain of happenings in a cheerful and acquiescent spirit, and his encounter now, with her, being the culminating event that settles and ends the whole affair. He interprets his father's promise made very long ago to grant two boons to mother Kaikeyi. As a significant turning point, and more evidently, in fulfillment of the two boons and as injunctions claimed by mother Kalkeyi, father has granted the throne of Ayodhya to Bharathan, and has involuntarily banished Him for fourteen years. Raman, however, seeks her assurance that she would in no way inflict obstructions and thwart His intention of carrying out His father's promises. Longingly, Sita launches her next move with overtones of inseparation, invisible bond of fidelity etc., suggesting that it would not augur well if He went away alone to the forest without her and proposes that also she should accompany Him. It pleases Raman to hear this. But He expresses verbal concern about His inability to take Her with Him into the dreadful forests abounding with ferocious and treacherous wild animals, reptiles, insects and demons too. It is troublingly clear that she would have to negotiate with bonafide dangers, live life under precarious and extremely fragile conditions unavailability of food, even sour and wild fruits scarcely to be found and undergo untold hardships traversing thorny pathways, sheltering only in caves and ditches and harbouring the lingering fear of losing life. He persuades her with the only viable option of staying back at home.

Necessitating a fresh appraisal of the situation, Sita, sick at heart, with a shade of anger in her voice poses yet another question. She is anxious to know how Raman being a good-natured, gracious and pietistic husband should entertain the preconceived idea of leaving behind a devote and dutiful wife. She queries whether some defect of guilt or weakness of hers should be the cause for His detraction.

The undaunted Sita pronounces that a life for her away from Him will be totally disintegrated and wholly miserable and not happy and peaceful. She infuses confidence in Him saying she can confront and cope with any difficult situation or hardship, as He, Raman, is her sheet-anchor, adding that even a mountain will turn into a molehill by his Grace. Further, the remnants of food left by Him will serve as nectarine food, sufficing as a sumptuous meal. She obligates to be helpful in some way, and not be a thorn in the flesh, even in a minuscule way, thus assisting him in discharging His mission assigned by God as presaged by an erudite astromancer; the heart is where the treasure is and she so chooses to die instantly if Raman does not relent.

Finally, in consonance with her wishes Raman softens his stand but eggs her on to distribute in charity her wealth and all her jewellery to the Brahmins and to Arundhathi, the preceptor's wife, to abandon royal life and its regal splendour and prepare to start the same day.

In the same vein, Raman pleasingly offers his wealth and riches to the Brahmins and servants and gets ready to take leave of His father and soon embark on His mission to the forest. Lakshman's action conforms to that of Raman's, giving away his belongings and wealth, and entrusts his mother Sumithra into the custody of Queen Kausalya.

Raman, the quintessence of Beauty, looking extensively glorious and resplendent as the expansive azure sky, treads his way, radiating all the directions, to his father's palace with Sita and Lakshman following close on his heels. Meanwhile the whole populace of the kingdom is grief-stricken, curiously, watching Raman as He cleanses and sanctifies the earth, His feet acting as the purifying agent, leaving behind foot prints of humility, renunciation, obedience, love and peace on the sands of time to be emulated universally.

Chapter - III

Raman's Departure to the Forest

News of Raman's deportment diffuses throughout the Kingdom. The grief-stricken citizens take to the streets; they gravitate towards the royal palace. Chaos and confusion prevail everywhere giving way to agitation. The tumultuous mob murmur, whimper and remonstrate against the injustice meted out to the royal couple. Prompted by love, respect and honour, that Raman commands, the people on seeing Him with Sita and Lakshman, make overtures to follow them to the jungle as they prefer not to live in Ayodhya, a sad testimony of desecration without Raman. They target their impassioned sentiments of ire, censure and abuse at Dasarathar and Kaikeyi for their inclement, impertinent coupde main.

In the interim, Sage Bama Deva addresses the turbulent crowd. He tries to narrow down their resentment by making them listen to reason. He expounds that Lord Vishnu, in the ancient past, under pressing circumstances had assumed a number of forms. Highlighting the ten far-famed manifestations to save humanity from the clutches of evil, Sage Bama Deva now acquaints the people of Lord Vishnu's power of yogamaya known as illusion. He adds, by this yogamaya, Lord Vishnu has willed himself to be born as Raman to venture into the forest for fulfilling the grave mission of exterminating diabolic Ravanan and his clan of demons who exasperate and torment the people, sages, saints and gods. It is also stated that Raman confided to Sage Narathar about His objective of going to the forests, when the latter had met him furtively.

Furthermore, Sage Bama Deva clarifies their misconceived illation about Dasarathar and Kaikeyi being blamed for manoeuvering Raman's ostracism by widely explaining that they too being overshadowed by yoga Maya were made to act in the manner they did under its influence.

Sage Bama Deva persuades them into believing the truth that no amount of sorrow or pain or trouble would affect Raman as he is really the Almighty

God. So to attribute personality to God in the sense in which we use the word in common parlance is childishly anthropomorphic and egotistic. Just the chanting of His name always, and loving Him and realising Him to be the incarnation of Lord Vishnu would make the chanter blissfully pious and peaceful. Even great sinners are cleansed by uttering His holy name.

Now focusing on Raman and Sita and Lakshman, they are in the presence of kaikeyi in her royal apartment. The natural proclivity of staying out of dangerous emotional waters makes Raman, with noiseless gracefulness, compatibility and modesty verbally inform mother Kaikeyi of their immediate departure from the Kingdom. Right-away, Kaikeyi prescribes the clothes they have to change into. Promptly, Raman and Lakshman disrobe their royal attire and clothe themselves with barks of trees afforded to them, Raman, makes the transition from Price to hermit easily in a manner which draws no attention to His regal background. The same mode of dress is ordained to Sita which is stymied by Vashisthar who confronts Kaikeyi, saying, she has no authority to banish Sita, for Sita is following Raman to the forests as a dutiful wife and therefore, she, Kaikeyi has no moral right to order barks for her.

Impressively, household women in their quarters are moved to tears at the heart-rending sight and with un feigned sorrow bid adieu to Devi Sita.

King Dasarathar is cut to the quick. His mental and emotional life as well is agonizingly devoured by deep and continuous grief. Notwithstanding this, he directs the minister Sumanthran to convey Raman to the forest by the grand imperial chariot. Ere long, Raman, Lakshman and Sita leave the palace and set off on their journey. In double quick time they are out of the bounds of Ayodhya with all the males, both young and old and even boys doggedly running after the vehicle to follow Raman and be with Him whereever He goes. That day they all reach the banks of Tamasa river.

Back at the palace in Ayodhya, Dasarather's grief escalates quantitatively since the exodus of Raman. The Monarch is entangled in a series of mixed emotions. He is now desirous of seeing Lady Kausalya; he wishes to make amends. Once inside Queen Kausalya's apartment, he is totally helpless on account of his grave afflictions and unsoundness, falling into a fainting fit, senseless, and unable to ambulate or even speak.

Meanwhile, virtuous Raman and Sita are escorted everywhere by Lakshrnan with his bow. Though without a morsel to eat they are still cheerful and doss down for the night beneath a tree with Lakshman safe guarding them. Raman and company decamp from the place early in the morning, hastily driven by Sumanthran towards the forest inorder to evade the sleeping citizens who are persistent in following Him.

The invisible bond of friendship is apparent when, Guhan, a very intimate friend of Raman, comes running with unbounded jubilance and enthusiasm to receive Raman, his friend and gracious master, at Sringaberpur his own kingdom. An inspiring illustration of true friendship is visible as Guhan offers gifts and delicious wild fruits. On the other hand, Raman, disinterestedly, lavishes embraces on his host friend.

Raman is a hermit to the core. He stringently adheres to the codes of hermits' life. As it is unconventional of hermits, He declines to partake of fruits offered by Guhan brought from the villages and cities. Again, using the juice of the 'Batha' tree he twists his tresses making a tuft on the crown of his head.

Guhan acknowledgingly accentuates the status of Raman as the Lord paramount scion of the Raghu race. With hearty pleasure he expresses that this meeting with and greeting him is the most opportune chance in his life. Most humbly he requests Raman to live on in his kingdom, which is but wholly His as He is the lord of the Universe, that everything he has and possesses is His, as He, Raman, is the creator of all that is in the universe, and then, to go with him into the city and sanctify his house there.

He complaisantly offers himself as a humble and obedient servant always at his service. Raman, in the capacity of an anchorite, expresses His inability to comply with all his requests, but assures Him of His friendship. Gradually, a blanket of darkness spreads over Sringaberpur.

They all spend the night only drinking pure water of the clear stream. Necessarily, Raman with Sita slumbers on a bed of Kusha grass which serves as a mattress for them, already improvised by Lakshman for the comfort of his adorable brother Raman and Goddess Sita. Meanwhile Lakshman is voluntarily awake keeping vigil over them all through the night.

Chapter - IV

Raman Meets Valmiki

Tearfully heavy-hearted at the sight of Raman and Sita slumbering on the grassy earth, while the gorgeous beds lie vacant in the palace, Guhan complains to Lakshman castigating providence as being the absolute entity in a man's life. Raman and Sita, the glorious royal couple, born in the lap of luxury should endure such misfortune is really the machination of queen Kaikeyi who has undeniably brought sin upon herself, egged on by Manthra.

Lakshman does not authenticate Guhan's statements, instead enlightens him with a rational explanation of the causes of misery or happiness. No alien force or person is responsible or blamed for a man's tribulations and disasters. It is his destiny that determines his life. Every individual is born under a distinctive set of circumstances; the set of circumstances which beset an individual's birth and life, is to be regarded as the result which originates from his own deeds of previous lives. Happiness is not a boon and misery is not a curse. Both are the natural and inevitable consequences of one's action in his course of life. Every action has a reaction. Hence no connotation should be attached to his life as being either prosperous or miserable. It is a foregone conclusion that man's life oscillates between happiness and misery.

It should not be erroneously understood that no one ever lives either happily or miserably for his whole life through. In the same vein a man's friends, foes or mediation are determined according to the appropriate result of his good or bad deeds of the past. In other words, reward and penalty are the inescapable consequences when they are deserved. So it should be rightly understood that it is utterly futile to be elated and intoxicated with pride at his prosperity or be nonplused and disconsolate at his woes.

A close scrutiny or introspection throws light upon the truth that misery is an admixture of happiness, and likewise, in happiness there is hidden a shade of misery. The two concepts are inseparable, a compound always mixed, similar to mud. Anyway, and individual has got to live his life though his life be affluent or impecunious. Lakshman advocates equanimity of mind both in success and failure, in opulence and indigence. Only if the individual is insouciant and abandons attachment he can be unperturbed in any condition of life. It is a certitude that he cannot find peace, but only loses it, if he lusts after happiness which is short-lived. Again, peace will remain with him only if he is not disconcerted in times of adversity. Conclusively, in this short journey of life, the interplay of sorrow and joy, fruition and disappointment and prosperity and adversity are but a natural phenomenon like the dawns and sunsets.

Even the dappled dawn does not yet put an end to the conversation between Lakshman and Guhan. But daybreak very gently awakens Raman and Sita. Guhan, with mixed feelings, gets ready a boat at Raman's request. In the intervening time Raman and Sita perform their morning rites. A lovely sturdy boat is brought and Guhan himself paddles carrying them all across the river quite safely, guarding them from all harm. Sita's instinctive reflexes sharpen when they reach midway of the Ganges. She communes with Mother Ganges asseverating that she would ritualistically and fervidly worship her if she would return with Raman and Lakshman safely from the forests.

The boat cruises along calmly and they reach the opposite embankments of the river. But Guhan is uncheerful and reluctant to leave Raman and Sita. He is far out of his comfort zone and implores Raman to take him with him or else, he would speculate on instant death. Compassionate Raman's reliable words that he would make a comeback after fourteen years of his extradition fleets away does in no way console Guhan. But, with a sagging heart he involuntarily bids farewell to Raman repeatedly embracing him. Later, the news of Raman's arrival at Sage Bharathwaja's hermitage, together with Sita and Lakshman, is communicated to the sage by a Brahmin boy.

The sage, whose heart is filled with immense joy welcomes and greets Raman, Sita and Lakshman respectfully adhering to all formalities, conventions and suavities. Sage Bharathwaja acknowledges to Raman that with his visit the penances that he has undertaken all these years have attained consummation. For though he is having prior knowledge of Vishnu's incarnation on earth, he is now fortunate to see the Supreme God in human form as Lord Raman, who has descended to obliterate Ravanan and his devilish clan. He also reveals that this was the request of Brahman the creator and this be the reason for his going to the forests. He expresses Raman's positive triumph over the demons for the good of humanity on earth. The sage verbally acknowledges that it is only by Raman's grace he is able to know the past, present and future of events. He is confident that all will go well according to the wishes of Sri Raman.

Despite his grand stature, Raman implores the graceful blessings of Sage Bharathwaj as any ordinary human would, and also reciprocates the homage paid to him in a humble way. The hermitage provides a safe refuge for the night. On the morn of the next day, Raman with Sita and Lakshman get set to cross the Yamuna. They arrive in Chitrakutha and proceed towards Sage Valmiki's hermitage, a delightfully sylvan place abounding with flora and fauna and luscious fruits.

Setting eyes on comely Raman, the fascinated Sage Valmiki gauges the resplendency of Raman in the garb of a hermit with twisted tufts of hair on the crest of his head. Raman is the subject of all attention. The sage's spontaneous overflow of rhapsody finds expression in his eyes welling up with tears to the brim as he embraces Raman. In an euphoric mood of worship he tenders delicious fruits to Raman and also entertains him.

Raman's humbleness becomes tangible to the sage, when with folded hands Raman requests him to direct Him to some suitable place of stay to pass sometime with Sita and Lakshman. Raman who acknowledges that the sage has prescient knowledge of the reason of their venture into the forest, just informs him that he is doing so inorder to fulfill His father's orders.

By this luminous exposition the Knowledgeable sage endorses Raman as the Universal Soul dwelling in all creatures of the world, they in him, and the entire creation to be His own right royal residence. His exceptional homes and temples, abiding in unison with Sri Sita Devi. His Divine consort, are the hearts of devotees dedicated with unalloyed love to Him alone, meditating on him every day and whose hearts are peaceful and free from vanity. Equanimity of minds, discrimination between real and unreal, detached attachment to worldliness and the consistent practice of penances are the qualities of a true devotee whose pure mind is anchored in Him forever. The sage proceeds to enumerate the true qualities of genuine devotees as being devoid of temptation and avarice, non-malignance, ambivalence, self-denial, renunciation, aspiration and meditation and being amicable and content. Those who cognize Raman to be immutable, immaculate, omniscient, omnipotent and omnipresent their pure hearts are the vibrant abode of Sri Raman as well as Sri Sita.

The sage unravels the mystical significance and degree of excellence he has gained by the chanting of Raman's hallowed name and glory.

He openly acknowledges that it truly enhances the quality of one's mundane existence too. He confesses to the all-knowing Sri Raman, that it was by the virtue of ceaselessly chanting and meditating on His holy name that a stunning evolution from a vile highway robber to a pedigree sage has taken place.

He ventilates how in the heydays of his youth, though born into the estate of a Brahmin, he had married a woman of low caste, associated with kiratas, a forest tribe and took to the base occupation of pillage. He was so brazen that he roamed about as a marauding plunderer, well armed, inorder to make his living and support his big family at the cost of robbing the life and property of others.

He goes on to relate a cathartic experience, when he happened to meet seven men whom he had decided to waylay. The seven men happened to be divine sages who were inciting him to a confrontation with his own sinful life. Knowing his ulterior motive to rob them they prodded him to gain an appropriate perspective of a new life by asking him to enquire from his wife and sons whether anyone of them was a partner to the nefarious crimes committed by him for their sustention. It was an unappetising reply in the negative, that they, enjoyed only his toil and labour and shared the fruits but had no concern for how and what he did for them. Overloaded by dejected sensations and emotions his mind seemed to blow a fuse; feeling hollow and dissatisfied, shame and guilt battle courage and love and instantly abandoning all his weapons, falls at the feet of the sages for his redemption. By this association with the saints a transformation by overcoming of the lower nature and a self-centered existence to an altruistic mode of life takes place; his heart is cleansed and made pure.

He discloses to Sri Raman how the sages were pleased to dismantle his illusive world piece by piece by their humane advice. He also reveals how they had given Him his name 'Rama', to be chanted in the reverse or opposite way 'Mara', ascertaining him to be a great sinner unworthy of chanting His holy name. Still the manthra echoes in his heart like the clear ringing of a bell.

He proceeds to relate that from the moment he had been initiated into chanting his holy name, he very earnestly and very soon found himself immersed in deep contemplation. He had made the manthra his article of faith, and had built on it, constantly pronouncing it and rising to the plane of bodily inexistence. Then came surreal moments. The ceaseless repetition of the 'Rama' manthra invaded and conquered his whole life that he remained in this condition for years together. Even then, he so doggedly pursed recitation of the manthra that his body was covered with the clay, accumulated over the years, by white ants. The cumulative effect of manthra chanting, over innumerable decades and centuries, again invited the seven sages, brilliant as the rising sun appearing out of the dark clouds, proving that the self that can acquiesce in its over degeneration can also reconstruct itself by effort. Such penances, when the divine sages got him out of the clay mould under which he was enveloped, deeply immersed in meditation, traces the opening of a transcendental possibility of being, a higher nature within the realm of ordinary human experience. Consequently, seeing that he had emerged out of the ant hill with a lofty form of the most exalted sage they christened him Valmiki. Thereafter, the sages disappeared into their celestial abode. And now sage Valmiki perfectly absolved of all sins, past and present, in an ecstatic mood visions Sri Raman Vis-a-Vis. He is a true paradigm to manifest the self that can concur in its own decadence and can also regenerate itself by effort. Offering due obeisance to Lord Sri Raman, the sage followed by his disciples takes Lakshman to an idyllic and shady strip of a riparian habitat by the Mandakini. Two cottages are set up, one stretching form east to west, the other form north to south.

Lakshman occupies a cottage; while Raman, who lives with Sita as merrily as Indhran with Sachi, lives very comfortably in the other. A remarkably and highly cherisable addition to their already prevailing peaceful and joyful life is the association Valmiki and the other residence have with Lord Raman and Devi Sita.

Chapter - V

The Demise of King Dasarathar

As dusk is gradually and silently cloaking the city of Ayodhya, Sumanthran duly returns to Ayodhya in his vacant chariot, after having set about undertaking the important but painful task of bearing Raman, Sita and Lakshman to their fate of banishment to the forests.

His healthy loyalty directly leads him straight away to visit the languishing Dasarathar, who is in an abject and reckless mood, to pay his respects to him.

The cumulative effect of all the grief sends the king raving as soon as he sets eyes on Sumanthran, calling upon the name of Raman repeatedly and uttering the names of Sita and Lakshman every now and then, he anxiously enquires about their whereabouts and welfare. Expectantly, he questions whether they have sent any message for him. He calls himself an accursed sinner and berates his own insensible action of driving the trio to banishment. Presuming to feel the tangible presence of Sita, he hails her as ocean of virtues, as the most truthful lady, and laments profusely, questioning if she too does not feel pity for him who is sinking as he is in the ocean of deep sorrow.

The grief-stricken king with necessitous sanity listens to Sumanthran as he reports details of his concluded task. He says he had taken them in his chariot upto Sringaberpur by the side of the Ganges where king Nishada, Guhan, had met and extended a warm hospitality to Raman to the best of his resourcefulness and status, to which Raman responded with gramercy He relates how they rested in the shade of a tree and twisted their hair with Botha Juice and knotted the same on the crest of their heads.

It is now that Sumanthran tries to ease Dasarathar's painful mind and moments. He informs the king of Raman's plea not to worry about Him, as He is quite happy and content as He was and would be in Ayodhya if He were present there. He conveys Raman's deference and homage to be paid to His mothers. Again, he conveys Raman's request to His mothers to take good care of His aged and wearied father and not to be distressed and disturbed about Him any longer.

Sumanthran further supplements his verbalization with Sita's humble entreaty to convey her due respects to her mother-in-law and, goes on to describe the unassertive manner-coyily blushing and looking up to the countenance of Raman alone and then gently bowing her head and walking away modestly in which she conveyed the message and the copious tears she shed. Finally, Sumanthran winds up his reporting by informing the king that he had seen Guhan ferrying the trio safely across the river and also disembarking, safe and sound, on the other bank of the river.

Queen Kausalya dissolving in tears and drawing on her reserves of fortitude and endurance cracks her code of long silence. She indulges in a tirade against King Dasarathar accusing him of hastily banishing innocent and noble Raman and now repenting in vain at leisure. She impeaches him that by gifting the throne to Kaikey's son Bharathan he has satisfied his over- riding selfish ends-fulfilling his promised boons to his amorous queen Kalkeyi without weighing Raman's authentic and legal ascension to the throne there by causing a permanent prostitution of the senses and spirit.

Cut to the quick by her speech, the King falls into a gaping abyss of anguish. Undoubtedly he is plagued with a foreboding sense of sinking into the bottomless pit of death. A tone of self-pity over shadows his loud wail to stop the vituperation as it is now, needless, because he is standing at death's door.

King Dasarathar journeys backward in time to the early years of his life and unbosoms the cause, the embryonic seed of his present grief stricken condition. A sage had once embittered the quality of his life with an imprecation, that he should in the evening of his life, with great lamentation and mental agony, die of heartbreak at his son's separation.

He narrates that in the prime of his youth he had a lust for hunting wild beasts. On one such expedition, he roamed the forests at night in search of some hunt when he heard sounds by the side of a river. He was of the belief that some elephant was slurping up water. Deceived by it, he instantly shot an arrow in that direction in the darkness. His deception was masked with an inequitable cruelty. The arrow had directly hit a sage boy who was filling his water pot by the riverside. The lad was writhing in great pain and he was, virtually, about to die when he reached him. The king not jolted out of rationalization despite his benumbed senses, submitted meekly, and apologetically begged pardon of him. The sage-lad laid bare his identity as Viasiya, and claimed that the arrow be pulled out from his organic being. He incorporated another claim to take the pot full of water to his parents who were aged and denied of eyesight, and have become frail due to a parched tongue, in a cottage at some distance.

Dasarathar hesitates to decry the lad's requisition as he saw foresaw a burning curse that would befall him. He was apprehensive of the incalculable damage the resultant situation would bring. He approached the boy's aged parents, who were great saints, to conciliate them. They were feverishly anticipating their son's return, when Dasarathar brought the mournful news of his death. They learnt that he had killed their precious son due to his inadvertent blunder, and were terribly hurt to the core of their being. Totally at their mercy, the king begged pardon. They were perturbed to know he was the king Dasarathar unbottling details of the fatal mishap. Since they had urged him, he took them to the site where they grappled the dead frame, and being greatly afflicted bemoaned the death of their precious son. The blind old sage, whose despair was transparent and whose rage suicidal, spat out the curse that he, Dasarathar, would face the same fate as himself; he would meet with no other sorrow but die in dire grief at the separation of his son. Eventually, the grand old couple had thrown themselves into the same burning funeral pyre hastily made by Dasrathar as a mark of respect for their dead son, and burnt themselves too.

Now, King Dasarathar is grasping at the threads of his aged life. After the lengthy effort at vocalization which seemed to sap the last gasps of his energy, the languid and pathetic king augurs his end, according to the sage's curse, connected with the boons promised to Kaikeyi. In utter finality, he cries out the names of Raman, Sita and Lakshman and forthwith gives up his spirit.

This heart-rending tragedy unfolds itself as the pangs of death play havoc on Kausalya and Sumithrai; extreme grief manifests itself, outwardly, by beating of breasts; thus, they wail and weep uncontrollably mourning his death.

Though time seems to slow down in a crisis, the sun comes up on another new morn that sets in motion painful preparations for the obsequies. Sage Vashisthrar arrives at the palace at the designated time. He visits the harem where the king's body lies in state, consoles and alleviates the sorrow and anguish that has plagued and wrecked the queens. He first prescribes the body to be embalmed in beautiful scented oil. The sage's emissary carried by horse riders with the message asking Bharathan and Sathrughnan to immediately reach Ayodhya is sent to Yudhajit's Kingdom.

With a heady rush of desperation and greater anxiety that some calamity or disaster has eventuated in Ayodhya, perplexed Bharathan and Sathrughan return as expeditiously as they can with the followers. When he borders on the outskirts of the city, he observes to his utter astonishment Ayodhya very desolate, bathed in gloom. He heads straight away to his mother kaikeyi's apartment. Surprisingly, Bharathan finds his mother in solitude without dear father and questions her on his absence.

Meanwhile, Kaikeyi turns a cold shoulder to such a poignant situation and neglects to assume even a fake posture of mourning. Instead, with unfeigned delight, she welcomes Bharathan affectionately, showers blessings on him and enquires about His parents' health and welfare. Inorder to break the news of his father's death, she designs her words in an improper fashion to incinerate she is blameless. Unscrupulously she says his father has taken, in good time, the same course that all pious kings who having performed Aswamedhas have to follow. Like a tree that is felled, Bharathan falls to the ground. He is rueful his father has passed away so suddenly even without entrusting him to the care of Raman. He questions whether the king has left any instruction for him.

Kaikeyi raises upweeping Bharathan who according to her is a sinless and dutiful son. Fearlessly, she informs him that his father died with only the names of Raman, Sita and Lakshman on his lips. At this Bharathan is caught up in a frenzy of sorrow and disquiet. Precariously, Kaikevi tries to placate him and deplete his heavily burdened heart. But in doing so she coaxes him into believing he is the most fortunate of sons as she has made all arrangements for his seductive prosperity. Regardless of what she is saying, Bharathan interjects a question about the whereabouts of the presence or absence of Sita, Raman and Lakshman at his bedside at the moment of his father's death.

At this juncture, Kaikeyi reveals to Bharathan how when the King was making preparations for the celebration of Raman's coronation, she snatched it as the most opportune moment to launch her audacious wager for the throne for him, Bharathan, and the life of a hermit in exile in the forests for fourteen years to Raman. This, was demanded in accordance with the two boons promised by king Dasarathar to he long ago. It is thus, in fulfilment of her immediate pressing demand, he, Bharathan, has come to inherit the glorious throne. She affirms Raman's punctiliousness in carrying out his father's injunction by venturing into the forest, followed by his chaste Sita and obedient Lakshman, and the consequent untimely death of the King due to extreme tomentation, guilt and mainly Raman's separation.

On hearing such shoking revelations, Bharathan keels over to the ground senseless like a tree syruck with a thunderbolt. Subsequently when he returns to from and Kaikeyi tries to assuage and pacify him, he surmises that in however sophisticated a fashion his queen mother may have masked her words, yet, they are brute expressions of her insidious nature which revels in power and domination. He wrihes in acute agony caused by the thought that it was for his sake Kaikeyi has committed the rave crime of banished Raman to the wilderness. Bharathan censures Kaikeyi for doing the most vile act that has resulted in the death of his beloved father, Dasarather. He, jolted into a rude awakening, considers himself sinful for having been born of such a sinful and repulsive woman who shall definitely meet with hell for killing her own husband. He is gone far out of his comfort zone that he speculates on ways he could die, either by buring or by consuming poison.

Giving ent to his explosive temper, Bharathan storms out of Kaikeyi's apartment and presently traces his steps to Queen Kauslaya's chamber. He finds Raman's celebrated, adorable and elegant mother so woebegone, sunk in the gloom of sorrow and made vulnerable by agony and despair.

In surprised silence but, with unfeigned delight written on her countenance, Lady Kausalya receives Bharathan into her arms. Unable to contain despair any longer, she loudly laments the separation of Raman, Sita and Lakshman, and their mode of living as hermits in the forest that has plunged her in the ocean of misery. In her hear she believes Raman to be the Supreme God. Yet, the human mind overwhelms her with grea affection and pain. Being incapacitated and also dependent, Queen Kausalya blames into being its own series of consequences and passes it into the Kaleidoscopic pattern of life.

Lady Kausalya's words, pregnant with meaning, hits innocent Bharathan lide a dart. Immediately going down on hi knees, he to, her feet and swearing upon his preceptor and his wife Arundhathi, pleads that he had no hand in banishing Raman from the Kingdom inorder to succedd to the throne. Kausalya's warm affection and tender emrace makes Bharathan see the right perspective, that he is unimpeachable. The apprehensions and doubts registered on his mind pass into oblivion. He surrenders to her without reserve of boundless confidence and affection.

There is an Induced need on the Part of Sage Vashisthar for dialoguing with Bharathan. Then in company with the councilors, the Sage fondly persuades him to comprehend the inexpediency on mourning for his dead father. He points out the futility of being buried in such deep anguish about the loss of his father. He unfolds the manifold good the king has accrued due to the many Aswamedhas he has performed. He has become very aged, is renowned across the length and breadth of the globe as a truthful and valiant king, has begotten Raman the Supreme God as his son and now, by his death he has attained equal status with Indhran in heaven. He divulges the truth that his father has now attained emancipation from the slavery of fleshy concerns, the thirst of the appetites and the poison of thwarted desires, and is very happy now. Further, the sage nourishes Bharathan with more conventional wisdom. In effect, he declares the Immortality of the soul. It has no birth nor death. The soul is every joyful, content, self-illuminating, enlightened immutable, infinite, without modifications and the prototype of the Supreme Lord. The soul is sue generis and immanent.

Hence the soul should be known. It is only by transcending the body can the individual focus shift on subtler levels of consciousness and realize the soul. The soul changes the body just as a person changes his dress. Therefore, the inferential conclusion is to dissuade men from grieving the death of any man, more so, their near and dear ones, as there is no ground for such strong harmful emotions to be experienced. It is only infatuations with the body with which an individual identifies himself that lies at the root of his ignorance. Again, it is only the material or gross body that perishes and it is only ignorance which exhibits such deep anguish at the passing away of family members, friends and such like. The wise develop detachment for the body and its afflictions, know that body is bound to annihilation with transmigration of life and death according to the merits and demerits of one's past actions. In as much, the sage concludes that knowledge of soul is the only real, tangible existence and that he, Bharathan, should pass his life peacefully, performing his duties at all cost.

Enlightening Bharathan on the transience of life, the emptiness and senselessness of grieving, sage Vashisthar thereafter directs him to remove his father's corpse from the oil tub, and with assistance from the ministers and with the sage's guidance, performs the funeral rites. Bharathan well advised completes all rituals according to Vedic liturgy, distributing benefits in cash and kind to Brahmins for the well being of his father's soul.

After a short span of stay, Bharathan, together with his brother Sathrughnan, feels ill-at-case to reside with family in Ayodhya; for, to him Ayodhya without Raman is a mute reminder of a wilderness. An unwavering resolve to meet Raman as early as possible in the forest crystallizes in his mind, as it is his top most priority to be able to render humble services to Sita and Raman, who with smiling countenances and auspicious appearance are his star celebrities. Moreover, his intention to evade the presence and company of his mendacious and fiendish mother Kaikeyi powerfully invades his mind.

Chapter - VI

Bharathan's Departure to bring Raman Back

Sage Vasishthar holds council with the ministers, learned persons and saints to deliberate on the installation of an heir to succeed King Dasarathar. They arrive at a general consensus, as the same thought crystallizes in the minds of others, and inform Bharathan that they are increasingly convinced to coronate him as the king, the very same day, in accordance with the wishes and orders of his late father, as he, Dasarathar, ultimately, fulfills his promise of the two boons to Kaikevi.

Politely addressing the great and honourable sage, Bharathan strikes a discordant note by refusing to accept the kingship. It is futile to accept, since Raman, the king of kings, who is the rightful successor, abides in the forest. He acknowledges himself and others to be mere slaves of Raman. His doleful yearning makes him resolved to take a gutsy chance into the forest and seek Raman out. It is his heart lived desire to bring Raman back to Ayodhya. He thinks aloud, that it would be an auspicious adventure to have the queen mothers, except Kaikeyi the fiendish woman, masquerading as mother, to accompany him to seek Raman in the forest and persuade him to return to Ayodhya. Bharathan is of the mind to slay Kaikeyi; however, he cannot afford the reckless luxury of allowing erratic emotions to get the better of righteous fear, the predominant alarming fear that Raman will not pardon him for such a heinous crime of killing a woman.

Bharathan avows to embark on his ordeal, despite the hazards lurking in a hermit's life in the forest, even if it demands risks like having to wear barks, he on sordid ground and eat only wild fruits which are all consistent with Raman's life. He ruminates that all these persistent hardships undergone by him will soften Raman's heart, to prevail upon him to make a come back to Ayodhya.

Bharathan's resolution is exactly appetising to the whole assembly gathered there, and all including Vasishthar, are in full admiration and appreciation of his lofty sentiments, his scrupulousness and his resolute fidelity to Raman. They are highly proud he has rejected a kingdom that has come to him unsolicited for the sake of his dear brother.

The next morning, Bharathan galvanizes into action taking out the four components of the army. Sathrughnan leads the army in proud array with the Queen mothers, Sage Vasishthar, Sumanthran, Priests and Brahmins following closely. The citizens of Ayodhya converge from different directions onto the main road and pathways and follow the royal troop with overflowing enthusiasm and fervour.

Bharathan and Sathrughnan wearing barks, with binding tufts of hair on the crest of their heads walk the extra miles on foot with others following and reach the banks of the river Ganges in Sringaberpur where they come to a grinding halt.

Guhan who learns of Bharathan's arrival is panic stricken; doubt and suspicion loom large over him; he at first suspects Bharathan's bonafides and thinks that Bharathan not being content with having driven Raman away from Ayodhya should carry his animus further and come on a man hunt to the forest, to either capture him or even slay him. He is casting about in desperation for the real reason for Bharathan's arrival. He considers it his right and moral duty to safeguard and protect Raman and so speculates on a crusade against Bharathan, if his intention to see Raman is painfully unwarranted, and force him to retreat; if otherwise, he would allow him to proceed further.

Inorder to get at the root of resisting Bharathan and his huge army, Guhan, as a precautionary measure orchestrates his boatmen to collect all the boats on the middle of the river and orders them to get ready with bows and arrows to await any eventuality that might ensue. Guhan's anxiety is tempered with excitement as he goes to meet Bharathan. But his heart is back in alignment on seeing Bharathan, contrary to his expectations, a replica of Raman, and a picture of grief. The cheerless face and the ascetic robes of Bharathan, convince Guhan that his presumptions were wrong. He is sorry for his hasty conclusions, for, what he sees is Bharathan sitting with Queen Mothers and Sathrughnan on one side and the councillors and the sage on the other chanting the name 'Rama' is symptomatic of Bharathan's profound devotion to Sri Raman. His joy and excitement ignite; presenting the scrumptious fruits and gift articles he has brought, he respectfully prostrates on the ground and pays homage to Bharathan.

A worldwide brotherhood is seen when Bharathan tenderly raises Guhan, addresses him as brother and with the same fraternal affection queries about his well being. He verbally recognizes Guhan as being really blessed and fortunate to have set eyes on Sri Raman, the erudite Ruler, together with Sita and Lakshman and, also, to have earned his approbation and grace by way of his kind embraces and sweet fruitful talk. He requests Guhan if, he would choose to show him and also take him to the locus where lotus eyed Raman had rested for the night and conversed with him before.

Bharathan's eyes misting over sees the piece of evidence the Khusa grass upon which Raman had slept. Through his tears of love, he sees shreds of gold embroidery threads from Sita's dress, a few pieces of her ornaments lying scattered there. He laments that the self-esteem of Sita, the beloved daughter of King Janahar, has suffered a cruel blow by condescending to sleep on the grass, for she has been born into privilege and is wont to slumber on gorgeously decorated bedsteads. He is consumed with a sense of guilt, surmising that his sinful self is the cause for her enduring such affliction. He calculates that Lakshman is happier and luckier to be with Raman, though in the forest. His own unspoken yearning to be with Raman surfaces in his outpouring, which expresses his fortunate desire to be even a slave of the slaves of Raman's devotees.

Guhan on seeing Bharathan cherishing and nurturing a deep throbbing love for Raman endorses him as a blessed soul. Bharathan's insatiable appetite to meet Raman is quelled as Guhan heartily acquaints him of Raman's riparian habitat the banks of the river Mandakini in Chitrakutha, and dwelling very cheerfully with Sita and Lakshman. With alacrity, he invites to take them there. At his orders, about five hundred boats are at their disposal to ferry the army and others across the Ganges. He takes upon himself the intensive task of rowing the royal boat carrying Bharathan, Sathrughnan, Kausalya and sage Vashisthar.

On landing, Bharathan and Sathrughnan instantly make it to Sage Bharathwaj's hermitage tucked away in the forested folds. The sage, who seems to them as brilliant as fire, is enthused by the advent of King Dasaratharar's sons, gleefully welcomes them and entertains them with due respect. After inquires about their health he switches over to the question, zeroing in on their being clad in barks and seeking reclusories instead of reigning over the country.

At this point, Bharathan's eyes do not hesitate to shed an endless stream of tears. He lauds the sage as an omniscient being who can read into the motivational vein of his unfeigned deception, attired as a hermit and coming to live as a recluse. He confesses that the mighty kingdom is worthless, trivial to him while Raman is spending his days in the forest. He swears upon the holy sage that he had no hand in Kaikyei's nefarious designs. Sathrughnan and their followers get scent of Raman's presence by tailing the bark dresses of Raman hanging upon the walls of the hermitage.

Chapter - VII

Bharathan Meets Raman in the Forest

A totally random landscape ensconced in the ruffles of the rugged forest is transformed into an idyllic habitation, which nestles the humble but pleasant cottage of Sri Raman.

The vicinity around the cottage is saturated with flavours, colours and fragrances. Flowering plants and fruit-bearing trees punctuate the enchanting scenic beauty of this piece of landscape. The sylvan beauty of this vicinity is enhanced by nature's abundant expression in its rolling meadows.

Raman, Sita and Lakshman are cocooned in the comfort of the cottage. Raman is engaged in a cheerful, thriving audiology with Sita and Lakshman and they all seem to share some lovely moments.

Being viewed by Bharathan from without, Raman's unpretentious dominating presence, looking illustrious as the brilliant sun enlightening all directions, reflecting glory and commanding such awe and respect, is a feast for the eyes.

Bharathan and Sathrughnan see the hides of deer, bows quivers planted with arrows hanging upon the walls of the cottage. From afar, they perceive imprints of Raman's footsteps on the ground at some distance of the cottage. As a proud reflection of culture, which stresses deference to elders and superiors, their promptitude to bow in deep reverence at the very sight of Ramna's foot prints, and pay their homage to them which bear divine impressions of conch, mace, disc and lotuses, sought for by even Brahman and other gods with devotion, speaks volumes of their stupendous fidelity and love.

As they draw nigh, Bharathan is inexplicably enamoured of the spectacle he sees-Raman sitting in the parlour clad in fresh barks, with his hair bound in a nice top knot on his crest, glancing towards Sita and permitting Lakshman to tenderly and fondly press his feet. Impelled by such a visual,

Bharathan respectfully prostrates on the floor and venerates Ramna's adorable feet. Raman, a captivating image of beauty and compassion, raises Bharathan and sits him on his lap. Streaming down tears of affection, Raman administers tender embraces to Bharathan, Kausalya and the other Queens, just like thirsty cows that run to drink water, rush very eagerly and excitedly to meet Raman.

The punctilious Raman, repeatedly acknowledges He has been blessed by their visit, observes the code of propriety paying obeisance to His mothers and due reverence to the preceptor Vashisthar Courteously offering them seats, he candidly wanders into verbal enquiries about King Dasarathar his father's welfare.

Dearly addressing Raman as Raghunadanan, Vashisthar feels constrained to inform Raman of the King's demise. However, in no uncertain words, he breaks the news that His father had passed away under severe pangs of longing and separation from Him. The sage continues to report His father's yearning and pining for His proximity, His long drawn thoughts about them ever etched on his memory and the constant uttering of their names Sita, Raman and Lakshman.

To Raman these reflections are not consoling in the light of his father's untimely demise. His composure shatters; his voice losing its edge, his eyes misting over he falls to the ground and in profound sorrow detonates a mournful cry saying all is lost, that, they have all lost everything; Sita and Lakshman too lament in the same manner. In a worldly-wise demeanour, Raman hopelessly wails that he has been left helpless by his dear father's death.

Momentarily the sage acts as a sources of consolation, bringing this painful ordeal to a resolution, taking them to the Mandakini River, to perform the customary funeral rites that every dutiful son should at the time of his father's demise; they take a dip in the river, perform the ceremony 'Sraddha' and offer water to their father's soul. Raman and Lakshman offer Inga fruit mixed with honey for appeasement of the soul. The Queens, Bharathan and Sathrughnan also take a dip. All members of the royal family observe morning fast and retire for the day.

The following day, Bharathan decides to rendezvous with Raman. Maintaining a humble exterior, he approaches Raman and floats his request. Very respectfully he importunes his brother to kindly return to Ayodhya and accept the throne. He woos Raman to this effect, saying that time is not yet ripe for him to take to the life of an anchorite in the forest. He falls prostate zealously entreating Raman to reign over Ayodhya and perform the cherished Aswamedhas and other ritualistic observations. Bharathan is actually quite cathartic to ventilate his remorse about Kalkey's sinful deed which has brought towering shame and pleads to be absolved of it.

Graciously, Raman raises Bharathan and seats him on his lap. While endorsing His gentle assertions, Raman peremptorily insists that they obey their parents; hence he, Bharathan, should govern Ayodhya and He Himself should live in the forest in conformity with the already concluded decree. He proclaims, the recalcitrant ones who act contrary to the will of their parents would suffer gravely in hell. In reply Bharathan pressurizes Raman not to lionize father, but to disregard his words as he always acted and spoke under a spell, gone crazy with lustful passion for his wife Kaikeyi.

Raman in a defensible attitude retorts that father had very faithfully and truthfully kept his promises. Falling in line with His father, Raman vouches to remain steadfast to His father's commands. And so, to keep up his promise He had committed Himself to live as a hermit in the forest (only) (for) fourteen years and then return to Ayodhya.

However Bharathan again pleads with Raman to return to Ayodhya now, and offers to live as a recluse in the forest for His sake. But Raman is tenacious in His commitment to carry out His father's edict. He articulates, if they were going to retract his order they would be impostors, since the monarch had bestowed the throne to Bharathan and had donated to him strict asceticism in the forest. Eventually Bharathan threatens to stay back with Him or even go to the extreme of embracing death should Raman reject his request of allowing him to follow Him just as He has licensed Lakshman a proximity to cherish his enfleshed presence, to bask in His blissful company and to serve Him.

Thus speaking he squats on the kusha grass meaning to die if Raman dismisses his petition. Sage Vasishthar intervenes at the behest of Raman who makes a silent ocular gesture to placate Bharathan. Consequently, inorder to school him privately, Vasishthar draws Bharathan aside and instructs him to shake of his mindless determination and obstinate insistence on Raman's return to Ayodhya. He divulges the genuine identity, not only of Sri Raman, the Tangible Manifestation of Lord Sri Vishnu, being born as the son of king Dasarathar, but also of Sri Sita to be Sri Lakshmi his consort, and Lakshman to be Sesha. They have descended to the earth on a mission as humans to exterminate Ravanan and his demon race, so as to return peace, harmony and well being to the Gods, sages and denizens of the globe.

Interestingly, Bharathan is astonished when Vasishthar makes a clean breast of Kaikeyi's inculpability. He adds that she had to succumb unknowingly to the royal prerogative of the Gods. If it were otherwise, she would not have made her presence right now. Bharathan is therefore, in turn coaxed by the sage to return to Ayodhya cheerfully, and should no more entangle Raman in controversy or irk Him further. Speaking positively the prudent sage assures Bharathan of Raman's speedy return; He would after fourteen years, having accomplished his mission on earth, undeniably, arrive at Ayodhya.

Vasishthar's honest assurance is refreshing to Bharathan. At once he hastens to Raman and translates his overwhelming choice of His sandals which he begs for as a token to represent Him in his absence. He vows that they deserve to be more intensely revered and worshipped than His lotus feet themselves. The loyal Bharathan agrees to wait upon them, as he used to do upon Raman, and declares to rule Ayodhya during His absence for fourteen years, keeping them on the throne until His home coming. It is a sign of a welcome proposition, since Raman pries off the gem-studded pair of sandals and bestows it to Bharathan, who had earlier on, with great devotion slipped the selfsame pair on to Raman's holy feet. He receives it with ostensible joy and respect, but resolutely intimidates Raman that he would leap into the uproaring fire, if even a single day expires after the lapse of the scheduled fourteen years. Instantly, Raman bathes him in an embracing reassurance and bids him farewell. He bids good bye to the others who have accompanied Bharathan. In the meanwhile, Sathrughnan makes all arrangements for the exodus of Bharathan and his royal entourage.

A deep self-examination is churning inside Kaikeyi. However, the penitent Kaikeyi approaches Raman and meekly tenders her heartfelt apologies. She craves pardon for her evil deeds. She declares that noble souls are really like Oceans; they can endure, resist the harm done to them. She accredits Raman as, undoubtedly, the Supreme Lord Vishnu and that the whole universe designed, engineered and executed by His unimaginable intelligence, is but His Illusion.

Like marionettes that dance to the fanciful music of the puppeteer by the pulling of the strings, all creatures animate, actuate and move to His own sweet will. It is apparent to Kaikeyi that her will and mind was constrained. She had acted upon Raman's will because it was His whole strategy to venture into the forest to accomplish the twin objectives of His incarnation, namely, the protection of the good and the establishment of Dharmam by destroying the evil forces; she realizes Raman as the infinite soul who is a mysterious vision, even, to the other gods who cannot have access to Him by their speech and mind. With unwavering optimism she takes refuge at the Holy Feet of Raman, the lord of the Universe. She commits herself into His hands and solicits Him to sever her undue attachments and the seemingly unbreakable link of bondage of false affection for sons and kith and kin.

Radiating warmth, smiling benignly Raman endorses her thumbnail sketch of Himself. He exonerates her from all incriminations, confirms her innocence and authenticates that everything has evolved from Himself alone.

Kaikeyi begins to see the daylight of recognition as she conceives Raman to be dispassionate having no attachment to His stunts of magic. She gauges Him to be non-discriminate, and benevolent to all. Kaikeyi would have remained ignorant of Raman's transcendental characteristics had not Raman revealed Himself to her. Furthermore, He declares He does not hesitate to instantly respond to a devotee's call, to those who need Him and ruminate on Him ceaselessly. Those who have the veil of ignorance drawn upon them cannot know His true form and purpose. She is indeed blessed for she has now come to cognize Raman in the right perspective. While directing Kaikeyi to return to Ayodhya, Raman puts forth a promising proposition that if she fervently ponders on Him constantly, she would be released from fleshy concerns, obsession for material objects and thwarted desires and would taste his pure love attaining salvation thereof.

The sense of guilt that Kaikeyi has been keeping too Iong inside her is now scorched by Raman's homily which has really tuned her into the rhythm of vibrant happiness. She is exultant at the happy turn of events, that she has found inspiration, clarity and focus and in this mood she takes leave of Raman.

On returning home, the compelling need to placate the subjects, however, weighs heavily upon Bharathan. He does pacify them all in a befitting manner, and then repairs to Nadhigramam outside Ayodhya to spend his days as a hermit, meditate on Raman unfailingly and be remindful of his mandate. Raman's pair of sandals is crowned with glory as Bharathan places it on the majestic throne, decidedly, the very parameters of His rule. Bharathan's ingrained love for Raman is highlighted as he worships His sandals very earnestly reminding him of what he had vowed earlier. He remains faithful to his purpose of performing all the religious ceremonies and discharging his royal obligations regularly, as if he were a devotedly, humble servant of the sandals. He attunes his mind to the incessant chanting of Raman's name, awaiting His safe return in due course. As for Sathrughnan he follows in the footsteps of Bharathan, living the life of asceticism consuming fruits, wearing barks and sleeping on hard ground.

Raman's name explodes into the public consciousness and touches all nerves, so much so, that people keep thronging, inordinately, to Chitrakula, day by day, where Raman abides for some more days with Sita and Lakshman. Inorder to evade the people they leave for the Dandakaranya forest and enroute reach the hermitage of Sage Atri who is illumious as the moon. The soft spoken Raman, modestly states that He is blessed to have availed Himself of the opportunity of seeing him on His way to the Dandakar woods in the course of his scheduled period of exile.

Greeting and entertaining the Divine Incarnations with delicious fruits, the exalted sage suggests that Raman should permit Sita to meet his dutiful old wife, Anusuiya. Happily, Anusuiya and Sita acknowledge each other, embracing and greeting, with Sita falling at their feet and paying her respects.

The delighted Anusiya presents Sita with earrings silk sarees and celestial face powder that would enhance and preserve her beauty. Also, she showers benedictions on Sita, pronouncing that Raman will very faithfully triumph in His mission and that she will return with Him to Ayodhya victoriously and safely and serve her husband blissfully, thereafter. After which, she serves Raman and Lakshman delicious food and eloquently praises Raman as the illusive power who fashions the whole Universe; He is an actor who assumes the forms of Gods, the forms of man, animals and all mean creatures as well merely to maintain peace, and for the welfare of all living beings in the world. Though He blossoms out as the very breath of all lives, yet, He stands apart from them; He emerges as the Enigmatic, Distinct one, with his Maya under reins, even as she deludes the whole universe.

Part - III
Aranya Kandam

Chapter - I

Life in the Forest: Annihilation of Viradhan

Raman, decidedly resumes His odyssey to the Dandaka forest the next day with Sita and Lakshman, with the supportive consent of the Knowledgeable Sage Atri. The sage sees them off after instructing the young lads, aspirants, to ferry the trio across the river.

They debark on the other bank of the river, meander through the thick woods on foot and then border on the impenetrable and caliginous forests which abound with heterogeneous species of wild animals. Repercussions of the sonorous chirping and singing of a variety of birds and insects reverberate though the forests. Lurking in this part of the earth's territory is the Dandaka forest, the dwelling place of the malignant spirits as well.

The gallant Raman divines that to traverse the dreary forests is a proven risk-factor. He articulates a forewarning to Lakshman; with preparedness and alertness as their watchword, bows and arrows are in readiness for use to encounter any casualty on the way. He insinuates Devi Sita to walk in between them, with Raman leading and Lakshman following close on her heels. Maya is masquerading as Sita. They come upon a beautiful lake which is engulfed by gorgeous aquatic blossoms all around. They quench their thirst with its pristine waters.

The trio linger a while; Raman perches himself on a rugged rock with Sita and Lakshman beside Him, and they ease themselves a little. In the meantime, a monstrous form confronts them holding a heavy spike on which many human corpses are pinned. Its protruding belly, its mis-shaped massive form and its long drawn out jaws devouring the flesh of wild animals speak of its fiendish nature. As the Giant approaches closer to them, Raman calms Sita's fears and alerts Lakshman to be loaded for action.

The thunderous voice roars out, precisely, questioning the identity of the beings clad in barks, but puzzles over the possession of bows and arrows like warriors in contrast to their attire, more so the unquestionable beauty of Devi Sita fascinates him; he threatens that the woman who has accompanied them, though, so extraordinarily beautiful, is at most a morsel for his big mouth. After smilingly introducing Himself as Raman and the lady, Sita as his wife and Lakshman as his brother, Raman makes a clean breast of His intentions. He establishes He has come there to stay in due compliance with His fathers' wishes, the sole purpose being to rescue the world from the acquisitive and the aggrandizing power mongers, the evil beings, prowling the earth. He adds that He has come there specifically to teach him a good lesson. Infuriated, the monster bellows egotistically that his dreadful form, undoubtedly, incites fear in the beholder. He yells his name as Viradhan, a notoriously popular demon of the locality, with an uncanny skill for devouring the sages in this part of the terrain.

Threateningly he flirts with the only viable alternative to slay and devour them if they do not flee from the place wishing to save their lives which is more precious to them. He commands them to forfeit their bows and arrows, and, more importantly to deliver up Sita to him. Saying this, he breathlessly runs to capture her, but soon Raman severs both his arms by a single shot of an arrow, but Viradhan with his mouth wide open, persists in his attempts and leaps towards them. This time Raman immediately breaks both his legs with another shot. Finding him still plunging forward with his torso to swallow Him, Raman fells the head from his body with the third successive shot.

A fevered excitement is distinctly visible in Sita to see the numbskull giant fall to the ground streaming in a pool of blood. She is extremely elated to see Raman's bravura, and in admiration for his prowess, fortitude and chivalry she gently embraces him too, is a moment of jubilation for the deities in heaven; drums are sounded, while Gandharvas and Kinnaras sing delightfully and fairies dance, all expressing pure joy.

After an infinite moment, out from the corpse of the fallen demon unfolds the vision of a handsome man as luminous as the rising sun, attired in raiments decorated with gold, and falls at the feet of Sri Raman. He announces he is Vidhyadharan whom Sage Durvasa denatured into a demon by an imprecation. His discernible mind hails Raman as the Supreme God. He longs for wisdom and new freedom from the malady of ignorance. He surrenders to Raman and begs to favour Him with a mind always absorbed in Him alone in love. He pleads for nothing more but a communion with

Him, spending the days of his life praying and singing His praises ever. To sum up he prays for life in paradise.

Sri Raman acknowledges his pleas and lavishes on him salvation, knowledge and aspiration desired by him. He uproots his evil desires setting him free to enter heaven. Most humbly and respectfully Vidhyadharan pays homage to Sri Raman.

Any person who has the names of Sri Sita Devi and Sri Raman pregnant in their consciousness, consistently, and sings the glories of Sir Raman who killed the most horrible demon Viradhan, exonerating him from the Sage's vituperation bestowing on him blessings, thereby, restoring him once more to the status of divinity, Bidyadharsan, is designated to the full attainment of all his or her desires and aspirations.

Chapter - II

Meeting with Sarabhangar

The illustrious Sage Sarabhangar is extraordinarily exultant when he steps into the presence of the Unfathomable Mystery, Raman, who together with Sita and Lakshman arrives at his humble cottage. He cordially offers his salutations to them.

He supplicates Raman to allow him to shake off his organic coil as he desires, in his prodigious presence as he has nothing higher or worthier or more important to accomplish in this world than to vision the tangible presence of the Immanent Raman, here and now, before his very eyes. He acknowledges that his sustained penances have now attained consummation and have served him the desired fruits. Modestly, he lays the sum total of all the accrued benefits of all his good deeds at Raman's Holy feet. He likens Raman to 'Kamadhenu', the divine cow, which fulfills ones desires, for Raman has condescended to call on him at his humble dwellings at the mere contemplation of him.

Eventually, Sarabhangar lights a huge pyre. Then escaping onto the plane of tranquillity, with his whole system silenced, deeply immersing himself in meditation on Sri Raman and Sri Sita, he enters the fire which consumes him. His radiant soul assumes an ethereal form and ascends to the abode of Brahman the creator.

Aspirants and Sages who are immersed in meditation, observing penances, learn of Raman's enfleshed presence in their landscape, and so, flock to pay obeisance to Him. In the same fashion as they would entertain human beings, the hermits accord a hospitable reception to Raman. Sita and Lakshman heedless of their divine incarnation. They acclaim Raman's manifest form and, correspondingly propitiate him to disentangle the whole monastic fraternity from the torture of demons for which purpose He has descended to the earth. Confidentially, the sages take him round the neighbouring reclusions, proclaiming him as Lord Vishnu, Lakshman as

'Sesh Nag', the Serpent God, Bharathan the incarnation of his mighty weapon, 'the Disc' and Sathrughnana as his 'Divine Conch'.

Astoundingly Raman queries about the catalogue of innumerable human bones seen during His ambulation, lying scattered across the region. The sages respond, painfully, that they are the remnants of saints and sages devoured by demons prowling the earth, when engrossed in meditation. Empathetic about the miserable condition, Raman imparts the rare mental solace by promising to put and end to the diabolic onslaught unleashed by the evil spirits.

After a long tenture of stay, Raman, together with Sita and Lakshman, in the company of seers, Saints and aspirants who wait upon them and minister to their every need with abundant veneration, leaves for Suthikshanan's monastic abode. The different seasons do not affect the location wherein Suthikshanan's hermitage is housed, for it is a paradisiacal dwelling place offering repose and tranquillity to sages and hermits perennially. Here, Suthikshanan greets Raman, Sita and Laskshman genially and receives them offering delicious fruits. Immensely monopolized by the tutelage of the exalted Sage Agasthlyar, Suthikshanan has risen to be one of his favourite apostles. Suthikshnan for the nonce has climbed the stairway of achievement to divinity by chanting Raman's holy name indefatigably.

Suthiskhanan's whole being, body, mind and spirit stands in awe at the faithful presence of the Immanent and the Invisible, as Raman, a visual image before his naked eyes. He kudizes Sri Raman as the comely, spotless, graceful Lord of Devi Sri Sita. His lotus feet, which the Lord Shivan, the creator and all other gods worship, act as the raft to discerning aspirants to cross the sea of bondage and morbid, mundane preoccupations of life. To make possible a visible apparition of the Reality which is Imperceivable and formless, is not impossible with Raman. Suthikshanan's overwhelming gratitude leaves him utterly helpless in measuring Raman's compassion in assuming human form and having come personally to visit him, a slave entangled in a network of earthly bonds with kindred.

Raman, though, is the in-deweller in the heart of every being, keeps himself out of view and cognition from those who do not search him but bestows rare mental solace on those who earnestly recite His sacred name. Like the sun reflects upon different pots of water and is the same sun and light in all pots, Raman, the source of all things is present in every form of creation such as man, animals, birds, insects, trees, plants etc.

Suthikshanan praises Raman as the Creator, Sustainer and Destroyer of the Universe, duplicating the forms of Vishnu, Brahman and Shivan respectively. His beautiful illusion called Maya with all her attributes such as quiescent, material and predatory dance only to His own sweet will.

Suthikshanan positively confirms that Raman has doubly blessed him. First since Raman is pleased He has condescended to grace his humble lodgings and secondly, He has provided him the golden opportunity to behold Him in the most handsome manifest form with bow and in the company of Sita and Lakshman. He adds that he adores Raman's charming visible physique when many spiritual seekers meticulously aspire to realise His supreme state of Brahmam, the infinite, limitless, formless, beyond space, time and nature. So he airs his cherished desire and importunes Sri Raman to patronize him with an inexpungible impression of His enfleshed personality on his mind and heart, so that he may constantly meditate on Him alone.

Sri Raman smiles appreciatively reminding Suthikshanan that unless he ceaselessly repeats His name and constantly ponders on His form, he cannot live in peace. He also reveals to him that by nature of his concentrated, endless chanting of His names He, Raman has ordained for him the physical communion with Him. He discloses the truth of His grace detaching him thoroughly from worldly attachments even in this life, and his mind being sanctified here and now. Further, more importantly, Sir Raman assures Suthiskhanan of the blissful union with His soul after death.

Sri Raman explicitly promulgates the only way to realise Him is to chant His names and practice yoga. He proclaims that when a devotee or aspirant follows this path he can douche the mind of agitating emotions and impulses and restore it to its pristine calmness and serenity. He emphatically ensures also the status to envision Him face to face and obtain His favour and benediction.

Sri Raman graciously proclaims that those who shall listen or read the invocation shall be dispensed with right knowledge and His pure love.

Suthikshanan floats a humble request, petitioning Sri Raman to go with him, for its long since he too has seen him, to visit his preceptor sage Agasthiyar's hermitage the next day. The following morn, Sri Raman, highly enthusiastic about dialoguing with the eminent sage, accompanied by Sita and Lakshman and guided by Suthiskhanan reach the hermitage of Agasthiyar's younger brother on their way.

Chapter - III

Sage Agasthiyar Meets Raman

After a very brief sojourn at the residence of Agasthiyar's younger brother' Raman accompanied by Sita, Lakshman and Sage Suthikshanan reach Agasthiyar's hermitage the following day.

The high souled Sage Agasthiyar is seated amidst other sages and his many disciples at his hermitage, earnestly educating them all on religious matters, also instructing them in the scriptures and as well, explaining the sacred significance of Raman's name, when Suthikshanan heralds the arrival of Raman himself. Exuding reverence and exuberance Sage Agasthiyar greets Raman, Sita and Lakshman without the hermitage and then taking Raman by the hand conducts Him inside proclaiming that he is very fortunate this day in receiving Raman as his beloved guest attributing this to the result of his good deeds and penances. As a sign of mutual respect, Raman Sita and Lakshman fall at Agasthiyar's feet paying their obeisance.

Agasthiar's whole being trembles with innermost rapture as he embraces Raman in ecstatic joy, and as if programmed, his eyes brim with beaming tears. It is a transfigured atmosphere of heavenly delight. The sage lavishes on them a hearty hospitality entertaining them with luscious fruits and offering them a variety of gifts and artefacts.

Worshipping Raman very earnestly as the Lord, Sage Agasthyar says that he is knowledgeable about Brahman the creator's request to Him, to descend to the earth. He also expresses that from then on he has been passionately yearning and eagerly anticipating His visit to his humble lodgings which has now been fulfilled. He acknowledges Raman as the Supreme God who is the sole existence prior to recreation. He observes that illusion or Maya called Avidya is His dynamic operation and static nature. His Maya is called nature, ignorance, the worldliness, and bondage and the creative energy yet, He is inaction and is detachable from all that He creates. He is always accompanied by His Maya like an unseen shadow.

Nature is the sum total of all elements that has its origin, in the fashion of primus in His energy which is superimposed on his will thus transforming itself into the prime author generating Mahatattva and Ahankara, the ego. The three fold attributes or natural activities of Mahattattva are quiescent, material and predatory (Sathvic, Rajashik and Thamasik) together with the intellect and five fine elements of matter created by nature namely sound, feeling, shape, smell and liquid, known as Sabda, Sparisha, Rupa, Gandha and Rasha respectively.

The astral bodies of jivas are created by Raman, the Universal Ego, by His Sathvic or quiscent attribute that is very peaceful and serene; by His Rajashik or material attribute He creates the five sense organs and by His Thamasik or predatory activity He creates matter and its five gross substances of nature-earth, water, liquid, fire, light and ether and air with sentiments and sensations. All these constituents intermingle together and through His influence they form an amalgam called Sukshma, the subtle body. God, the mystic Master, and His creation, the whole universe inclusive of all creations, animate or inanimate, is Vishwa or Virat.

Raman is Lord Vishnu as the Sustainer; He is Lord Brahman as the Creator; and He is Lord Shivan as the Demolitionist of his own creations. Raman, Lord, of the universe has condescended to manifest His own self in all creatures of the universe. He abides in the sanctum of each soul, the source of all life; but is inert, and yet, dwells as the witness within the nucleus of every being; though He is the same self dynamic in character, existing beyond the sphere called mind, and sustaining the three states waking, dreaming and deep sleeping of existence which are considered to be the whole of the individuals existence. And His Maya comes to the fore when masquerading in human form, He plays His part in the worldly drama of life. Therefore mind that is endowed by Nature plays a dominant role in a living being, being activated accordingly by the three attributes or Gunas-quiscent, material and predatory; hence the soul or God only grants prana or energy or consciousness to the body and it does nothing to activate the organic frame.

The individuals power of discrimination is choked or obfuscated by his Maya or illusion, which performs dualistically dispensing knowledge or abetting ignorance known as Vidya or Avidya. It follows, inevitably that the Individuals saturate themselves in worldliness due to nescience and conclusively acquiesce in their own degeneration. They can also reconstruct themselves and aspire for liberation acquiring true knowledge of discrimination and detachment and attain peace and salvation, the goal of human life. Unchallenged, Raman exists perennially as the subject of understanding, as the richest body of learning and knowledge. The acquisition of right understanding and knowledge cannot be secured better and sooner than those who chant His hallowed name, whose faith in Him is vibrant and whose love for Him is expensively blemishless. It is vain to try to gain knowledge that leads to emancipation through the senses, as it is a very difficult hardship which calls for concentrated devotion to Him alone.

Equilibrium of intellect forms the bedrock of the spiritual life of true saints, sincere devotees and discerning aspirants to triumph over the world of distinctions. They ascend the plane of the incorporeal state, exempt from all changes, ever satisfied, content and blissful, in which neither good nor evil nor cause or effect, nor past, or present nor future has any place, keeping mind imperturbed under the varying conditions of pleasure and pain, gain and loss and maintaining evenness of mind in favourable and unfavourable situations. This engenders in them a spirit of detachment from things worldly and from the anxiety of materialistic prosperity. All their desires are fused into one, directing it towards the Absolute, Raman. Every activity is an instrument of worship, therefore, there is no distinction between one activity and another. Their yearning for Him makes them utterly indifferent to all else.

Saints, sages and devotees are masters who have maneuvered the oscillations of mind to a one pointed static state, with the reins of the sense and sense organs under stringent subordination. Substantially, it is their spiritual endeavour to resourcefully and consistently pursue the seemingly thorny path of salvation. In fine, association with and the company of the aforesaid saints, sages and devotees is to be sought with assiduity, regarded as the best modus operandi to attain salvation.

Enunciating the prime significance of Lord Raman's manifestation, Sage Agasthiyar beseeches Raman for a boon, as he so heartily wishes to live amidst or merely to have constant acquaintance with such god-drunk saints and devotees forever and wherever he lives. Agasthiyar asserts that his penances and his life's vocation have been fortuitous only now, by virtue of his meeting Raman and worshipping Him this day. Addressing Lord Raman as the greatest of the Raghu race, the sage begs Raman to concur with Him in treasuring him, Raman together with Sita, in the sanctum of his heart so that He becomes the inescapable reality whom he may never ever lose sight of.

It being the most evocative moment of his life, sage Agasthiyar savouring the boons, and simultaneously, satiating Raman with his sincere invocation presents and requests Raman to accept the bow, quivers and sword with a gold handle, left in his custody by Indhran for his use. He requisitions Lord Raman to wield the weapons against the lupine demons and evil doers who unleash terror with a global reach, so as to annihilate them entirely from the face of the earth for the good of its people. Inorder to consummate the secret assignment, Agasthiyar courteousy suggests that they sojourn at a lovely habitat called Panchabathi, circled by a silver coil of the river Gautham, as long as the task on hand demands. Charmed by Agasthlyar's kind and significant advocacy, the omniscient Lord Raman recommences IIis journey, faithfully taklng to the itinerary as proscribed by the exalted Sage.

Chapter - IV

The Philosophy of Life

Raman on landing Panchabathi, erroneously perceives Jatayu the vulture, because of its gawky body, seemingly, disguised out of shape, looking like a hill, to be some ferocious demon. He espies Lakshman and instantly calls for His bow and arrow to shoot down the weird creature impeding His path.

Hastily the vulture introduces himself to Raman as his father, King Dasarathar's friend, Jatayu, and also His Bonhomie. He pleads to Raman not to slay him, but commits himself as a sentinel to guard Sita until their stay there. An invisible bond of friendship is born. Tenderly embracing Jatayu, Raman consents to his continuance in the vicinity of their cottage and requests him to befriend them in times of need.

A healthy locale, at close quarters to the Gauthami river, pleasantly sprawling in tranquillity, richly laden with excellent fruit trees, is selected by Raman where two cottages beneath canopies of new born leaves are erected dexterously by Lakshman. They dwell in this haven of peace in which situation Lakshman has the good fortune of serving Raman and Sita, performing the daily chores of bringing water, collecting fruits and gleaning flowers from the forest. With daily bath in the river and wild fruits to consume they bask in the irresistible serenity and beauty of the landscape. Particularly Lakshman revels in keeping vigil over them with bow in hand all through the nights. Invariably, he is delighted in seeing himself in the role of an obedient ministering angel.

The ambience of Raman's humble residence is luxuriously peaceful and conducive to Lakshman for commencing an open verbal communication with Raman. The throbbing echoes of the inner realities of Spiritual doctrine lying deep in his heart find expression. He initiates by genially requesting Raman to enlighten him with true knowledge on the moot points of transcendental truths, spiritual discipline, right effort and mindful practice.

He begs to be gifted with devotion, experience and detachment from morbid and mundane preoccupation with materialistic life, the means to eternal salvation, which he categorically desires to attain. He envisions Raman to be the Supreme Evangelist to expound and illuminate him on the elevated subject.

In response to Lakshman's enquiry, Raman settles down to endearingly catechize him about the mysterious philosophy of spiritual life by which an aspirant can conquer nescience. The elemental necessity to know about the true concepts, the first being Maya or ignorance and its operation, then, the assiduous means to attain knowledge with live mystical experiences to follow-experience, the best teacher is a quiet personal epiphany that fuels knowledge leading to self-realisation and also about the supreme soul, whereby, the astute aspirant transcends worldly fears and delusions perennially.

The concept of Maya or ignorance which occupies a pivotal position is delineated as having two aspects the first being dynamic operation and the second static. By its dynamic operation it creates a pseudo influence between the soul and the body and by which the entire world of phenomena, the scene of life, its bondage, sufferings and liberation all fall within its boundless realm. It projects the cosmic manifold and builds castles in the air. By its static function, Maya conceals the nature of reality, conceals real knowledge or the Supreme Soul like that of the appearance of the snake in the rope.

Understandably, the individual therefore, cannot cognize the soul, the inner self which is the real self; he identifies himself as corporeal matter, is steeped in ignorance, is nonplused and impotent in discriminating the reality from the ephemeral external objects. This subtle nescience does not exist in reality; it is mere illusion akin to dreams and daydreams. So long as ignorance overshadows the individual he is immersed in illusion and is said to be worldly, fettered by the recurrent cyclic births and deaths that ensue. All the actions and mundane pleasures mixed with pain and agony, illusions, transience and impermanence are operated by the body and not by the soul. Congeneric ties, attachment and relationships pertain to only the body. The five gross elements of Nature-earth, water, air, ether and fire and the five intriguing phenomena- sound, touch, form, smell and liquidness and the ego with its ten sense-organs and intellect-go into the making of the body. The soul though encased in the body is a separate entity detached from the medley of these material instruments. The impression caught by these instruments reach the soul through mind and intellect, and the soul perceives them and gives suitable orders. So to say, the soul manifests the Ego, Intellect, Mind, the senses and the external instruments. In truth, the living self cannot be anything different from the Divine Self, God.

The virtues that an individual should cultivate to achieve knowledge of the self are: renunciation of objects of the senses, seeking forgiveness, candour, kindness, cheerfulness, contentment, fidelity to truth. Added to these qualities are freedom from self-importance, unpretentiousness, non violence, patience, service to parents and preceptor, cleanliness, steadfastness, self control, abhorrence of sensuality, self-effacement, realization of misery in birth, death, old age and sickness, detachment from one's kith and kin and one's belongings and equanimity of mind. More are the study of philosophy and the Holy Scriptures and the practice of yoga. Above all, the blossoming of love for Raman or God is the bedrock of liberation.

The faithful adherence to these characteristic virtues, which should serve the proper role in the enhancement of practice, is the gateway to transcendental knowledge. Otherwise, spiritual illiteracy and sterility will result eventually if backsliding sets in. Nothing more is imperative to prepare for the great passage to freedom of the soul which is ever self-governing. The individual's nexus with the body is sundered and dark ignorance dispelled, when he cognizes the soul as being omniscient omnipotent, omnipresent, immortal, immutable, self existent, free, without mutation and eternal.

Self-realization, humanity's main goal, a dispensation unique to humanity alone, an enterprise open to every human being is the means to God-realization that is Salvation. When the factor of the self has come to be realized then everything about the true nature of the soul, the past, present and future, that is blemishless, pure, all potent, unbounded and eternal can be realized. He alone who armours himself with robust faith and unalloyed love and wholehearted devotion can succeed in negotiating the spiritual goal. Just as darkness, devoid of light makes it impossible for a person to see anything, so too, he cannot gain lofty spiritual knowledge and cannot know his soul or god without devotion and love, for the human soul rests ultimately in love. The light can be lighted from light alone. The soul cannot be concealed by any power. It is ever shining and the glory of the self's light alone makes the individual to cognize his own self.

Every act or action is yoked to the self. Hence, Lord Raman exhorts certain guidelines for engaging in such action that would positively lead to eternal salvation. Extraordinary emphasis is laid on rendering service to

His dear devotees, worshipping Him or His image with faith and love, singing and praising His sacred names, reading the written description of His Divine Life, observing fast and penance on the eleventh lunar days and holy days dedicated to Raman, solemnizing holy festivals and doling out in charity to the destitute and the deprived, discerning that every individual is a replica of the cosmic self, and as a natural result being dispensed with the heart anchored in Raman in timelessness.

Raman fondly counsels Lakshman to treasure these seasoned niceties, dwell on them, so that they have a direct bearing, accordingly, on his practical, spiritual tenor of life. Further, he vehemently appeals to him to withhold these privileged spiritual facts from the nothingarians and the uninitiated, but to inspire His devotees and aspirants with invaluable advice whenever He lights upon them. Raman gently reiterates His assurance of a rich harvest-the realization of salvation, which is within reach, pulsating in the core of one's own being or is instantaneous to the dynamic men of action in search of sustained intimate company and administering to the devotees, to the pure hearted and realized souls who keep the torch of knowledge and spiritualism ablaze, as He is always tangible and can be seen face to face by them but never by those who are spiritually arid and impotent.

Chapter - V

The Episode of Surpanakhai

Surpanakhai, the sister of the Demon King Ravanan, espies august Raman in Panchabathi. She plans to give him a dramatic welcome; so she transforms her weird structure and assumes the physique of a beautiful girl. She approximates to the omniscient Raman and vocalizes her preying mind questioning Him as to why so handsome and young a gentleman as he should wrap himself up in hermits garb and come to live in the feral forest, leaving the comfort and luxury of the home in the prime of his life.

In temperate words He announces Himself as Raman, the son of king Dasarathar of Ayodhya. He further enunciates that His wife Sita and brother Lakshman are with Him, to expend fourteen years in the forest in complaisance with their father's decree of banishment from Ayodhya.

Surpanakhai garrulously makes overtures to Raman by introducing herself as king Ravanan's sister, living with her younger brother Khara in the forest. She gives a pointer to her sole authority over the forests. An insight into Surpanakhai's superlative vicious character is seen as she intentionally spits out her insatiable appetite to devour saints and sages whenever she sets eyes on them. Now her lasciviousness surfaces as she, fascinated by Raman's youthful and suave bearing, overtly allures Him to appease her selfish desire that craves for sensual gratification.

The apathist Raman, unperturbed, addressing Surpanakhai as a, gentle, lady gesticulates towards Sita and gives her the high sign that she will feel forlorn to cohabit, happily and peacefully, with his beloved wife from whom He cannot part, as she is part and parcel of Him. He directs her to approach Lakshman who has no wife, there, with him. Surpanankhai draws near to Lakshman. Informing him that she has been sent by Raman, she puts forth her proposal going back to square one. Lakshman buttresses Raman's stand and turns down her advances saying he is a devote slave of Raman and so she would, unquestionably, be unhappy in slavery. Infuriated, Surpanakhai returns to Raman. She demands why she is being irked and sent running from pillar to post in vain. Boisterously she intimidates to make a meal of Sita, if he, Raman, does not yield to her desires; she makes a plunge towards her. Lakshman simultaneously catches hold of her and severs her ears and nose, the right royal punishment she so utterly deserves, on a cue from Raman. Unable to stomach such maltreatment, for coquetry is a costly mistake, Surpanakhai flees away howling and crying loudly, and reaches Khara, her brother, the mighty leader of the demons.

Khara anxiously queries about the unfortunate assailant who has invited death at his hands. And Surpanakhai weeping bitterly replenishes him with particulars of Raman living with wife Sita and brother Lakshman in the forest, the brother being the author of this bloody attack at the instigation of Raman. She pleads to her brother for the immediate death of Lakshman, and his flesh and blood to be brought as food to satiate her ravenous appetite and explosive anger, or else, she threatens to kill herself instantly.

Khara, Dushana and Trishira commanding an array of fourteen thousand soldiers march to war against Raman. The two mighty warriors, Dushana and Trishira, leading the army attack Raman atrociously and brutally hurling boulders, hillocks and large trees on him.

Raman directs Lakshman to give them a wide berth and enter the nearby cave anon. He advances single-handed to counter the attack. Miraculous indeed is His feat, when, a battery of a thousand arrows together is discharged in one shot from His mighty bow killing them all including the powerful leaders Khara, Dushana and Trishira in a trice. Sita is extensively amused at this phenomenal deed of Raman and on His return visibly rejoices over the victory and tenderly attends to the wounds received in the encounter.

Concurrently, Raman's miraculous deed takes Surpanakhai's breath away. She is overcome by an expansive fear; an uneasy sense of frustration creeps into her being. Provoked by revenge, defeat and humiliation at the hands of Raman, she runs away helter skelter to the comfort zone of Ravanan in Lanka. Ravanan is taken aback by her disfigured face; it is frighteningly clear to him that something has gone awry. It is a severe blow to his vanity, the king of demons, to see his sister's nose and ears mangled and supportingly elicits the author, however great and valourous he may be, of the misdeed, who certainly merits death at his hands, and also, the wide range of happenings that have led to this terrible debacle.

Surpanakhai retorts with such resentment calling him, Ravanan, a numbskull, carousing, so luxuriously obsessed with inebriates and drinking pots. She points an accusing finger castigating him for the dismaying lack of authority, misrule and disregard for the serious happenings in his state. With yet another allegation against him of negligence to appoint state spies or sleuths, she briefs him, very importantly, about Raman's fearless stay with his wife Sita and brother Lakshman at Panchabathi, a prohibited area, in Dandaka forest. Surpanakhai entices Ravanan with her sweet description of Sita as the most beautiful Lady in the world and narrates her unsuccessful attempt of abducting and bringing Sita for a wife for him, when Lakshman at the instigation of Raman axed her nose and ears. Nevertheless, with the military assistance of fourteen thousand soldiers from Khara together with Dushana and Trishira, Raman, who retaliated single-handed could not be vanquished. She expresses her bewilderment at Raman's prowess and potentiality to kill the whole army. Though superficially Ravanan assuringly placates Surpanakhai with unstinting succour and solace, he becomes introverted and pensive on hearing her baffling audiology. In the secret recesses of his mind he ruminates that no mediocre mortal could have single-handedly and fearlessly killed Khara, Dhusana and Trishira and therefore, Raman is, conclusively, God incarnate having descended on earth at Brahman's obsecration, for, he Brahman, has stamped his doom at the hands of a supreme human being for redeeming the earth from his evil clutches by killing him and his fiendish clan and thereby establishing peace and prosperity.

Ravanan is of two minds due to a collision of ideas whether to boldly wage war against Raman or not. He collects his thoughts and weighs the pros and cons of a battle; if he triumphs he will continue in the garb of the king of demons, still holdingg on to having sway over the globe and additionally, thrive in the pleasures that exclusively kingship offers; and if he is slain by Lord Raman, he would enjoy inheriting the royal exalted privilege of a life in heaven.

He does not want to damage the prospect of a crusade against Raman, because he can in no way easily appease Raman, neither by servitude nor devotion to Him nor by any other peaceful means. In his heart of hearts, he fathoms Raman to be none other than Supreme Vishnu Himself, and to encounter death at His hands would merit him the highest bid, a status and celestial life in the abode of Gods, including mighty Khara, Dushana and Trishira in a trice. She wonders if this is evidence enough that Raman is the Omnipotent to annihilate the Universe.

Chapter - VI

The Episode of Moreeson

Mareeson, once a demon turned hermit now, is on the path to straighten up and strengthen his spiritual life by absorbing himself in uninterrupted meditation. At this stage, in the on-going process of meditation, Mareeson is intruded upon by Ravanan the mean being with a big ego. Mareeson is unnerved at his unheralded appearance but, however, respectfully receives him with grace. In total readiness to execute his orders, only if they are not unrighteous, he seeks to know the objective of his visit in such a mirthless and dejected mood.

Ravanan informs Mareeson that at present, Raman has come with His exotic wife Sita and his brother Lakshman to dwell in the forest at Panchapathi by the side of the Gauthami river. He cautions Mareeson not to take Raman and Lakshman lightly, but substantially highlights their valour, narrating how they have so fearlessly and so soon severed the nose and ears of Surpanakhai and have even killed Khara, Dhusana and Trishira along with fourteen thousand soldiers. At this Juncture, Ravanan seeks the help of Mareeson and in league with him conspires to kidnap Sita. So he weaves an elaborate charade; accordingly, Mareeson should assume the form of a beautiful gold deer and lure Raman and Lakshman far into the forest, away from their cottage.

Mareeson is grieved to know that Ravanan, the Mighty king of Demons, is facing acrimony, enmity and umbrage, at the hands of a mere mortal being who is mightier than him. He is also astounded to learn that Ravanan's enemy is the invincible Raman who is the cause for taunting him with such a perilous idea. Mareeson who had earlier seen and tasted a wee bit of Raman's tough mettle trembles all over at the very thought of Him. He rakes up a past incident at Sage Vishwamithrar's yajna ceremony which he essayed to foil, when all at once he was flung thousands •of miles away into the ocean by a shot from Raman's blunt arrow. Subsequently it was then, disguised as a deer he had attacked Raman, intending to kill Him with his strong and sharp horns, when again, he had met with severe punishment by being hurled up into the sky.

Mareeson asserts that the aforementioned incident has since kept him behind doors in his hermitage, undergoing a gradual renaissance through the overcoming of the lower nature from which he habitually operated. Therefore, he pleads with Ravanan to waive the irrational appeal to kidnap Sita; also to give up the idea of enmity with Raman as it cannot be effectively countered. He confesses he has been unnerved and chilled to the bone by Raman's deeds that even the first syllable of His Name instils fear in him. He admits he is perpetually conscious of Raman's pervasive presence whether asleep or awake. He requests Ravanan to evade confronting ugly realties inorder to safeguard his long established dynasty functioning from ancient times. Mareeson subserviently suggests that he, Ravanan, should instead enroll himself as a devotee of Sri Raman and enchant his various names without intermission.

Epitomizing Raman's noble qualities, Mareeson advocates a radical change of heart in Ravanan as it is only Raman who is the saviour to redeem him from any vulnerable situation. He quotes the predictions of the sages of Raman being the enfleshed form of Lord Sri Vishnu, having descended upon the earth at Brahman's request to retrieve the earth from the quagmire of sin, eliminate the evils of terrorism unleashed by demons and to annihilate him Ravanan the Monarch of the devilish clan.

Ravanan downplays Mareeson's observations and exhortations; with unprecedented ferocity he draws out his sword to put an end to him instantly if he does not stop his mouth and execute his bidding instead of trying to derail the whole process with supplications for his conversion. Becoming increasingly aggressive, he further says he is on safe ground, if, as all sages declare Raman to be the incarnation of God, then Raman would go ahead with his mission and, consequently, he, Ravanan would be emancipated. Lust rears its ugly head making Ravanan so increasingly convinced he could easily have Sita without any resistance, if Raman were only a non-de-script mediocre mortal being.

Mareeson cannot come to terms with Ravanan's threatening negotiations, and so decides to operate with impunity, but in short order ruminates that he would suffer hell if he be killed by Ravanan now. On the other hand, he would feasibly attain salvation, a priceless reward, If obliterated by Lord Sri Raman later. Apparently apologetic, Mareeson judiciously consigns himself to carry out his orders and wishes.

Mareeson, a protagonist in the diabolic operation, harnessing all the expertise, transforms himself into a fictitious deer fair of form, with a body of gold speckled with silver dots, with hoofs and horns of precious stones and eyes of sapphire. Instantly distinct, he struts about proudly in front of Raman's cottage. Meticulously he begins to gambol and romp around in the spotlight of Sita's vision so as to capture her attention.

Chapter - VII

The Abduction of Sita

Raman is clouded with the presentiment of Ravanan duplicating himself as a monk and arriving there to kidnap Sita. In the seclusion of their humble cottage, the Omniscient Raman interprets his insights into the future of events and its for reaching implications into a verbal tête-á tête with Sita. Hence he counsels Sita to maintain a fabricated illusory form of herself on this earth and to live concealed with her real self in fire until He effaces Ravanan from the face of the earth, who is to undoubtedly gain access there inorder to carry her away presently.

Sita resigns to His bidding, disassembles her real self to live in obscurity in the fire, the most compelling testimony to Sita's chastity, and fabricates a fictitious, delusive form of herself. Moments later, the fake Sita espies a deer of gold frisking about in the foreground. She draws the attention of Raman to this extraordinary creature by cajoling him into securing the hide of the fantastic deer for her.

Raman hails Lakshman and enjoins him to keep intensive vigil over Sita so as to facilitate Him to hunt down the deer and kill it. He also exhorts him of the vicious demons sneaking about in the forest.

Lakshman voices his skepticism though; he questions how a species of nature can don a decorative garb of gold such as this. He discerns it is Mareeson denatured as deer Raman strongly predicates his suspicion, and still, is resolved to embark on His mission, launching the first step in this dangerously duplicitous situation, to hound the deer, namely, Mareeson and kill it. However, He imposes on him stringent security measures to protect Sita against any kind of undesirable contingency. Subsequently, Raman goes in hot pursuit of the deer, which entices him to tread vast stretches further into the dense wild woods.

In the stream of one's thoughts, that Raman, the Omniscient, Omnipresent and Omnipotent Supreme God, should pursue a deer strikes and inharmonious note which runs clear in the mind. Greater clarity should be ingrained in the mind to know that Sri Raman does so as a human being, inevitably, only to vindicate the authenticity of His promise to His sincere devotees. When Raman is far gone into the forest, He aims a shot at the deer which falls dead instantly. At the same moment, Mareeson's clever deception of transmutation is exposed as he rises from the carcass of the deer. Then, parodying Raman's voice Mareeson vociferates the name of Lakshman sending a long moan, as If trapped in the pangs of death, to come immediately to his succour as he is dying.

As Mareeson is in the very presence of the Almighty Raman, his soul coalesces with Him, the Universal Self, and attains the highest status of salvation. Mareeson's death exemplifies a sinner's attainment of a blissful life in paradise wrought by the constant uttering of Raman's Name. So anyone, at the last moments of death, simply uttering the name Raman is certainly entitled to final liberation, for he, Raman, remains the eternal ideal for mankind to aspire to evolve to higher degrees of perfection. All the celestials in heaven bearing witness to the death of Mareeson are profoundly awe-struck at the transforming power of Raman's love and Grace, because Mareeson an evil demon as he, with his cumulative malignities of the past, should all at once take to a life of repentance, uttering the Lord's name Raman constantly, effectuating his own salvation.

Raman conjectures the unfortunate concurrence of foul play by the evil demons back at his cottage. With this uppermost on His mind he hastily makes His return to the cottage.

Meanwhile, Sita, presuming that Raman's call for help has fallen on deaf ears rebukes Lakshman for not responding to his call. Lakshman addressing Goddess Sita humbly replies disclaiming it to be Raman's verbal cry, but some demon ejaculating in pain at the moment of death. His emphatic assurance that no disaster, in any form, can even supervene or approach Sri Raman who is so powerful as to demolish the three worlds goes unheeded by Sita.

A shadow of doubt lingers in Sita's non-verbal subconscious darkness resulting in reprimanding Lakshman for harbouring ill will towards Raman, secretly desiring His death and artfully dreaming, there by, to take possession of her. Shedding copious tears, she reproves him for such an infamous action and voices that she will neither touch him nor Bharathan but permit only Death to lay his icy hands on her that very moment.

This verbal friction emanating from Sita hurts Lakshman to the core of his being. He is simultaneously enraged to hear such profanity being pronounced by the one whom he worships as Goddess. Unable to assimilate any more of it, he shuts his ears and in turn snipes at her that she shall, in the long run, suffer much for her thoughtless ignobility and unkindness. Leaving her behind, Lakshman then makes haste to meet Raman.

Ravanan impersonating himself as a Brahmin mendicant dressed in ochre robes, holding a staff in one hand a bowl in the other arrives promptly at the cottage. His attire lends credence to Sita to mistake him for a saint and so extends an implicit invitation into the cottage. She respectfully pays due homage offering fruits and a suitable place to recline and rest until such time her husband and her brother-in-law arrive to entertain him in a felicitous manner Ravanan smitten with Sita's fresh-faced innocence and charm deftly initiates a colloquy with her. Showering accolades on her ethereal beauty and hailing her as a lotus-eyed gorgeous, exquisite lady, he enquires of her identity. She interjects she is Sita, daughter of Janahar, the king of Mithilai and the wife of Raman, who, in compliance with His father King Dasasrathar's decree, has come with His brother Lakshman from Ayodhya to stay there in exile for fourteen years. Having introduced himself as Ravanan, King of Lanka, his most cherished opportunity of exposing his intentions of abducting her having arrived, he candidly states he has arrived there only to carry her off with him. Categorically he requests her to follow him without much ado. He insinuates the futility, hopelessness and ineffectiveness of living in the forest with nothing better to benefit her other than pain, misery and an indigent life with the hermit Raman.

Sita flares up instantly and excoriates that he deserves instant death by Raman's arrows. She distressfully retorts that a mighty lion's wife cannot be entrapped by a poor inferior rabbit With his ego bruised, his adrenalin shooting up, and dissipating his saintly mask, Ravanan in a potent rage transmutes himself into his real form, appearing before Sita with ten heads and twenty arms, as colorless as the darkness, a horrifying visible apparition more dreadful and more monstrous than a hillock.

The helpless deities seeing this run pell-mell in fear. Ravanan opts for only a lump of soil dug from the earth upon which Sita was standing, soon galvanizes into action lifting Sita onto his chariot and placing the lump of soil beside her, flies, away in the sky while Sita, tears streaking her cheeks, in full cry is appealing for help; loud pitched, she hails the name of Raman and Lakshman wherever they are, to come to her rescue. She now turns penitent for having mindlessly cast a shadow of doubt and suspicion on Lakshman's spotless character and personality.

The vulture king, Jatayu, espying Ravanan's chariot flying in the sky, seizes it and interrogates the villain as to where and why he is forcing Sita away like a dog stealing away the oblation from the sacrificial spot. He intercepts the chariot and rocks it with all his might throwing Ravanan and Sita onto the ground. Furiously, Ravanan draws his heavy sword and mutilates the vulture's wings and takes flight in another chariot leaving the bird bleeding profusely and short-winded awaiting a tragic end.

All the way through, Sita is beside herself with grief, regretting for being irresponsible in thought, and silently begging Lakshman to forgive her for her slanderous words. She calls upon her Lord Raman to extricate her, a helpless victim in the hands of Ravanan, from this predicament. It dawns on her when she catches sight of monkeys on a hill top to wrap up her ornaments in a piece of cloth and fling it at them, nurturing the massive hope that they would, sooner or later, meet Raman some day.

Eventually on reaching Lanka, Ravanan, as a strategic sequel to the elaborate charade engineered by him, places Sita in his gardens named Asokha, in the shade of the Sinshapa tree. She is heavily guarded by demonesses who also serve and do her bidding. Though she is treated and protected like Mother, she lives unhappily and agonizingly in the forlorn hope, lamenting the name of Lord Raman, that he would unquestionably come to recapture her.

Chapter - VIII

Jadayu's Meeting with Raman

Raman's act of chastising Mareeson is a benign act of grace. While returning from the forest after having vanquished Mareeson, Raman mentally reviews the priorities dividing his attention to be duly fulfilled. Increasingly a spark of doubt generates in Raman's mind about Sita's presence at the cottage. His feelings of despair and apprehension are palpable when he chances on Lakshman half way. The clairvoyant Raman deprecates Lakshman for leaving Sita all alone back at the cottage. He articulates His trepidation about her predicament that some misadventure has befallen her. He further chides Lakshman for the erroneous move of leaving Sita even while she insisted on his going out to seek Him when she misconstrued the unknown voice as his calling for help.

With not a moment to lose Raman quickens His pace towards the cottage. His presage of the catastrophe is validated; the cottage and its surroundings wear a deserted look, as Sita is nowhere to be found. His feigned sorrow becomes instantly distinct as He begins to bewail her disappearance akin to ordinary mortals. Raman and Lakshman venture out immediately on the intensive task of finding Sita. With an overpowering feeling of sadness they roam hither and thither aimlessly.

Raman is afflicted so much that he is teetering on the brink of a complete breakdown. Seeming to lose His sanity He behaves and talks like a common man, sometimes embracing beautiful flower plants and addressing other beautiful objects of nature around the place. At times he laments loudly. Also, He cries out the name Sita noisily and unproductively. The fearful uncertainty of never knowing her whereabouts grips him.

At a lengthy distance they come upon a potentially startling breakthrough. They see a fractured bow and a scattered chariot upon the ground. Raman divines some strange creature to have snatched Sita from her abductor, from the cottage. At the outset, lack of hard evidences adds stress to His already excited mind. They are propelled to abseil further. At length, in the background they see the vulture King Jadayu lying helpless, bleeding profusely to death.

The fears that this diabolic creature should have devoured Sita provokes Raman to summon Lakshman with his bow and arrows inorder to shoot the creature.

Raman's consternation wanes as the sadly crippled vulture king verbally acknowledges his identity as Jadayu, who is on the brink of death, being fatally wounded by Ravanan in a fight against him to retrieve Devi Sita. At this moment, Raman's painful mind is eased. The euphoria generated by Jadayu's visible demonstration of good will impels Raman to embrace him. In this infinite moment, He simultaneously expresses His heartfelt sorrow to see him in such a dire condition. Further, He enthuses Jadayu to replenish Him with every detail of the combat.

Jadayu relates what transpired between him and Ravanan since the moment he heard. Sita's loud resistant cry and espied Ravanan flying speedily in the air with Sita in his chariot, his intercepting the vehicle, the struggle between them, the breaking of the bow, his smashing and toppling the chariot together with the pair onto the ground, Ravanan chopping off his wings with his heavy sword and resuming flight in another chariot bound southwards with Sita Devi wailing bitterly.

Jadayu is conscious he is breathing his last. Hence, he pleads with Raman to touch his body, as His divine touch would suffice to liberate him. While speaking and at the same time feeling solace and comfort at Raman's supreme touch, Jadayu respires the last breath.

Raman in His standing as Jadayu's camaraderie and more as his kindred mourns his demise greatly. Accordingly, He makes arrangements for the funeral rites, which pave the way for Jadayu's liberation, to be performed punctually and appropriately. At this, Jadayu's divine form is made manifest in Sri Raman's enfleshed presence. Subsequently, he dedicates a plethora of praise to the sacred feet of Sri Raman. He bows subserviently to Lord Raman, the most virtuous, illuminous, matchless creator, sustainer and annihilator of the Universe. He lauds Sri Raman as Supreme God whom he incessantly realizes to be the greatest human incarnation of Lord Sri Vishnu. He acclaims Sri Raman as Devi Laskhmi's beloved consort. He extols Sri Raman as the saviour who alleviates the anxieties and misfortunes of Brahman and all other Gods.

Jadayu hails Sri Raman as a stronghold in whom he takes refuge as he is Supreme God who is most handsome and more luminous than a thousand moons. He is the one who unfolds within the hearts of His aspirants fulfilling even their every unborn wish too, and being adored by all the deities and Lord Shiva as well.

Jadayu falls at Sri Raman's feet whom he praises as Raghunathan who is blue hued as the Yamuna river. He is the supreme one who is imperceivable, inaccessible and unobtainable by those who have no spiritual moorings in Him and are lost in the complex sensory activities of mundane pleasure and pain. He acknowledges Sri Raman as the authority of the Raghus, abiding in the hearts of Shivan and Parvathl. He is the most dependable mighty ship which carries discerning aspirants and eminent savants and stalwart seers across the sea of worldly bondage. Sri Raman's inscrutable form is worshipped by God's, demon Kings and Sages. Sri Raman's happiness is a benign virus infecting others who come to Him, extremely ecstatic and prosperous by bestowing on them boons galore.

As Jadayu perceives the exceptionally handsome divine personage, with love eyes and captivating smile, the bearer of Govardhana hills, and as he cognizes the amalgamation of the three different personalities creator Brahman, Vishnu, and Shivan as one glorious form before his eyes as his Salvager, he is sweetly intoxicated with heavenly joy. Finally, as Jadayu's citation concludes, Sri Raman empowers him to enter the doors to heavenly glory, paradise, and, by His grace transforms him into a luminous and divine form, restoring him to his original completeness, replica of Vishnu's form holding couch, mace, disc and lotus in His four hands respectively; he, Jadayu ascends the heavenly abode by a fanciful air chariot chaperoned by Lord Vishnu's devotees and sages.

This commendation of Raman by Jadayu is numinous. By the wide generosity of Sri Raman's grace the reader is dispensed with Supreme Knowledge when read in the context of implicit piety and untainted love for Him.

Chapter - IX

Kabandhar's Supplication to Raman

The disheartened Raman and Lakshman wistfully resume their search for Sita, when, they are accosted by a very outlandish and grotesque demon in whose arms, that are about ten miles long, they are entrapped The ugliness of this freakish demon is conspicuous; he has a big cavity on his own stomach for a mouth. He has neither ears nor eyes and so, uses his ten-mile-long hands to ensnare creatures. Thereupon, Raman and Lakshman too happen to be thus inveigled and find themselves entrapped within his arms. Extricating themselves from the demon's clutches is onerous; consequently, the only way out is they sunder his very long hands.

The demon named Kabandhar reveals the hypothesis brewing in his mind, that the ones who have severed his arms must be Gods. But Raman unpretentiously laughs it away and answers the demon's queries by introducing themselves as king Dasarathar's sons, having come to stay in the forest in exile in deference to their father's orders. He further briefs him about the abduction of Sita from their cottage by a perverted demon in their absence and their extensive dogged wandering in quest of her.

While he is trying to retrieve his lost status, Kabandhar, the erstwhile King of Gandharvar, has reasons to be in high spirits for he declares he is blessed to meet Raman in his manifest form. In the presence of Sri Raman, he wails about his transformation into the present demon state. In the long distant past, an execration by Sage Astabakra who was aggravated by his facetious laughter had forced him to suffer a truncated body. Further more, Indhran whom he had chased dropped his thunderbolt upon him consequently jabbing his head and feet under his abdomen abbreviating his body. Fortunately, he did not die because he has been immortalized by a boon from Brahman. Taking pity on him Indhran shaped his mouth on his stomach by burrowing into its and also extended his arms ten miles long so that he may by ensnaring his prey sustain himself. Eventually, when Kabandhar begged pardon and prayed to Astabakra to be kind enough and purge him of all worldly dross, the sage enunciated he would be liberated when Lord Sri Raman cuts his arms asunder.

Kabandhar supplicates Sri Raman to incinerate his body so that he may have access to his original form and by that he could primarily apprise Him of his insights into the direction and place where His beloved Sita is harboured.

Accordingly, when the body of Kabandhar is set ablaze there rises from the flames a figure most handsome having earmarks of the God of cupid. He pays his respectful homage to Sri Raman and with unconfined joy paeans Raman as Lord who without an equal beyond words is beyond the range of all knowledge and sight. He transcends the limitations of mind, intellect and nature. He is like a myth in the minds of all, yet stands as a living witness in every individual being, and the spirit or Jiva is simply his own Imprint superimposed upon the intellect. All creatures subtle and indescribable are entities not separate from Him.

Kabandhar is rueful of his illusory knowledge which precludes him from describing Lord Raman comprehensively. Yet he perceives and designates Raman's subtle form "Hiranya Garbha", and as "Birat" in his grand and universal structure. His indistinct form is the intrinsic cause for the rich variety and complexity of the particulars manifest by the past, present and future creations. Kabandhar's long striving for one-pointed awareness of Raman's ethereal form is beneficial and ever rapturous as he pours forth his transcendental knowledge about Lord Raman as an ever fresh, lengthy, verbal garland of praise. He comprehends that the six spheres of 'Brahmanda' For grand universe, such as Bhu, Bohuba, Swa, Japa, Jana, Sathya, Maha Lokhas or worlds, which are subsumed in his grand form Birat, are constituted by the elements of Nature and phenomena. He proceeds to describe the nether world, patal, as his padal base; Mahatul as his anklets; Jatalal his legs; Bhutal the lower part of his thighs; Bital his upper thighs; Atal and the earth, his waist; Bhulok, his naval; Swargalokha or heaven, his breasts; Mahalok, his neck; Janalokha his face; Tapalokha his forehead and Sathayloka, his head. He is ecstatic to perceive Indhran and other deities as Lord Raman's arms and directions; Aswin Kumar to be his ears; fire, his nostrils; the sun, his mouth; the moon, his eyes; Time, his mind; the eyebrows his movements and Brishaspathi, the God of wisdom, his intellect; God Shiva is designated as his egoism; Veda, his speech, Yama, the God of the Death, his teeth; the innumerable stars, his petite teeth; Maya or Illusion, his smiles; the creative energy his looks, religion and piety, his foot side;

sin, his back; day and night, his winking; seven oceans, his belly; rivers, his sinews; trees and medicines, his hair; the rains, his semen and wisdom, his glory.

Meditating upon the universal form of the Lord which is the easiest path, expedites immediate salvation, is granted to seers, sages and serene devotees. Such a boon bestowed on Kabandhar to envision Lord Sir Raman's Transcendental Universal Apparition is not only feasible to meditate upon Sri Raman, but also overwhelms him with profound exuberance that is boundless. Yet, though not satiated comprehensively by this boon, he craves for Sri Raman's human form with bow and arrows in hermits garb, followed by Lakshman in search of Sita, and so, prays to almighty Raman to imprint, it indelibly, indeniably on his heart so that he may contemplate on it ever.

Lord Shiva's silent mission in 'Kasi' is unveiled to Sri Raman by Kabandhar. Lord Shiva is wholly and delightfully engaged in eternally preaching Raman's hallowed name to all who come to Him. Further, Shivan is preoccupied in scrumptuously enjoining, especially, the dying individuals to chant this holy name for their substantial and effortless passage to salvation.

Kabandhar acknowledges that Lord Raman in human form cannot be even conceptualized to be the Supreme Almighty God by the mediocre organic beings, for they are all the time befouled and befuddled by Him by His illusory deeds. For fear of being beguiled by Raman's illusions, Kabandhar together with Lakshman repeatedly bows and prays and implores the Lord of Ayodhya, the compassionate Sri Raman, to favour him and kindly save him so that his chicanery do not have any sway over him.

Lord Raman exonerates Kabandhar of all his sins; past and present, and he becomes sanctified and sinless. As He is ultimately pleased with him, Raman authorizes him to enter His divine abode. Again he unequivocally promises that individuals can in the same manner share his glorious abode with Him if they happen to even read this invocation with piety. Also, he stoutly proclaims that at the same moment they will be purged of sins and dark ignorance and be united with Him eternally in death.

Chapter - X

Sabhari's Salvation

Kabandhar unburdens himself of the obligation not to enlighten Raman on Sita's whereabouts. Instead he olans to make Raman have a strategic rendezvous which, perchance, has a twin purpose to serve with Sabhari, a genuine and ardent devotee of Raman. So he humbly proposes to Raman to call upon Sabhari, a lady who has fore knowledge of his visit, inorder to be updated on Sita's emplacement and state of affairs; perhaps this is one of the twin purposes. With this Gandharva chanting the holy name of Lord Raman the bestower of cosmic blessings, and by Raman's generosity alone, ascends to heaven on an effulgent plane.

Sabhari inhabits a rock shelter in a dense forest infested with untamed brutes. She is a woman of advance years. The anxious years of waiting for long have made her frail. But she is keeping alive cherised hopes of meeting Raman vis-a-vis some day. When she is zealously anticipating His visit, Raman with Lakshman arrives at her cave. The visible presence of the lord Raman at her dwelling ignites Sabhari's unbounded joy. Very enthusiastically she entertains Him offering nectarious plums which she had processed for such an auspicious occasion.

She worships Raman and Lakshman wholeheartedly and with great sincerity. Her expectation, anticipation is realistic, productive and worthy; for despite her poverty of literacy and her plebeian class and her gender complex, being a female, too, she has an upfront interaction with Almighty Raman. She pours out her heart to Lord Raman apprising him about her master sage Mathang's instructions to anticipate His advent patiently. She had struck a receptive chord when the Sage, who had lived there long ago, before leaving for the abode of Brahman, explicitly endorsed the good fortune of having her fleshy frame cast of purely by Raman's grace so as to attain his heavenly kingdom; and this perhaps is the second of the twin purposes. Now, though having been born into the low caste, an ordinary woman, she rejoices and thanks her stars for beholding Raman in person face to face. She asserts that her preceptor's words have come to pass. However, her sterility of spiritual knowledge and illiteracy and her inferior status are feeding self-doubts because she fumbles for the ways and means to adore and invoke the Omniscient Raman. Feeling a sensation of queasy helplessness and confusion she solicits him to patronize her.

At this juncture the all-pervasive Raman proclaims He cannot be seen or found or trapped by anyone who has not cultivated in his heart pure love for Him alone. He also enunciates that He is attracted to, irrespective of caste and race and regardless of gender and literacy distinctions, His discerning aspirants and ardent devotees who cherish and nurture flawless and unflinching love solely for Him which He prizes the most. Further He goes on to enumerate the nine expedient steps leading to devotion to Him which delight and appease Him endlessly, such as, sustained affiliation with His aspirants and true devotees, constant study and reflection on His life sagas, singing His glorious deeds in melodious hymns, imparting spiritual knowledge, service and obedience of the highest order to one's spiritual mentor, self-discipline leading to a chaste and holy life and worship of God, self-restraint-leading to control of mind and sense organs, ceaseless chanting of His varied names and sacred manthras, self abnegation and detachment from worldly bondage, obeisance of the highest order to His devoted followers more than Himself, equanimity and equilibrium of mind and doggedly pursuing truth thereby abiding in peace and bliss. It never fails to please Him when one with profound loyalty and perseverance takes to such a life of devotion and worship.

Raman categorically pronounces that achievement of salvation is near at hand, only if the individual in this very life span establishes and fosters such immaculate love for Him by cognizing His true self. Thus, significantly, Raman asserts that the prerequisite and consistent means for securing His love and liberation is the association with high-minded sages and saints.

Magnanimously Raman singles out Sabhari as a true-blue aspirant and guarantees her of positive salvation. Raman, now, broaches the subject of Sita's present emplacement. He requests her to tell him of the whereabouts of his beloved wife Sita, who was abducted by a wicked demon.

Though hailing Raman as the Omniscient Lord, Sabhari remarks it is His worldly wise anxiety, in the manner of nondescript human beings, that makes her respond to his queries. She has not much to say except that Ravanan has carried Sita away to Lanka that she has been placed well, and right now, she is safe and well protected. In addition, she entreats Raman to advance beyond her habitation to the hills of Rishyamuksha where the highly nervy Sugrivan is abiding with four of his gallant ministers. She pleads Sugrivan's cause requesting Raman to befriend him since he is living in hiding there for fear of his brother Vali. Glowing with understanding, she stimulates His hopes of finding Sita with the help of Sugrivan and achieving remarkable success in his endeavours. Interestingly, Sabhari rapidly graduates with the totality of her organic being, to invoke Raman to be compassionate in allowing her to shake off her material coil. She implores Him not to proceed until she has done so and ascends heaven by his benign grace. Her faith makes present the grace of Raman and the prudent Sabhari enters the fire and burns her frame thus getting detached from anxieties, illusions and the throes of worldly life; she soon attains divine form and mounts to Raman's abode.

It is but mandatory that discerning aspirants should with their whole being love Raman alone so as to be purged of all sins and be sheltered from worldly attachments. If the saintly life of the low born Sabhari, who was ignorant and unlettered, stands out as a perfect paradigm teaching lessons to all, irrespective of caste, gender, education, creed, race, colour, social standing etc., for the attainment of the highest place, Elysium, then, how much more will the magnitude of the task of attaining salvation be for the aristocrats and the pure hearted persons. It is neither confounding nor strenuous when such landmarks to guide us in our quest for truth are a prerequisite.

To dynamize the emancipatory impulse, Individuals should stop spending energies in frivolous and frothy talk, and should fathom that salvation is fostering a judicious combination of deep impeccable love and unswerving devotion to unparalleled God Raman, whose splendorous, charming, azure sheened form has a shoreless loveliness which steals even the celebrated heart of Lord Shivan where in He abides permanently.

Part - IV
Kishkindha Kandham

Chapter - I

Raman's Fraternity with Monkeys: Sugrivan's Bond of Friendship

The instant response to traverse beyond prompts Raman and Lakshman to meander further through the forest and arrive at a region wherein flows the Pamban, a beautiful waterscape of untainted waters. The elegance of this lake is enhanced by the different hued lotuses which perfume its crystal clear waters, in which graceful swans glide noiselessly and other amphibious birds swoop in and take to flight, a lovely feast for the eyes, The peerless essence gladdens them to quench their thirst after which they reach the foot of the Rishyamuksha hill.

The arrival of Raman and Lakshman is instantly distinctive, creating a furor, because of their ascetic attire, hairdo and the carrying of bows and arrows, among Sugrivan and his ministers residing there.

Sugrivan seeing them approaching towards their abode is on the verge of panic, that he immediately deputes his chief Minster, Hanuman, to know their mind and intent of arriving there, for the reason, that he fears his brother Vali would have delegated these valiant lads to slay him. Hanuman masked as hermit meets Raman and Lakshman and initiates a dialogue humbly questioning them on their identity, so starkly different, and requests them to inform him of the purpose of their unforeseen visit. Hanuman voices his percipience establishing them to be incarnations of God, having descended on earth in the forms of spectacular, inimitable youthful warriors to bequeath boons and shower blessings on distinguished aspirants and to annihilate the sinful, and the nefarious demons thus defiling the earth.

After evidently witnessing Hanuman's eloquent verbal display Raman in low tones to Lakshman ratifies Hanuman as a very intelligent and well-grounded lad at that. Then, basically, He modulates they are sons of King Dasarathar having come to live in exile for fourteen years in the forest at their father's behest. Further, he explains the abduction of His beloved Sita by a demon in their absence and eventually has arrived there to make a laborious and extensive quest for her.

Hanuman reciprocates Raman's query pronouncing His name, saying he is the son of the God of Wind and Sugrivan's minister. Beforehand, he draws Raman's attention to a collateral situation plaguing Sugrivan's life for which he seeks redress. He unfolds the events that led to Sugrivan's extradition from his own kingdom, Kiskindha, and presently residing on the hill tops, by his elder brother Vali, who also, coercively and powerfully, deprived him of his wife too. He entreats Raman, that His visit augurs well, to scrupulously befriend Sugrivan and to right all wrongs. Raman expresses similar sentiments, acknowledges Hanuman's supplication and assures to bring peace accordingly.

Hanuman, with Raman and Lakshman poised on his broad shoulders, and in just a single stride, bounces atop the hill in a second to join Sugrivan. He informs Sugrivan of the closely woven pattern of friendship that is in prospect between the two sides. With this Sugrivan's fears are extinguished, and thereafter, hastens to welcome Raman and Lakshman. Exchanging pleasantries they seat themselves merrily on the branches broken from the trees, after which, Sugrivan, has the specific aspects of Sita's kidnap detailed to him by Lakshman. At this moment, Sugrivan is reminiscent of a bundle of ornaments that had dropped from a flying chariot in which a lady evidently much against her will and consent, was being carried away by a demon, and which he preserves even to this day. Presenting it to Raman to examine and confirm if they belong to Sita, Sugrivan simultaneously pledges also his best supportive efforts and endeavour to trace and find Sita.

On seeing Raman weeping uncontrollably as would a common man, unlike a transcendental being, at the very sight of the jewels, both Sugrivan and Lakshman try their best to conciliate him in the manner of worldly men. Reassuringly, Sugrivan reiterates his commitment to the cause of rescuing her safely with the help of the monkeys from the evil clutches of Ravanan. As a visible sign of good faith, Hanuman blazes a fire and Raman professes a vow of sacred fraternization with Sugrivan before it; thereby, they enfold each other in a warm embrace. They are both radiant with love for each other and this event cements a bond for eternal friendship.

Thereafter, Sugrivan opens up his heart to Raman; he goes back to the mental attic where he has stored away the events of his eventful life, relating how a mighty giant, the son of Maya, had challenged and also lost to Vali in a duel at Kishkindha. The giant had taken to his heels since he was defeated and wounded by Vali's hard percussions. Vali relentlessly chased him on followed by Sugrivan, up to a cave into which Mayabi and Vali entered. He, Sugrivan, had waited for a month at the entrance for Vali's return, when, one day he only saw blood flow out of it. Presuming there was no denial of Vali's in existence, he had placed a huge boulder across the mouth of the cave and returned to Kiskindha in deep grief and announced to its citizens the sudden death of his brother Vali. The councillors counselled him to take the throne. Yet, unenthusiastically and unwillingly, and even at the consensus of the citizens, he took over the reins of sovereignty.

But all was not well for Sugrivan. Incrediulously, when, after the lapse of a few days, Vali arrived unexpectedly to the great consternation of everyone. Vali's resentment at finding Sugrivan holding the reins of power as king provoked him to misconstrue that Sugrivan had hoodwinked him completely in his greed for the Kingdom and so meted out the same treatment of thrashing him with heavy blows. Such intimidating handling had forced Sugrivan to flee the country inorder to save his life. Unabated Vali blinded with rage pursued him on a wild hunt, wherever he went throughout the whole globe. Finally, the exclusive zone that could give him solace and refuge was the Rishyamugha hills, where Vali still could not dare venture owing to a malediction by a sage in the past. Consequently, Vali had expropriated his wealth and property and abducted his wife also.

Sugrivan laments that the internecine conflict has only purchased years of frustration and adversity. But he takes immense comfort in knowing that the return of peace, happiness and prosperity are no longer a remote possibility, for, Raman, while expressing sympathetic sentiments about Sugrivan's present deplorable condition promises to kill Vali. Yet, Sugrivan, in some corner of his mind doubts Raman's prowess to slay Vali. He cites an incident in point to substantiate Vali's invincibility. Once, when a mighty giant named Dundvir engaged Vali in a combat in Kishkindha, the latter had severed and flung his head some ten miles away landing by accident at the hermitage of Sage Mathanga, and contaminating and desecrating the premises with its blood.

The enraged Sage had imprecated him then that he would meet the same fate, if he ever went near Mathanga's hermitage at Rishyamugha hills. Conclusively, Sugrivan points to the skeleton of the giant's head, which is a big as a hillock. Though Sugrivan together with his ministers cheers Raman for effortlessly tossing the head some hundred miles away with just His toes, he is still neither convinced nor does he endorse Raman's valour.

Further, Sugrivan in preference, points to seven Tal trees which Vali used to shake, all at the same time, thereby, making all the trees shed all their leaves completely by the shaking, thus trumpeting Vali's mettle. He is till inspired to test Raman's invulnerability and intrepidity! Hence, pointing to the seven same Tal trees again Sugrivan floats an audacious wager defying Raman to pierce them all with an arrow in a single shot. If he succeeds he will be absolutely ascertained that none mightier than Raman could kill Vali.

Admiration and stupefaction is written on the face of Sugrivan and all other monkeys as they witness amicable Raman performing the prodigious feat of releasing an arrow from His bow, which, inevitabiy, pierces all the seven trees simultaneously, and instantly returns to his quiver. And what is more, the confidence engendered by Raman's successful execution is visible in them that they are all amazed at his marvellous titanic strength. The moment the truth hits Sugrivan, he explodes with strong emotions of joy and faith pronouncing Raman as the Absolute Reality whom he has encountered this day, a sequel to the upright deeds performed in the births gone by.

In the light of Raman's preceding adventure, Sugrivan unequivocally declares he has secured an esoteric treasure, namely, a life of sanctification with Raman's benedictions just as a person' while digging the earth unexpectedly happens on a very fantastic bulky treasure, would undergo any discomfort or trouble to annex it. Hence he does not demand creature comforts or opulence or high living from Raman. He chooses to walk in the footsteps of the Saints and Sages who love Raman undividedly for their salvation. Since he has found the most invaluable treasure, Raman, all other things-a big intimate family circle, prosperity, wealth, kingdom and the ambiguous realities of daily existence, which are His plausible creations, are distasteful and trivial to him. Because, he is anxious, just as an individual is entangled all the more resolutely in worldly existence by his sacrifices, austerities and other pious deeds, that he too may be embroiled in such egocentric travails. The incessant chanting of his umpteen names, the chanter, he be a murderer of Brahmins or a wicked dipsomaniac, shall be liberated at once from his sins. Moreover, liberation of an individual from ignorance, and the perishing ills of existence can be achieved by even a moment's association or contact with Raman's benign touch.

Sugrivan realizes and acknowledges that it is only now his mind has emerged from Raman's illusion which had thickly clouded him so long, resulting in discriminating individuals as friends, foes and neutrals. But now his transformation makes him believe and cognize that there is no distinction, that everything is God. Therefore, he expresses no desire for worldly properties nor makes claims for the retrieval of his wife, for they are all the transitory creations of his illusion. Only, he craves for Raman's love alone as it disintegrates the manacles of birth and death for ever Sugrivan necessitates the beneficent Raman to bestow on him such favours as to live with Him consecrating his mind, heart and all organic senses and organs to His service day in and day out, with deep-rooted belief that the whole universe is His tabernacle, to untiringly chant His names and be ever mindful of His glorious deeds in His different incarnations.

Chapter - II

The Emancipation of Vali

Benevolent Raman, invariably, accredits the friendly Sugrivan's foregone sentiments. Furthermore, He sends the pure-hearted Sugrivan into raptures by His enthralling, captivating yet, deceptive smiles, thus substantiating that blessed individuals on earth can visualize god face to face and still live most happily which is no exaggeration. At this instant, Raman, acting as a strong influence instigates Sugrivan to proceed to Kiskindha and incite Vali to a challenging confrontation. Likewise, He asserts that it would be unreasonable in the light of worldly opinion if He does not persevere in His promise to kill Vali to Sugrivan's advantage.

Sugrivan and his retinue are bound for Kiskindha with Raman at the helm of affairs. He reaches Vali's palace without Raman, and detonates a loud reverberating bawl inviting Vali to a fight. As a quick reflex response, the estranged Vali indignant at Sugrivan's irksome roar instantly appears on the scene to confront him. But quickly enough, without giving him time to gauge the situation or even defend himself, Sugrivan treats him to a spate of cruel blows. Soon Vali gains the upper hand retaliating with heavier blows thus, over powering him. At a distance Raman is astoundingly perturbed at the identical appearance of Vali, a spitting image of Sugrivan, so much so, that He cannot tell them apart. Hence, Raman desists from striking with his bow and arrow, lest His misconception should kill Sugrivan instead of Vali, inadvertently.

Routed by the undeniably mightier Vali, Sugrivan is forced to retreat and flee to where Raman is stationed at a distance. He accusingly questions Raman on the punitive action of sending him to encounter Vali when, He Himself could have killed him if He so intended. He dolefully remonstrates that had he not taken to his heels he, otherwise, would have been slain by Vall.

Raman cordially sympathizes and soothes the disconsolate Sugrivan telling him He eschewed killing Vali because He was perplexed at their indistinguishable identities. He effaces Sugrivan's inertia to resist, inspires hope and encourages him to venture on a second challenge, this time garlanded, so that He may single Vali out and kill him eventually. On Raman's order Lakhsman arranges a garland for Sugrivan.

Loaded with a strategic sequel to Raman's significant move, the garlanded Sugrivan storms into the premises of Vali's palace and bellows a resonating roar, more formidable than before, challenging him to a daring duel again.

Vali's spouse Tara, hampers his preparations for a confrontation with Sugrivan. She is inclined to fear that an all-powerful force is his main stay, buttressing his endeavours in his mission and making him emerge victorious at every step. For the horrifying disclosure by her son Angadhan, who once during his hunting spree had heard that Raman and Lakshman have met Sugrivan at the Rishyamugha hills and have established a friendly bond with Him that, thenceforth, Raman has promised Sugrivan all prop, invariably, in his efforts to retrieve his lost property and his wife. She adds that Raman has also assured Sugrivan of the Kingship and kingdom of Kishkindha by dethroning him, Vali, to the extent of killing him.

In conclusion, Tara voices concern for her dear Lord Vali; she pray to him to renounce this confrontational life and hostility towards Sugrivan. She pleads for initiating and sustaining a compatible relationship, a highway for the return of peace with him. Over shadowed by fear even now, it becomes her to tearfully request Vali not to disparage her humble suggestions whlch would otherwise jeopardize the interests of her son Angadhan and the Kingdom of Kishkindha.

Contrary to her anticipation, her deeply felt sentiments go unheeded. Vali spurns her words as coming from that of the weaker sex who merely entertains fears without any rhyme or reason. Resting on his laurels, he prides himself in being a much-publicized warrior and vanquisher, blatantly refusing to be untrammelled and remain subdued indoors. Since he has been favoured with a good position, ability and proclivity, he is determined to go all out and kill Sugrivan in the encounter if he has come all alone.

Further, Vali tries to quell Tara's fears about Raman being Sugrivan's bulwark. He conceptualizes Raman as a divine being, the incarnation of God. And if he happens to meet Sri Raman now, he would please and gladden him by using the currency of love and devotion to Him. He is intrigued by the enigmatic Raman, yet cognizes Him as being equitable, bestowing favours to only the ones who nurture unimpeachable love for Him alone. In this fashion Vali augments his self-image and is all set to encounter Sugrivan. Thereupon, Vali rushes out and fights against Sugrivan with all his might and power. In the interim, Raman who does not expose Himself to Vali snipes a powerful shaft striking and piercing his breast straightaway. The wounded Vali experiencing agonizing pain twists his torso, leaps up and then buckles to the ground senseless. Gradually regaining consciousness he returns to normalcy and visions Sri Raman and Sri Lakshman standing at his side. By nod and nuance, Vali makes it clear to Raman that he deprecates his action.

Vali, who is struck off guard feels he is wronged, censures Lord Raman for having done him serious injustice of shooting an arrow when he has not committed any crime; he acknowledges to be a sincere devotee of Raman; he discloses his knowledge of Raman making Sugrivan His confidant and the secret alliance of committing him to bring back Sita from Ravanan's custody. Vali continues his vocalization underlining Raman's lack of confidence in him, and boasts of his own potentiality to bring back Sita together with Ravanan in a split second had Raman commanded him to do so. Again, Vali probes into the propriety of Sri Raman hiding, like a thief, behind a tree and shooting him from a distance. Moreover, he blames Raman for stigmatizing the Kshatriya race into which he has been born by His cowardly attack; he continues, if Raman had contrarily encountered an attack against him, His nobility as a Kshatriyan would have been distinctly evident far and wide. He cannot conjecture why Sri Raman had drawn this line of distinction between them, himself and Sugrivan, and preferred to choose only Sugrivan and befriend him, isolating him out. He concedes he belongs to the species of Monkeys and even his organic frame will not in anyway be acceptable or useful to human beings.

Lord Raman, however, out of His infinite compassion, chooses to answer all the queries put forward by the fallen King Vali in a manner that fully convinces him of the fairness of His action. He reprimands Vali not to brag too much in the fashion he has just been doing, as he truly merits death. Sri Raman constrains Vali to confront the enormity of the untruth that underlies his life; a sinner, being guilty of abducting his younger brother's beloved wife and depriving him of his wealth and property. He again constrains Vali to realize that he as a monkey cannot understand, and does not have regard for Virtuous people like Him who traverse the length and breadth of the globe only to resurrect such wrong doers from the quagmire of sin.

Vali regrets that he has been so foolish as to challenge Sri Raman's action and thereupon seeks His pardon. He confesses his sins and prostrates at the feet of Lord Sir Raman, acknowledging Him as Supreme God and begs to be forgiven for his audacious belligerence.

His holistic perspective recognizes Lord Raman as Sri Vishnu and Devi Sita as Sri Lakshmi and that their incarnations are intermediary for bringing peace and re- creating the power of love on earth as the human soul rests ultimately in love.

Vali humbly requests the benevolent Raman to remove the arrow from his chest and bless him so as to overcome the final power of death. He pleads to Sri Raman to be gracious to his son Angadhar When Lord Raman plucks out the arrow, Vali breathes his last.

Vali's sucombing to death takes place in the context of Lord Raman's love, just by a touch, that he instantly attains a celestial form. By the Lord's grace, he, beyond question, secures a very illustrious station like that of Indhran the king of Gods in paradise which even great saints crave for.

Chapter - III

Solace to Tara and Enthronement of Sugrivan

Vali's attendants are terrified and traumatized by Raman's bravura which felled their invincible warrior king. They, apprehensive of increased trouble from Sugrivan's quarter, immediately, approach their queen Tara and break the sad news of Vali's tragic death at the hands of Raman. On hearing the news, Tara is swayed by distress. Bitter grief assaults her senses that she swoons to the ground senseless. When she recovers from the fainting fit, the attendants adjure her to instantly invest the Kingdom in the hands of Angad her beloved Son.

They supplicate her to immediately instal him on the throne while they guard the city with all the main entrances firmly shut.

The bereaved queen, unable to come to terms with the unfortunate blow, in bitter sorrow articulates that the thought of self-immolation is predominantly plaguing her abject mind, as she perceives the triviality and uselessness of all this opulence, the kingdom and even her son Angadhan, when her Lord Vali the invincible King of the forest is no more. She swears to unite with her dead husband by killing herself.

So saying, with loose strands of hair, she rushes out of doors and arrives at the spot where Vali's corpse is doused in a pool of blood and dust. She eats her heart out; loudly wailing and striking her breast' as she, through her tearful eyes sees Raman standing by her side. At once she exhorts Lord Raman to do away with her life also with the self same arrow with which He has slain her husband who is suffering an inner sense of alienation and cannot enjoy bliss even in heaven due to his forceful separation from her. She implores Raman to be merciful to her by alleviating the painfully insurmountable grief, which she is intensely experiencing in mourning for her Lord Vali.

Tara labouring under a cloud of injustice that has been meted out to her, scoffs at Sugrivan saying that it is his turn now to command prosperity and affluence and be convivial with his wife since Raman has thus favoured him by killing Vali.

At this moment, Raman unobtrusively instructs Tara on the indigenous perspective of the soul, which, he says, is immortal, omnipresent and spotless. To reinforce His import, He points out to the hollowness and senselessness in being so much heart-broken at being torn apart from her husband's organic body which is evanescent and doomed to perish. Moreover, every individual at every moment of his life is confronted by his own mortality. Hence, there is no misgiving for separation in anyway as his soul is deathless and pervasive. He requests her to take heart as only persons steeped in dark ignorance mourn profusely and elaborately at the death of their kith and kin.

The lucid explanation of the conception of the soul leads Tara on to request Raman to further enlighten her on the uninterrupted interplay of happiness and misery in this world and the inter twining of joy and sorrow experienced by an individual in his life; even the soul is ever euphoric and eternal and the body having no sense is gross and mortal.

Sir Raman explicitly expounds that by the combinations of the intellect, the senses and mind the ego in the individual is born. By the synchronizing of the eternal subtle entities such as the Senses, Mind, Intellect and Ego in the individual, the Ego thinks itself to be happy or miserable because it alone is predominantly acting in the body through the sense organs.

Wherefore it expresses itself as "I". Owing to the soul's reflections, the spirit or Jiva of an individual in his egoistic form integrates with the intellect and mind, which alone is the enjoyer or the victim in life. The soul wholly pure and real has no nescience and disorientation whereas, it is only simply through his egoism and mind that the individual thoroughly experiences worldliness and its enjoyments.

Dreams are insubstantial; like wise, all creations of the Universe are flimsy and false like dreams. The soul manifests the Ego, Intellect, Mind, Senses and the external instruments. The soul, like a catalyst, is not affected by the recurrent cycles of birth and death together with worldly bondage and revulsion; but it is mind which runs into the labyrinths of worldly pleasure, enjoyment pain, sorrow that is intertwined with them. In as much, man's soul is only a silent spectator in the mind and it is only mind that operates in him and through him.

Subtle ignorance makes man believe that the doer, enjoyer and suffer is principally his gross body and not his soul. Veritably the body is non-intelligent and is just an instrument; the soul is inoperative, performing just as an agent which is the real perceiver or the knower, granting energy to the ego and the intellect which work according to the three gunas - Sattva-enlightenment. Rajas - exertion and Tamas - ignorance. The impressions caught by the other instruments and the senses reach the soul through mind and intellect.

Everything is a product of the three attributes or gunas Sattva, Rajas and Tamas, incorporate in man. When the Sattva or peaceful guna is preponderant in an individual at such times, it is said to be influencing his mind, initiating him into virtuous deeds of worship, meditation and the like. Similarly, other worldly activities get underway when mind is predominantly influenced by Rajasic gunas, and Thamasic gunas trigger off such predatory deeds like murder, inebriation, licentiousness etc., when the mind is strongly under its influence. Consequently, this leads to the concept of the Rule of the Law, from which arise the doctrine of Karma and the doctrine of Rebirth, the former hinging on the conviction that there exists an order which may be described as universal justice. The doctrine of Karma stands for the principle of necessity operating in the moralistic life of an individual. It stretches the relation of cause and effect from the physical plane, where the determination is external, for every occurrence is determined by something other than itself, to the moral plane where the moral determination is self-determination for the individual decides the actions and is bound to experience the results of his actions. This leads to the concept of the doctrine of Rebirth where the individual is a programmed creature with a set of circumstances besetting him at birth and in life, showing certain advantages and disadvantages at birth itself; these are to be regarded as the result of his actions in previous lives which involves him in worldliness so long as his egoistic connections with deeply rooted worldly impressions prevail. The doctrine of Karma seems to be an impediment to the cessation of rebirth. But then, the individual can override the impediments constraining him to live in a quandary of worldliness conducive to recurrent births as Lord Sir Raman cultivates the optimism and hope of the individual for attaining salvation. The crux of Raman's declaration for attaining salvation is the realization of the Self by transcending the ego with the acquisition of transcendental knowledge, devotion and worship to Him solely.

Sri Raman discloses to Tara his immense pleasure at being propitiated by her in her previous life and now He has sought to divulge to her the most sacred philosophy, which effectuates complete liberation to His aspirants. Further, He enjoins her to follow His injunctions with her mind concentratedly focused on Him. In doing so Sri Raman maintains she will visualize her inner self and attain salvation even in her present life time, though being engaged in the manifold and multifarious phases of worldly existence.

Tara is beside herself with joy on hearing Lord Sri Raman's homily. Her association with Sri Raman instantly releases her mind of all grief and is filled with peace, utterly by His grace. She has also promptly acquired indescribable knowledge of the inner self and her malady or ignorance takes flight immediately. She extols Sri Raman as none other than the Supreme Almighty Authority, the sole refuge for those who seek recovery of possessions lost and more importantly or those who aspire for prosperity.

Thereafter, Vali's corpse is taken out in royal procession with all pomp and show to the sounds of trumpets and other musical instruments, accompanied by Sugrivan, Angadan, the attendants and the citizens to the river side and consigned to flames following due rites of the funeral ceremony.

Subsequently, as a reciprocal gesture, Sugrivan proffers the kingship of Kishkindha to Lord Sri Raman entreating Him to accept the throne and pave the way for him, Sugrivan, to serve Him as a mere slave. Sri Raman cheerfully repudiates the offer saying it is of little significance as to who rules the kingdom since there is no difference between them as they are both one and the same. He ordains Sugrivan to go immediately to Kishkindha to take over the reins of royal power and declare himself as the king making Angadan his next successor to the throne. As with the onset of the monsoon, Raman suggests that they defer the search for Sita until the rainy season passes and proposes to sojourn at the top of the hills with Lakshman until such time.

After paying due obeisance in the most humble fashion, prostrating at the Lotus feet of Lord Sri Raman, Sugrivan, accompanied by Lakshman is bound for Kishkindha where the coronation ceremony is performed, accordingly, as Sri Raman has prescribed and ordained. On Lakshman's return, Raman and he wend their way to the distant Pravarshana hills. Atop the hills they find an ideally comfortable cave. The idyllic sylvan spot, abounding with streams and fruits is really delighting and cheering, as it is a sanctuary for various kinds of beautiful birds and beasts. Enchanted by the beauty of this scenic place, they begin to sojourn here with peace and cheer abiding in their hearts.

Chapter - IV

Raman's Preaching to Lakshman or Raman's Injunctions to Lakshman Raman or Enlightens Lakshman on the Efficiency of Praver and worship

Raman and Lakshman are passing the rainy spell by basking in the tranquillity and calm prevalent among the Pravarshana hills. The Kaleidoscopic spectrum-huge grey clouds pregnant with rain changing shapes and sizes as they float along green mountains, undulating and swelling rivers and boisterous cataracts lustily cascading its waters-showcase the grandeur and sublimity of the monsoon season. These changing scenes are a cheering sight being relished by Raman with great pleasure. Supplementing this blissful aura, comely and chubby deer, frisking merrily in the rain, delighting the onlookers, converge near Raman's cave. Sages and even saints who yearn for a close proximity to Raman, disguised as deer approximate as close to Raman inorder to be touched or caressed by Him.

It is against this back drop, Lakshman, one day, encounters Raman in a secluded retreat where a spate of curious sentiments emanate from Lakshman's maturing temper of spiritual life. He articulates that it is by Raman's Grace alone he has emerged spotlessly uninfected from the unfathomable abyss of illusive bondage. He calls for a fruitful communion with Raman to have knowledge of the best procedure and sequence of worshipping Him in His true essence. He exposes the fact that even illustrious sages take to the path of worship and devotion to Him alone for attaining salvation. Here, Lakshman exerts his personal and private opinion as worship and devotion being the surest, the easiest and the quickest channel or mode to delight Him.

Raman, at the outset, acknowledges the practice of worship as being intrinsic to the life of spirituality. Though He enunciates that there are innumerable ways to worship Him, He deigns to disclose the easy way to attain Him. He promulgates manthra chanting, with sincerity and devotion, an arbitrary frill by which the aspirant should first sanctify himself. Primarily, all worship and prayer should begin after cleansing the body with a bath with holy water. Worship of his idols or images, a concrete necessity, is permitted till the devotee is able to transcend the preparatory state of mind regarding worship, according to the devised system of tenets under which each individual should follow, prescribed for him by his preceptor whom also he should worship. The devotee may worship Him in the form of any idol, better an idol in Saligramam, a sacred stone. His concentrated effort of mind may be directed to worship Him within his own heart or even in fire, water or in the sun as there exists no special entity as matter, for all that manifests is the Lord and he alone.

The devotee should perform the daily ritual practices or spiritual duties, on his seat, having great disciplinary valve of acquiring perseverance and sustained devotion, and if persisted regularly and systematically with devotion and faith, are good for the body, mind and soul, with his mind rightfully concentrated on yoga pranayama - systematic breath control, inhaling and exhaling breathing exercise. Then he should worship the image or idol of the Lord, Sri Raman, very fervently, smearing it very carefully with holy ingredients, pure sandal paste, holy ashes etc., and decorating it with garlands, flowers, perfumes after having bathed it in pure holy water or cleaning it in case of it being a picture, Lord Sri Raman openly asserts that He is highly satiated by any individuals whole hearted worship and guileless offering of even moderate articles of food and simple fruits, notwithstanding his inability to ostentatiously offer expensive articles and food extravagantly. He underscores that a little water, some flowers or even a leaf, if offered to Him exclusively, with sincerity and faith are bound to delight Him sufficiently. The devotee should perform Nyasam, Dhyanam or meditation, and offer water, Madhuparka, it being mixed with milk, curd, honey and refined butter and sugar. But if he opts to worship Him in fire, he should offer oblations, and if he chooses to worship Him in the sun, a surya chakra the picture of the sun on metal plate or metal foil is required. It follows the necessity that at the time of completing the worship, for arrangement of light with burning cotton sticks soaked in ghee. This form of worship is called "Nirajan".

Dhyanam is concrete meditation on the image or icon of the Lord. The devotee with steadfast conviction should believe that the image that is meditated on is not a symbol merely, but he, who is everywhere, his very form appearing before his mind's eye. The devotee should constantly repeat a chosen manthra called Japa, which is the necessary intermediate step to meditation. Through Japa he gets the ability to fix his mind on a single thought track combining His name and His form, after which he performs Havana, if the method is known to him, the best method to be followed being the one prescribed by sage Agasthiyar. At every moment of repetition of the Manthra, His name, the devotee should offer into the blazing fire rice prepared in milk and sugar or till and barley soaked in ghee. The pit or altar for performing havana should be assembled according to vedic injunctions and methods. In course of the worship the devotee should glorify Sri Raman highlighting His names and deeds in soul-stirring music and song. Such miscellaneous items as camphor, sandal-wood paste, fragrant powder, kum-kum, agrau, incense, betel leaves and betel nuts, coconut milk, ghee, honey, specific sweet smelling flowers, variety of fruits, fine, rich silk material are indispensable for idol worship. The devotee should fall prostrate at the Lord's image and invoke His abundant blessings at the consummation of his image worship of the Lord.

Finally all the offerings made unto Him, the idol of the Lord, take the name of 'Prasatham' of which the devotee should partake a small portion of the edible items-fruits, coconuts etc., and put to use the non-edible items. He should be, in toto, content to etch and register the thought and picture of the Lord on his soul through the idol.

But Lord Sri Raman unequivocally states, though, this external worship so expensively performed with a huge measure of riches will please Him little, tending to border on pride, pomp and extravaganza, if, internally the heart is barren, devoid of love, piety, solemnity and truthfulness. Sri Raman again asserts emphatically that the devotee will without an iota of doubt, reach paradise at his death by His grace if he consistently worships Him with love and conviction conforming to the path and instructions propounded by Himself, and even reads or hears His infallible and enduring words. Further, He promises to dispense him with a life of happiness and prosperity throughout his life.

Now coming down on to the plane of worldly existence, Raman's composure collapses as he weeps, a fine play-acting, bethinking of Sita, and continues weeping throughout the night as any ordinary moral would do. These touching sentiments vibrate tugging at the heartstrings of Hanuman at Kishkindha, who, in the meantime, is negotiating with Sugrivan on the issue of setting up a search mission for retrieving Sita. Hanuman reprehends him for his irreflective and inconsiderate behaviour in not living up to his promise made to Raman to search for Sita, till now. He urges Sugrivan to keep up his memory against defecting neurons, and reminds him of Raman's altruism in restoring the kingdom, the kingship and his wife to him by slaying the unconquerable Vali to his advantage.

He warns of the same outcome, death, at the hands of Raman, if he relegates the pledge to the shelf as quaint and neglects his commitment.

Sugrivan, jolted out of his epicurean spell, affectionately addresses Hanuman, requesting him to depute the chief officers to the different parts of the globe to bring all the monkeys there immediately. He delegates Hanuman to issue stringent orders to them to reach Kiskindha within a fortnight failing which they will be done to death for disobedience of the decree. Hanuman fuels Sugrivan's resolve, accordingly, commissioning all the intelligent and valourous monkeys by bestowing on them due rewards and honour for their disposition and purpose.

Chapter - V

Lakshman Cautions Sugrivan

Raman's cumulative despondency surfaces whenever He reminisces about Sita Devi. He misses her increasingly as the days go by One night. His reflections on His consort Sri Sita Devi are not consoling, though he thinks on her moon like face, a captivating image of beauty and modesty, her mystical virtues and fresh-faced innocence. Eventually He flees into a conventional escape of dejection and explodes into a verbal violence, promising Lakshman to annihilate the demon Ravanan together with his progeny as he has stealthily taken possession of Sita. But He intones that He would find her as nectar extracted from the ocean.

Raman remonstrates that Sugrivan whom He addresses as brother seems to be ungrateful and oblivious of His asseveration to track down and recapture Sita. He is anxious that time is slipping though His fingers; the rainy season has stretched into the autumn which has Just commenced, and thus far, Sugrivan has not focused his mind on such deliberations to initiate the search mission. He presumes that Sugrivan, unmindful of his oath, is extensively engaged in revelling in the just inherited affluence and prosperity and seems to be tied to his wife's apron strings indulging in titillating pleasures. Nothing annoys Raman more as want of gratitude, for gratitude unlocks the fullness of life. He fires away His indignation at him for his alleged lack of reverence to his pledge, involving the danger of punishment, death at His hands for his ingratitude.

Soon Lakshman is infected with anger and prays to Raman to permit him to, immediately go to Kishkindha and kill the ungrateful wretch Sugrivan. Raman subscribes to Lakshman's encounter with Sugrivan only to reprimand him and not to slay him as the invisible bond of friendship exists and is still vibrant between them. He asserts that the future of action will be determined by the tidings that he brings from Sugrivan after his return.

Base minds, speculating on Raman's worldly-wise demeanor of dejection and woe at the separation from his divine consort Sri Sita Devi, who is goddess Lakshmi, only expose their stark ignorance and spiritual insanity. It is indispensable that the Supreme Lord Raman chooses to be grief-stricken and woebegone, virtually, play acting, conforming to human nature and manners, so that the world might evidently perceive him to be a human person. Raman's life saga called 'Ramayanam' is the fountain-head of spiritual heritage, with an elaboration of even the minutest details relating to several and miniscule facets of life, offering eternal knowledge to the world at large for the attainment of salvation. It is the quintessence of self-emancipation, freedom and perfection of every type of activity to all on earth preserved for posterity.

Lakshman arrives in Kishkindha. Not surprisingly, inorder to announce his arrival and make his presence felt very much and, more so, to unbottle his vehement anger, he resonates an explosive sound with his bow sending an alarming note as if he were meaning to kill all the monkeys. This reverberating sound forces the young and brave Angadan out of his quarters and immediately hastens to receive Lakshman reverentially, with all respects.

Lakshman's hard-edged formality sends Angadan back into the palace to immediately inform Sugrivan of his arrival, as he has come as a harbinger from Raman to deliver a message tipped with wrath and caution. Sugrivan showing signs of fear and apprehension, instantly sends Hanuman with Angadan to invite Lakshman with due honour and respect, to meet him. He requests Tara who has got the hospitable frame of mind, to welcome Lakshman on the way, so that she mitigates his anger to some extent. The inflamed Lakshman is met by Tara and her maids, while Sugrivan emerging from Ruma, his wife's inner apartment, hails Lakshman with great respect and delectable words, offering himself as his obedient servant in full readiness to do his bidding always.

Inconsiderately, Lakshman bawls out angrily at Sugrivan, briefly referring to his shocking sense of betraying Raman, and for his lack of awe and reverence for Him. He swears to punish him for his breach of promise and ingratitude to Raman.

At this moment, Hanuman, intercedes with Lakshman on behalf of Sugrivan, telling him that Sugrivan's devotion to Sri Raman, no less inferior to his, should not be belittled as he has engineered all preparations for Sita's search mission. He apprises Lakshman of the contrivance and strategy of innumerable warfaring, competent and sturdy monkeys in readiness to set in motion the search for Sita. Hence, Hanuman requests Lakshman not to become enmeshed in unhealthy doubts about Sugrivan's loyalty and sincerity.

Lakshman's ire evaporates; in friendship, he apologizes for his uncivil speech as it is only concern and affection that made him speak so. To endorse he bears them no animosity or malice, he invites them to meet Raman promptly. Sugrivan, on the other hand, undoubtedly reaffirms his docility and servitude, always his topmost priority to tender his all to the service of Raman. Being only a designated aide, Sugrivan, yet again, acclaims Raman's prowess who in the batter of an eyelid can conquer numberless worlds by dint of His innate effulgence.

On nominating Hanuman to take charge of all the monkeys to be pressed into the service of searching for Sita thoroughly, and thereby succeeding in the mission, Sugrivan assents to proceed to meet Raman. Sugrivan and Lakshman set off for the Pravarshana hills in a gorgeous chariot attended by Hanuman and his retinue of monkeys, numerous followers with mighty bears, and bands of monkeys, blowing trumpets and sounding other musical instruments to meet Raman.

Chapter - VI

Monkeys' Search Mission for Sita Commences or Commencement of Monkeys' Search Mission for Sita

Raman, delightfully greets His friend Sugrivan on his arrival, tenders him a hearty welcome and a generous embrace. Voluntarily, Sugrivan humbly briefs his Lord Raman of his preparedness to embark on the diplomatic search mission for Sita with a collection of millions and millions of mighty, potent monkeys who are all set, awaiting orders.

Sugrivan, deeming it a great privilege and honour introduces Raman to his assemblage of monkeys. Then, successively, he acquaints Raman of the valvour and merits, highlighting the achievements of his chief leaders Hanuman, Angadan, Nala, Neela, Gabya, Gabaxa, Sushena, Tara, Keshhari, Hanuman's father, Panas, Balmikha, Dashimukah, Sarava, Manideva and others. Forthwith, Raman is exceedingly pleased at Sugrivan's sincere commitment to the cause. Delighted to see the huge congregation of monkeys, He instructs him to dispatch them accordingly, to their assigned tasks.

Before long, Sugrivan issues standing orders to the task forces as they set off, under the august leadership of Hanuman and Angadan, to accomplish the assigned mission within a month's time or else they would have to face death. Raman's decisive mind fathoms Hanuman's positive accomplishment of the hard task of tracing out Sita, and so, furtively meets him and hands over, secretly, a talisman, his own ring of gold with His name inscribed on it, so that he might deliver it to Sita. He resolutely believes it would act as a token of identity, driving home to her the comforting truth that the emissary, Hanuman, is none other than His friend sent by Him to locate her placement and situation. Raman bestows His blessings on Him, and wishing Him well directs him to proceed ahead.

Bound southward, the battalions of spirited monkeys follow their leaders, Hanuman and Angadan in an up-beat mood. On their way they meet with a huge, monstrous demon whom they deduce to be Ravanan and so kill him fearlessly.

As they proceed on their way, the monkeys go on a laborious quest running hither and thither for water to moisten their parched tongues, slake their thirst and cool their heels. Eventually they spy aquatic birds swooping in and out of a cave's door. Once, in there, they light upon a tank of crystal clear water encircled by fruit laden trees, plants and an elegant cottage, maintaining a humble and tranquil exterior, and in the interior, dwelling a hermit girl of unparalleled beauty.

Discreetly, the maiden initiates a dialogue with Hanuman questioning their identity and purpose of their imposing mobilization. Hanuman regales her with the saga of Raman's life in detail and concludes that they are in the process of their search mission for Sita. The maiden requests them to replenish themselves with the luscious fruits from the trees and quench their thirst after which she would disclose her status and circumstances. The whole retinue of monkeys in passive obedience help themselves.

By now, becoming less shy and more willing to communicate, the maiden opens up pronouncing her name as Swamprava, the daughter of Gandharva. She articulates that celibacy has ruled her life in this hermitage inherited by Hema, Vishwa - Karma's daughter, from Lord Shiva as a recompense for propitiating him by her dances. Since then, Hema had lived there for thousands of years performing penance's when she, Swamprava, joined her as her maid in waiting, attending to all her needs. Her father, Gandharva, at the infinite moment of attaining Salvation, before ascending to the abode of Brahman the creator, had counselled her to continue abiding at the hermitage as a celibate, performing penances till the Almighty Supreme Lord Sri Vishnu incarnates as Raman in tangible form, and monkeys would be in his servitude, as a sign. He had assured her that Raman, inevitably, would visit the hermitage and meet her veritably. Now on learning that Raman has descended on the earth, she expresses her enhanced desire to see Raman in good time, and wishes to leave the cave immediately. At this instant, Hanuman and the monkeys leaving the cave wend their way southwards.

Swamprava straight away arrives at the Pravarshana hills and cordially offers her respects and salutations to Lord Raman. Being a rustic, she laments her ignorance and incompetence to perceive the Lord's transcendental form. And the only thing that she can happily perform to the best of her ability, as her aspiration is successfully crowned with a priceless harvest, is to humbly bow to Him repeatedly. She is on cloud nine as her vocation in life, by her sustained penances and austere sacrifices, has attained consummation now with the desired golden opportunity of visioning the enfleshed form of Lord Vishnu manifest as Raman, who has deigned to descend to the earth for dispensing boons to the righteous and extirpate the unrighteous.

Swamprava sagaciously acknowledges this as the most cherished opportunity of praising Sri Raman alone as the only anchorage of the impecunious and the weak. She solicits Sri Raman to favour her with the perpetual presence of His blissful human form ever to be enjoyed in unfailing and unfading richness and freshness, so that it can really make her blessed through eternity, attaining salvation and peace by His benevolence. She admits that she has had previous knowledge of how Lord Raman has accomplished now in the present births of Dasarathar and Kausalya, their wishes of the past birth, to be born as their son, and also He has incarnated for the purpose of killing Ravanan. She is unhappy that only a few are cognizable of Sri Raman being the manifest form of Lord Vishnu and His delusive play acting cannot be precisely conceived by even an expansive stretch of one's imagination. She, therefore, implores Lord Raman to terminate the deceiving effect of His illusion on her, instantly, so that, by His favour, she may be free to shake off the yoke of recurrent births and deaths and thereby be unrestrained to cross the endless ocean of materialistic living perennially.

The lady Swamprava is instructed by Lord Sir Raman to go to the forests of Badrikanatha . in the Northern Himalayas where she shall rid herself of her fleshy frame and attain restoration of her indigenious luminous form. With Lord Sri Raman's benedictions Lady Swamprava pursues her way to the Northern Himalayas and accordingly attains salvation by the Lord's. Grace.

Chapter - VII

The Episode of Sampathi

The monkeys on the other hand, are experiencing some low moments. A heaviness, a weariness settles on their camp along with the grim reality that they could die at Sugrivan's hands as, their hopeless incompetence to narrow down the location of Sita taunts them.

As days stretch into near completion of the month's deadline to trace out Sita, set by Sugrivan, the monkeys who have been so perseveringly looking for her are disappointed with their unsuccessful attempts. They fear the wrath of Sugrivan, which threatens their very existence. Angadan, in particular, fears Sugrivan the most for he suspects him to snatch this opportunity for killing him as he nurses some kind of animus against him, though, he fully entrusts himself in the hands of Raman who, beyond doubt would save him. The monkeys enjoy listening to Angadan's pitiful complaints as he incriminates Sugrivan of being sinful, because of his eroticism to take to his brother's wife who is even like his mother. He is decisive in returning to Kishkindha at any cost, but, instead swears to stay behind and end his life there.

Without a second thought all the monkeys in unison concur with Angadan to stay back with him in the cave and serve him as the cave is as beautifully prosperous and palatial as Indhran's palace.

Hanuman overhearing Angadan's conversation with the monkeys counsels him to rid himself of such misconceptions and offers some bits of wisdom in his interest. Hanuman makes him see Sugrivan's love for him as he is Tara's most dear son. With a gradual change of emphasis, Hanuman acquaints him of Raman who loves him even more than He loves Lakshman, whose might and power can obliterate all the beings in the three worlds with a single arrow. He wheedles him to see reason by pointing out the hypothetical assurance of the monkeys to live with him back at the cave for his sake when, they too have families and cannot part from them. Hanuman pronounces to be his well-wisher and promises to stand by him whenever his assistance is obligatory and however grave the situation may be.

Buffered by a warmth, Hanuman unravels to Angadan a hidden secret from the deepest chambers of his heart. He declares Sri Raman to be the enfleshed incarnation of Supreme Lord Vishnu who has deigned to descend on the earth to accomplish God's mission. Further, he reveals that it is by sheer dint of their devotion to Sri Raman in their previous births that they have manifested in the form of monkeys to play attendants to Sri Raman for achieving His purpose. Again, he declares that Sri Sita is the incarnation of Sri Mahalakshmi, the divine consort of Lord Vishnu, and at the appropriate time, they would en masse return to their original abode, Paradise, with Sri Raman.

Hanuman infuses Angadan with courage and also steadies his hopes. In turn, Angadan's resolve steels the crew and thus they all resume their search mission for Sita. Their enthusiasm is again crippled and hopes shattered when they reach the seashore at the foot of the Mandarachal hills. Their search mission comes to a standstill because they are helpless at the sight of the vast and unfathomable sea. They are frustrated at their inertia, unable to come up with solutions for crossing the sea. Moreover the fear of death at the hands of Sugrivan, on their return to Kishkindha consumes them. Disappointed, they prefer to fast unto death, instead of being done to death by Sugrivan. This fear is fuelled further by the immediate fear of falling prey to a huge vulture which emerges from the Mandarachal cave while sitting on the kusha grass with the determination of death upper most on their minds.

The vulture while alighting in the midst of the monkeys, thanks his good fortune for the bonanza of so many monkeys for him to make a good meal of. Concurrently, the monkeys opine they are star-crossed beings to be killed even before the completion of their assigned task. They vocally begrudge Jatayu who was really fortunate in dying in action for Raman's cause.

The very mention of Jatayu's name is a great find, as nectar, to Sampathi the majestic vulture. He allays the fears of the monkeys and requests them to furnish him with more details about Jatayu.

Angadan relates the role of Jatayu as a warrior wounded to death in a fierce fight with Ravanan, the Demon King, who made good his escape in a chariot with Sita after abducting her, the beloved consort of Sri Raman' son of King Dasarathar, who in compliance with his father's edict had gone to live in exile in the forest for fourteen years. Angadan supplements him with a comprehensive retrospective of Sugrivan's bond of friendship with Raman who annihilated Vali and consequently bestowed the throne of Kishkindha to him. Anxiously, he prods Sampathi to acquaint him with knowledgeable details about Sita Devi. Without reserve he confesses their inability and their futile aspirations in tracking down the location of Sri Sita Devi. He lays heavy emphasis on their contemplation of a fast unto death rather than return to Kishkintha empty handed to face a death sentence as decreed by Sugrivan.

Sampathi is overwhelmed by deep sentiments at the hard news of his brother Jatayu's death. Ritualistically, he takes a dtp in the sea, and then offers holy water to the departed soul of his dear brother. Subsequently with inspiring authority he articulates to Angadan his visionary, as well as his keen and penetrative visual perception of Sita, because, undoubtedly, vultures do have very sharp and long eyesight, from where he is stationed, seated under the Sinsahpa tree in the city of Lanka some hundred miles away across the ocean. He provokes anyone of them to jump across the sea and take a look at Sita. Sampathi is wistful of his past prowess which would have been powerful enough to vanquish Ravanan had he not, unfortunately, lost his wings. He positively persuades Angadan and the rest, that in course of time, Raman would assuredly kill Ravanan and redeem Sita. But then, he floats a proposal to winnow from among themselves the tactical champion who can arrive at Lanka, rendezvous with Sita, parley with her and return safely.

All the monkeys fantasize about this mighty Vulture that they become increasingly curious to know about his life that has slipped into the shadows of the past. And Sampathi replenishes them with vivid memories of how he and Jatayu once flew some thousands of miles away from the earth, a daring feat, towards the sun. In the process he had his own wings burnt off by the Sun's rays while trying to save and shield Jatayu whose wings were about to be burnt, and in the negotiation, how he happened to fall on Mandarahcal hills, senseless. As he was hit seriously by the fall he was incapacitated to fly and so had to grovel miserably on the ground.

Eventually, in this sad light he had reached the hermitage of sage Chandrama who was petrified at his deplorable predicament and enquired how he was denuded of his wings.

The woebegone Sampathi reported all that had happened and lamented that he wished to reduce himself to ashes than live in this opprobrious condition without wings.

Reckoning to console and mitigate Sampathi's torment, Sage Chandrama had injected him with a heavy dose of invigorated and sublimated pansophism. He had enlightened him about the material body which is dispensed to an individual's conforming to the cumulative result of the deeds of his precedent births. The individual is attachment to and repugnance for worldly objects are inherited from his embodied self of Jiva, which alone feels pleasure and pain. Individual ego is emphatically not the real self, but is infact delusive shadows reflected by only God or the Supreme Soul. So the identity of pure self with the reflection on the body is the cosmic world.

The exiting of Jiva, which embodies the ego, from the material body is death, after which, with its elemental or causal bodies it ascends to heaven or to other astral abodes such as 'Petri Lokha' etc., or descends to hell in respect to his good and bad deeds of his previous births.

The Jiva, endures in these abodes until his merits or demerits or goodness or sin are exhausted, returns alone with the descending fog and mist to the earth in the form of liquid elements such as rain and is ingested into the saturated soil where it fructifies into food grains. The whole process being a cyclic programmed development, the food grains are assimilated into the blood when eaten by anyone; again, appearing as Spermatozoa just to be married in the natural plan of intercourse with the ova already formed in the wombs of women. Thus, in a day it is conceived and acquires a marginal fixity facilitated by uterine covering all around it. In five days it evolves into a big, thick clot of blood in the womb and in seven days moulds into a very tender egg like shape.

In this fashion, it progresses and develops gradually into a babyish symmetry in the course of ten months time. Generally, in eight months, the complete body with all its organs and constituents is formed. In five months, the diminutive babe attains nebulous consciousness which goes on mellowing till it revives the past-life experiences-events and happenings of its foregone lives. Then cloistered in the womb, its suffering, drastically, from the immense heat of the womb commences and also its praying to god for its accounchement becomes an arbitrary frill. Its many petitions are tuned with copious penitences and replete with conditional promises; it atones for its past deeds and travails; its tentative tall promises that, if emancipated from the hell like uterine abode, it would ever love and adore God after its immediate and safe birth.

But no sooner when it's born than all such recollections and reflections fast fade away from the mind and the individual is overshadowed by ignorance. Infancy is always a despicable state for, when born as baby, it has to cruise along being at the mercy of others for everything and having to pass time in a squalid and unhygienic state of insects, viruses, worms, bacteria etc.

Correspondingly, in youth, and even in senectitude, the individual leads a life of instincts, emotions and passions. Though superficially his big family of members, wealth and prosperity, kith and kin are a source of joy and pleasure, he seems to be cheerful and happy. But their transient nature ultimately gives him no satisfaction. He is beset by diseases, indigence, anxieties, incertitudes, troubles and difficulties and is made unbearably miserable making life at the most unhappy from the very beginning. By long experience he gets discontented and discouraged by earthly happenings. As the Vulture King is cognisant of his past-life experiences, the Sage illumines the bird that sometimes the individual who undergoes unnumerable troubles and hardships in the present life, is dragooned to linger from one bodied life to another. He reveales that so long as the ego embodied in the jiva is unconquered and the individual is an ignoramus who lacks knowledge of his soul, the sequential manacles of births and deaths persist as a vicious cycle, never broken.

Peace within the heart can be attained only if he sets his heart and mind on the acquisition of wisdom and right understanding of his real inner nature and the perfect soul which is immortal, residing within his mortal frame too. A distinctive pattern of circumstances under which every individual is born is the scheduled way of life which unfolds in a natural way and which course, no creature on earth can deflect from or evade. For this reason the sage had counselled Sampathi to pass his time somehow and not brood over death, because he too would have to harvest the fruits of his previous life.

The realized soul is neither tantalized nor agitated about the time span to be spent on this earth to lead the embodied life because he fathoms the acquirement of transcendental knowledge and the eradication of nescience from the mind to be the prerequisites, which is the only solution to life's serious puzzle or question, in knowing his real self, the soul. Hence, sage Chandrama had persuaded Sampathi to abide at Mandrachal hill with his body as happily as a snake with its slough till monkeys arrived there. The sage had foretold of their noble endeavour of embarking on a search mission to an alien land, for Sita who would be kidnapped by Ravanan from the cottage when all alone.

Moreover, the sage had augured that he would repossess his wings by the benign Grace of Sri Raman when He happens to encounter the monkeys and apprise them about Sita Devi and her placement. And now, Sampathi taking a trip down memory lane, while concluding his clearest memories associated with powerful emotions from the pages of his life's history, gives a rhapsodical portrait of Sri Raman and Sri Sita, and while relating Sage Chandrama's contemplative exaltation of Life's philosophy and its goal and his predictions, miraculously, his wings begin to grow by the mere uttering of Raman's name and by the power of the sage's instructions. Then, Sampathi, enhancing their self confidence, blessing them and wishing them well in their endeavour, opens out his wings and takes flight, soaring high.

To cross the ocean of worldliness for the eternal abode easily, Raman's name helps even the sinful individual, if uttered sincerely. For these monkeys who are devoted messengers, who proclaim their servitude divinity is to be found where and when they most need it; so there arises no misgivings that they cannot cross this vast ocean to fulfill their search mission.

Chapter - VIII

Deliberations on Crossing the Ocean

Following the departure of Sampathi, there is a discernible common thread of brotherhood among the undaunted Monkeys which strengthens their prospect of finding out Sita. Their hopes soar high. But still, the monstrous waves and the aquatic creatures affect them with anxiety and fear.

It is of course imperative that they go to Lanka to see Sita. Angadan hits upon a specific idea and discusses it with his animated monkey friends. Preferably, he decides to select one among them to accomplish this onerous task. Silence, the sign of acceptance, prevails at every quarter. He surveys an evaluation of who amongst them would be able to leap and jump the longest distance. That not one among them is well suited to fit the critical parameters appropriate for crossing the ocean is unsettling, though each monkey prides himself of his ability to jump twenty miles or more.

Jambavan trumpets that in his youth he had at a stretch made twenty-one rounds of the early-like foot of Lord Bikram, but now, the underlying factors of venerable senectitude and feeble health debilitates him from crossing the sea. A lurking sense of diffidence whether he would make a comeback from Lanka safely, impedes his essay to go ahead there, though crossing the ocean lies in his power. Jambavan judiciously cautions Angadan against going to Lanka. Even if he possesses the wherewithal to go he should use his discretion because, primarily, he, the heir apparent is to succeed Sugrivan as the ruler.

Angadan, on being downcast at not ferretting out an expedient person to carry out the task is enthused by Jambvan who identifies the most dynamic monkey to accomplish the mission rewardingly. He singles out Hanuman who is very humbly quiet. He acknowledges him as the mightiest of all monkeys. He distinguishes him as the son of the God of Rains; exalts him as being prodigiously chivalrous and puissant as the mighty winds.

Jambavan's judgment of a person's personality being forged by events and people in early childhood, accredits Hanuman's precocity and capacity with a stunning proof of parachuting nearly five hundred miles above the earth in the sky, when he was just born, with an infantile intention of swallowing the sun deeming it to be a fruit. He exclaims that his exploits are so voluminous that none can compute or delineate. Thereby he directs Hanuman to psyche himself up for fulfilling the select assignment.

Thus encouraged, Hanuman exudes confidence and is incredibly soulful, willing to give himself whole heartedly to the endeavour. As a significant move he aggrandizes his biological frame as huge as a hill and with verbal violence he rebounds so loudly as if he were to rent the sky to shreds, and requisitions whether he should bring Sita back by annihilating Ravanan and his ilk and also reducing Lanka to ashes. Again, he bawls out if he should enfetter Ravanan and haul up the whole island on which his Lanka is situated, so that he may transport everything on his left hand and lay it all at the holy feet of Lordly Raman or should he return after meeting only Sita, the celebrated Lady.

Jambavan bids the illustrious Hanuman to venture into Lanka, rendezvous with Sita and talk to her only since he would be challenged to exhibit his mighty valour at a later date, when they all go to Lanka. Hanuman at once climbs atop the hill by the seashore and homing his skills stretching out his arms and enlarging his body immensely, an out of this world sensation, looking as resplendent as the rising sun and as gigantic as a mountain, midst loud cheering and benedictions from all sides, showcases his qualification and strength.

Part - V
Sundhara Kandham

Chapter - I

Hanuman Traverses the Ocean

Hanuman is a living demonstration of exuding remarkable inner strength, confidence and dedication in his vocation to champion Raman's cause. Exceedingly desirous of traversing the vast ocean, he is self-assured of success in his mission despite the odds and obstacles he has to encounter, especially the seas abounding with crocodiles and other dreaded creatures. Immediately before his departure, Hanuman is once again vocalizing with the monkeys, homing in the certitude that even a mediocre being too is empowered to effectuate liberation from the worldly labyrinths and convolutions if only he utters, even once, the holy name of Lord Raman. Further, Hanuman presages he would in no way founder in his quest for Sita because, he is a veracious and resolute devotee of Raman, ever in perpetual thought of Him, bearing a throbbing profile of Him etched in his heart and carrying the finger ring designated to be delivered through Him to her.

Hanuman programmes himself with a workout and a warm up to synchronize the movements of his limbs so as to make a fine take off. Facing south, at once he essays a marvellous bouncing parachuting several meters high above sea level into the sky and piloting himself smoothly in his flight thereafter.

In the heavens, the prying deities were quering if Hanuman would successfully enter Lanka. So, as to put Hanuman's ingenuity and competence to the test, they instigate Surasha, the Mother of Snakes to baffle him causing some kind of mischief to him to see whether he would beat retreat.

Accordingly, Surasha, the serpent queen-mother intercepts Hanuman and intimidates to devour him as she is ravenous. On the other hand, he endeavours to lighten her spirits. He requests the Mother not to forestall his volation, and attempt to eat him inorder to satiate her ravenous appetite. He expresses his inability to halt there and assuage her hunger as he is on his way to fulfill the Lord's mission. He professes to offer himself for her food, on his return, after accomplishing the Lord's mission and thereafter meeting him duly. The serpent queen mother impetuously pressurizes him to enter her mouth, or else, she would definitely swallow him.

Mutely challenging her dictates, Hanuman, requisitioning her to open her moth, inflates his body ten miles broad and ten miles long. In conjunction with his exploit, Surasha also elongates her jaws fifty miles wide. Hanuman, anew, magnifies his biological frame two hundred miles. Wherefore, in this fashion, they go on lengthening and broadening, increasingly, in competition and on the defeat and discomfiture of the other. The nimble-witted Hanuman, then deflates into the tiniest form, enters into her stomach, comes out of it, and bowing to her, the serpent Queen Mother, announces that he has just egressed from her stomach. He seeks permission to be allowed to go since he presumes he has slaked her hunger by swallowing him.

Filled with remorse for being ignorant at not knowing how Hanuman had entered and came out, equally eyebrow raising feats, of her belly, she confesses that it was at the behest of the deities who wanted to ascertain his commitment and capability that she had disported with him for discerning his sapience and puissance. Begging pardon for her dalliance, and, besides offering a profound reconciliation she permits him to forge ahead wishing him success in seeing Sita and suitably returning to Sri Raman. The set back doesn't dampen Hanuman's enthusiasm. He restarts his flight over the sea. On his way over the sea he is met by the brilliant God of the Hills, Mainka, who greets him as solicited by the God of the Seas. Therefore it is feasible for Mainka to welcome Hanuman to get to the zenith of his fructiferous island where he resides. As ordained by the Sea God, he proffers delicious refreshments and a delightful haven to recline for sometime. Mainka articulates that by his visit, being a predecessor of Raman and more importantly his ardent devotee to visit this place, the sea is now raised to the rank of an ocean. Hanuman thanks Mainka profusely for his many kindnesses but declines the offer of relaxing as he has not time to lose so long as he is engrossed in Raman's mission. Once again thanking him for his reception Hanuman proceeds further. Whilst nearing the shores of Lanka he senses the precariousness of his movements being stymied by some umbrageous object, his perspicacity determines it to be the demoness Sinhika, lying over the surface of the water and magnetizing him towards her by her mesmerizing power. Backlashing her to death with his foot he reaches the shore safely.

Hanuman spends the whole day on the outskirts of Lanka by the shore, and at night, assuming an infinitesimal form enters Lankini only to be captured by Lankan, the city guard. Mistaking Hanuman for a villain, she kicks him hard and interrogates him on his identification to enter in to the city. In compliance, Hanuman responds with a hard blow on her mouth, and bleeding excessively she satisfactorily concedes to his entry into the city freely, because by this incident, she cognises the end of Ravanan which is fast approaching. Lankini explicitly elucidates Brahman the Creator's prediction that when Raman's messenger, a monkey, named Hanuman strikes a blow on her face on his entry into Lanka, then, at that moment Ravanan's doom at the hands of Raman has been sealed.

She apprises him of her knowledge about Sita, and reflects on how fortunate enough she is to ponder on Raman perpetually in her heart. The vibrant pulsating of the eyes and the arms of Sita, Raman and Ravanan simultaneously is accelerated in a pronounced manner, a sign of spelling good omen for Raman and Sita alone, and evil omen for Ravanan, at the time when Hanuman is crossing the Ocean.

Chapter - II

Sita's Placement in the woods of Ashoka

Hanuman in his assumed infinitesimal form enters the city of Lanka to track down Sita. He forages all the hideouts and nooks and corners of the city. As a last resort, he ventures to enter an area which harbours perilous vulnerability - Ravanan's Palace, and searches every cubbyhole there, but in vain.

At long last, inspired by Lankini's audiology, Hanuman catches a glimpse of Sita trapped in the remote woods of Ashoka' sitting under a Sinshapa tree, heavily guarded by demonesses. The propound power of his intuition ciphers her to be enervated, depressed and plagued with doubts and anxieties. Her disquieting passivity casts the spell of a feeling of the precious moments of solitude to chant the varied names of Sri Raman. He retreats into the shadows and hides in the foliage of the trees with the objective of observing her with the astute sense of perception of his being, providential in his great achievement.

Simultaneously, the potentate Ravanan too is mystified and solicitous as to why Raman has not yet reached Lanka even after the elapse of a lengthy span of time. Anxiety invades his life. He has in a reverie come to apprehend that a certain monkey has arrived in Lanka and has covertly met Sita. Therefore, attired elaborately in royal robes and trappings, together with Mandothri and other women, Ravanan presumptuously calls on Sita to reinforce on her the designs of his affairs d'amour, whereas, he veraciously warrants his death at the hands of Sri Raman, at this moment.

Brushing aside Sita's comparative indifference with which he is greeted, but consumed with his own importance, he questions her as to why she is still vacillating and skeptical to accept his love. Dissipating his royal mask and stooping to conquer the heart of another man's wife, he Is trying to skew her mind by verbally drawing a distorted picture of Raman as being worthless, loveless, loathsome, ungrateful and only too proud. Undermining her confidence, he points that Raman has still not condescended to even search for her He gibes at Raman's non-existent conceitedness at being learned, supercilious and wise; though, he declares that Raman is really inane and distrait. He is accusing Raman of being unsympathetic, impervious and sometimes ceasing to be. After this much of railing, suddenly, he intones Sita to accept his love, as much as, he would raise her to the status of his crowning paramour while other women cannot hold a candle to her, if only she concedes. There are no arguments that can move him from his consuming passion for Sita. His lust blinds him to the terrible consequences that would ensue, sooner.

His words infuriate her extensively that she places a piece of grass as a curtain between herself and her implacable foe Ravanan. Equally alarming and enraging to her is his characterization of her Lord Raman in such contumely language that she bawls out with verbal evidence calling him a villain who is still bragging inefficaciously about abducting her like a dog stealing the oblations from the sacrificial altar. Shrugging away his mean notions and words, she swears that he would be torn to pieces by Raman's arrows, who would in all likelihood, arrive there with Lakshman at any time either by drying up the ocean or constructing a bridge of arrows. She condones, that, he so well deserves punishment, seeing that he is undoubtedly a mean creature. Sita's sparked rumblings of dissent and rancour provokes Ravanan into striking her with his sword-a vestal virgin on the point of being sacrificed for honour's sake when, Mandothiri restrains him not to harm her in this unbefitting manner. She quizzes as to why he is hankering after Sita who has a razor thin body, lacks the extra dash of glamour, and unsuitable for him, although he has so many young wives. Intimidating her that he would devour her merely for his breakfast if she does not yield to his whims and fancies within two months, he returns to his palace. Eventually, Sita is hemmed in by demonesses who keep strict vigil over her.

These demonesses victimize Sita inorder to persuade her to concur to Ravanan's words and accept his passionate love because, they have been demanded to win her over to Ravanan's side either by coaxing or cajoling or threatening or by any of their worst tactics known to them.

But soon the demonesses are enjoined by Trijata, one of the guards to cease persecution of Sita; they are directed instead to pay deference to her, reverentially. The justification being he narrates as fluently as a film, visions of a dream he has had; Raman's arrival on the island Lanka to retrieve Sita; Ravanan's nakedness, his body completely bedaubed with cow dung and going away southwards and Vibhisanan sitting happily with Raman. Trijata interprets that it indicates Raman killing Ravanan and bequeathing the throne of Lanka to Vibhisanan and Raman returning with Sita. Therefore all the guards desist from hurting her and retire to bed, while Sita weary from the hours of intense harassment and pain weeps copious tears; fatigue hits her like a hammer on the anvil. Forlorn and forsaken and unable to keep herself in this precarious situation, she evokes a possible avenue of an absurd error' self-destruction. She is trying to do away with her life as she has been tortured and beleaguered by the demonesses.

Chapter - III

(Encounters) Hanuman Meets Sita

Hanuman has been closely observing the scenario from his hideout in the foliage of the trees. His keen penetrative perception has gauged Sita's definite inclination to commit suicide, and so, is anxious and nonplussed. As it is, he is also painfully aware that it is necessary she maintains a resolute attitude to the end of the struggle. He is inspired to recount in soft soothing words the life history of Sri Raman to effectuate a change of mood Not surprisingly, Sita is astounded on hearing the incorporeal voice, as it were, relating the saga of Raman's life, and hails the narrator to come into view so that she may deduce the authenticity and intensity of his sincerity. Hanuman shows up, relatively truncating his form to the size of a tiny water bowl and pays obeisance with great reverence. Earlier, being skeptical of Ravanan transforming himself into the form of a monkey to see her, Sita stoops to peer down at him, when Hanuman articulates he is undeniably her humble servant and presents to her Raman's finger-ring as proof, beyond question. Her mortifying moments vanish and this lovely moment lifts her off her treadmill and quickens her pulse that she becomes deliriously happy and delighted at seeing Raman's ring as dear to her as her life. She expresses her unbounded gratitude, offering thanks and widely appreciating his visit after a long search fraught with untold troubles and pains. Working steadily towards disclosing her mind, she requests him to apprise Raman with the present scenario and the difficult straits she is in, and to prevail upon Him to arrive there at the earliest for rescuing her from Ravanan who threatens to kill her within two months. She is happily curious to know the identity of Raman's top-flight confidant whom He trusts implicitly.

In devoted response, glorifying her as mother, he declares he is Hanuman, the Paramount Minster of Sugrivan, King of Kishandha, who has newly forged a bond of friendship with Raman, promising to rescue her by obliterating Ravanan and his ilk with millions and millions of his race all psyched up and disposed to fight for Raman's sake.

Sita's verbal reflection, a fascinating factor, as to how such miniscule monkeys as him would be able to counter, comparatively, ferocious and mighty demons is settled as quickly as Hanuman enlarges his fleshy frame in dimensional proportions as huge and mighty as a hill. She is transfixed by the sensory input through her eyes - this fabulous hero - something she had never seen before. His tour de force pleases her extremely that she is now self-assured he is the mightiest being. The question still lingering on her mind as to how he shall bring Raman and all the monkeys, millions and millions of them, to Lanka is again clarified as soon as Hanuman assures her that they would either construct a bridge or jump and leap as he has done. The imperceptible nuances of her impatience, expectancy and restiveness prod Hanuman to quickly go and persuade Raman to reach Lanka at the earliest opportunity.

Sita relates to Hanuman with joy and pride, to epitomize Raman's zealous Guardianship and His extraordinary prowess, an incident from the memories of those by gone days, when, once, He was taking a nap on her lap, Indhran's son Jainta in the guise of a crow had pecked and wounded her foot severely. Raman coming to know of this, just like that, picked up a straw and at once released it in the manner of an unflinching arrow in Jainta's direction. The arrow -like straw was intently pursuing Jainta wherever he fled, but none throughout heaven and earth could save him from Raman's arrow. Involuntarily he was proceeding to take refuge at Raman's arrow. Involuntarily he was forced to take refuge at Raman's feet and implore Him to compassionately spare him his life.

Regardless of his supplication, Raman notified that he had to pay the penalty to His inerrable arrow by losing his left eye. Thus Sita unfolds with this incident Raman's unfathomable and incredible valour, convincingly declaring, by which His arrows will absolutely exterminate Ravanan together with his race of ferocious demons, but frets about her inability to comprehend his long tardiness in arriving there.

Before Sita could descend further to the doldrums Hanuman stops her short with comforting words disclosing the sequels the pledging and initiation of a search mission to trace her, task forces comprising millions and millions of monkeys set up and despatched to all the nooks and corners of the globe-following the alliance between Raman and Sugrivan, a unanimous decision of the monkeys and all the chiefs, which has resulted in his arriving there, earlier than Raman to tract her down, converse with her, assimilate the situation and then return to Raman forthwith and apprise Him of the whole. At Hanuman's request, Sita, glowing with enthusiasm, hands over a radiant hair clip, the surest talisman, a credential attesting their interaction, to him to be given to Raman and also conveys through him her salutation and veneration to Him.

Hanuman's shrewd and restless inquiring mind reflects on the ways and means of meeting Ravanan, also, as a truly devoted servant, and set the thames on fire in Lanka before his take off to meet Raman. Immediately he requests Mother Sita for some fruits as he is famished.

Heedless of Mother Sita's injunctions about the wrath and anger of the guards, Hanuman, nonchalantly, uproots not only the fruit bearing trees, but also other trees of the Asokha garden haphazardly and mindlessly kills the guards too. On hearing this, Ravanan sends a million followers, servants and guardsmen all of whom are killed in a trice. Again, Ravanan despatches a larger number of soldiers and five sons of his minister, who cannot overcome Hanuman. They too are killed as quickly as the former batch of opponents. Next he sends Akshaya Kumar, his own son, and a still larger composite number of mighty soldiers under his command whom Hanuman pounces upon in one leap and levels to dust with a huge iron rod.

Back at the palace, Ravanan unable to contain his exploding anger at the sudden spurt of havoc being caused by Hanuman, has willed himself to go out there and exterminate him outright, but is checked by his son Indrajit assuring him that he would go instead to bind Hanuman, and bring him alive before him. Eventually, a fierce single-handed combat ensues between himself and Hanuman who could finally be bound by the "Brahmastra" a divine and foolproof noose dispensed to him by Brahman, the creator.

The efficacy of the divine Brahmastra on the knowledgeable Hanuman is only temporary. Even then, uneager to extricate himself for the reason that he is desirous of meeting Ravanan, he feigns captivity. In as much as he is provisionally bound and is carried by Indrajit to Ravanan's palace.

That even Hanuman can also be bound up is the conjecture of only the indiscreet. Hanuman is perennially conscious and ever devoted to Sri Raman that he has been emancipated from the shackles of delusive Maya. It is such individuals who constantly chant Lord Raman's names, that their fetters of worldly bondage are cut asunder. Hanuman willed himself to be taken captive in the interest of interacting with Ravanan and offer some sane counsel and conventional wisdom; therefore he stands face to face with Ravanan.

Chapter - IV

Lanka on Fire

Temporarily bound Hanuman stands face to face with Ravanan, the Mighty King of Demons. Indrajit informs his father that the ape which he has bound by the Brahmastra, the divine noose, is no mean or ordinary creature to be taken lightly, but should be dealt with diplomatically and judiciously.

As commanded by Ravanan, his minister's Prahasta interrogates Hanuman as to why he has come to Lanka and his ulterior motive in visiting the Ashoka woods. He assures him that if he states the truth he would be disentangled from the noose and exculpated.

Acknowledging himself, first and foremost, as Hanuman, the humble servant of Raman and then as the chief Minster of King Sugrivan of Kishkindha, he forthrightly announces that he has arrived in Lanka on a search mission to ferret out the placement of Sita whom Ravanan had stolen like a shameful, vile dog. He replenishes him with the preceding details of Raman's arrival in Panchabathi with his brother Lakshman and wife Sita to live in exile for fourteen years in compliance with his father, King Dasarathar's edict, presently staying at Prabarshana hills and being taken care of by millions and millions of monkeys, himself being one of them to arrive in advance in Lanka for the aforementioned purpose, and their preparedness to invade Lanka before long.

In addition, he confesses he has now seen Sita and in the process destroyed the garden of Ashoka, as is instinctive of a monkey and also decimated the armies of demons in legitimate self defense. Finally, Hanuman speaks his mind making his intention very clear about deliberately reaching there to meet and interact with Ravanan, despite the fugacious effect of Brahmastra, the divine noose by which Indrajit bound him and from which he could have easily wriggled out and freed himself, but did not, solely in the interest of a well wisher to tender genuine and wholesome advice to him for his own good, though, invariably, it is likely to be disliked and rejected by him.

And now, addressing Ravanan in particular, Hanuman makes a categorical statement inducing him to cognize that he is the progenitor of the renowned and pious sage Pulastya and Kuberan also is his brother. Hence, he makes him realize that his body is therefore not demonic. Hanuman offers Ravanan an ounce of transcendental philosophy accentuating the truth that he is not the body and the sense organs; he is the pure soul which is immortal, immutable and one with the whole universe without a second. It is only ignorance known as illusion or Maya or God which perdue, and unceasingly creates all the apparent material organs, subtle senses and the gross body.

Hanuman continues to enlighten him on his divine nature. The sky though immanent in the whole Universe is always separate and free. Analogous to this point, the soul which dwells in the body is immanent everywhere, is always distinct and cannot be defiled by the worldly matters. The soul is none other than God himself and is the creator of these perishable entities such as body, intellect and mind. Infallibly it is the ego that influences mind and the intellect, feels happiness or misery, pleasure and pain, heat and cold etc. Hanuman pressurizes Ravanan to resurrect the goodness dwelling in his heart. He instructs there is a higher transcendental nature within the realm of ordinary human experience, and adds, just as fire ignites into a blaze, burns unwanted and impure things to ashes, the fire of devotion to Raman extinguishes all evil, purifies even the lowest and cleanses the sinner of all his base thoughts and deeds.

Wherefore, he exhorts Ravanan to consecrate his mind and all to Raman, Omnipotent, Omnipresent and Omniscient God, the incarnation of Lord Vishnu in tangible form and Sita, his divine consort, the incarnation of Lakshmi Devi.

Hanuman cautions Ravanan against the twin evil forces of pride and arrogance which upset mental equipoise. Just as light and darkness cannot cohere, noble deeds and sinful comportment cannot co-exits. To the extent that one is a champion of Dharmam, he will obtain the obligatory reward but the sequel of his noble deeds will be obliterated the moment he intentionally indulges in unrighteousness. Hanuman, underscores that to seek a woman other than one's wife is a heinous crime entailing severe punishment.

Again, he reiterates that regardless of his erudition, penance and observance of codes contained in the scriptures, by his abduction of Sri

Sita, the results of his good deeds are nullified. He admonishes Ravanan not to incur the enmity of Lord Raman whom he can please effectually and feasibly by love and worship; otherwise, it would be a great folly and would have to face dire consequences.

In view of setting up a new direction to Ravanan's life, igniting the inner quest for achieving the highest goal of human life, Hanuman implores Ravanan to restore Sita to Raman, beg pardon of Him for his abominable crime and thus save himself and his tribe from Sri Raman's wrath, failing which, the pangs of conscience will, growing worse and worse with each passing day, torment him making him split and sick and unhappy and insecure.

Ravanan's blinding humiliation is unconcealed as he blows a fuse castigating Hanuman as a proud and stupid monkey, and reprimanding him for the homily coming as it does from a mere monkey, which he cannot endure, obdurately swearing that he who is unlimitedly potent will indubitably slay Raman, Lakshman, Sugrivan and all other monkeys, and immediately unseats himself to strike him dead.

Simultaneously Hanuman's feathers are ruffled at the instance of Ravanan's insolent statement. Seething with rage, as if to scorch the demon with his anger, he retaliates defiantly declaring that he, Ravanan, a vile demon, should reckon that crores and crores of demons like him cannot prevail against him, the humble and faithful servant of Raman and his shoreless puissance.

Immediately Ravanan explodes with anger ordering one of his attendants to severe Hanuman's head with the sword for his impertinence, whereupon, visbhishanan intervenes to stop this demeaning act on the ground that it is not fair and square to kill an alien emissary. He instructs Ravanan to penalize him in some other way for the nonce and to permit him to return to Raman for conveying all the happenings that have transpired here.

A momentary spasm of goodness prevails over the iron willed Ravanan. Agreeing with Vibhishanan's judicious suggestion that the envoy should not be killed, he orders his soldiers to burn the tail of the mischievous monkey and drive him away.

Hanuman's deceptive frivolousness enhances him to sport with the soldiers when they by the orders of Ravanan try to burn his tail. In the process of trying to wrap the tail with cloth soaked in oil, Hanuman enlarges his tail, growing it thicker and longer to the extent that cloth, oil ghee etc., are ail exhausted and unavailable no longer. Vexed, they some how or other, bind the tail with ropes and rags and set it ablaze. Then gargantuan demons carry him around the city in the midst of abuses, threats and blows emanating from the public. Hanuman choosing this as the most enticing opportunity bounces off on to the terraces and the roofs of houses and buildings with his blazing tail igniting every place, generating fire. This sudden. conflagration reduces the whole city to ashes except Vibhishanan's mansion, which alone Hanuman spares. Contrary to Ravanan's expectations he has destroyed the whole city. He is suddenly apprehensive of Sita's presence, regrets his own rashness and curses himself for losing his temper. He immerses his tail into the sea to extinguish the fire and then wends his way to visit Sita and see if all is well with her.

Since Sita had been praying for Hanuman's safety all the while even natural fire could do no harm to Hanuman's tail.

Fortunately, Hanuman is the chief envoy of Sri Raman. He is always free from any kind of threat to life even by the natural elements like fire, water etc. Likewise, by relentless and icy concentration on Raman or the mere mention or the careless utterance of Raman's holy name by even ordinary beings, will have their burning cares, overwhelming anxieties and gross deeds absolved by Him.

Chapter - V

Hanuman's Return to Raman

Hanuman races frantically to Sita's dwelling place and assures himself that she is safe. Offering his humble salutations to the Goddess Mother, Sita Devi, he informs her of having completed his assigned mission fortuitously. He solicits, graciously, to take leave of her, so as to return, forthwith, and meet Raman and facilitate him to arrive there at the earliest with Lakshman and Sugrivan's. Sita is felicitous to see him again and stands in awe of his commitment and perseverance. She assures that his successful mission is a victory to him, having the remarkable inner strength and faith to keep forging ahead.

Hanuman's departure is sure to jar Sita's equilibrium. She has to endure under an overpowering feeling of loneliness in a hostile environment. She expresses her disquietude at having to remain sunk in the gloom of her own solitude. Soon Hanuman vocalizes that there is hardly any cause to feel disheartened on the grounds, if she approves, he is predisposed and fortified to pilot her safely on his shoulder to her Lord Raman. By her heartening conclusion, she touts son Hanuman to go alone and beseech Raman to come there by any means, considering the mission as crucial, to extricate her from the evil custody of demonic Ravanan and slay him together with his demons and his armies. Clairvoyantly, she opines that Raman shall walk the highway to glory from there achieving universal renown and honour, bequeathing to the world at large, by the quintessence of human experience of every aspect of His life, a glorious and abiding paradigm for posterity.

Hanuman bursting with pride takes off with a tremendous leap over the sea into space. As he is sailing along he is resonating a loud roar in the sky. On hearing Hanuman's loud sonance spelling victory, eclat and jubilation, all the monkeys who have been all along anticipating his return on the sea shore are streaming with joy. They receive him with a riotous ovation. On learning that the accomplished mission is a gusty triumph they emanate a deafening applause that leaves them breathless with delight Thus in this jubilant mood, with a flurry of renewed interest they are returning with Hanuman to the Prabarshana Hills thereafter.

On their way, they wander into Madhubana, Sugrivan's orchard laden with fruit trees and honeycombs galore. Angadan authorizes them to help themselves to the fruits and honey so as to refresh themselves. Providentially. Sugrivan divines the message of the successful completion of the search mission, when Dadhimukh his maternal uncle and guard of the orchard complains angrily to him of the monkey's-millions and millions of them - offensive and disrespectful behaviour of voraciously eating, drinking and making merry in the orchard. Sugrivan surmising that the monkeys would have seen Sita so ordains Dadhimukh to direct them to Raman hastily.

Exploding with good tidings, the point man, Hanuman, together with Angadan and all the monkeys reaches Prabarshana Hills very happily. The finesse and the flavour of Hanuman's nuances in acquainting Raman with the good news radiantly reflects the ecstatic joy of his meeting and communing with Sita in Lanka. Synchronously, Raman undergoes a cheerful metamorphosis as Hanuman narrates his rendezvous with Sita. An exuberant optimism and confidence overwhelms him now. The positive valour and commitment Hanuman has displayed reveals his bravura, which procures for him Raman's unstinting praise and thankfulness. Raman is increasingly convinced that the amazing performance of Hanuman's deeds is most envied by the Gods who are incapable of performing even half of what he has accomplished. Solicitously he enquires whether Sita is keeping well and avidly requests him to furnish Him with all details.

Glowing with understanding, Hanuman segmentally relates beginning with his entry into Lanka, espying the Holy Mother, Sita Devi woebegone, thin, emaciated haggard, fatigued, despicable in the Ashoka woods, under the Sinshapa tree, under strict vigil by patrolling demonesses and his informative, encouraging talk about Him, His well being and His assurance, to Sita. Hanuman then conveys Sita's impatience and yearning for His immediate arrival in Lanka, and her respects by handing over the hair-clip as a token of remembrance and proof of their interview.

Furthermore, Hanuman apprises Raman of his composite dialogue with Ravanan the braggadocio, who crows with hubris, is arrogant and vicious, and truly warrants nemesis, death at His august hands. Along with this, in a related development, he relates he had caused substantial damage by incinerating Lanka to ashes.

Donning the garb of an ordinary human being, Raman is virtually moved to tears by Sita's miserable plight and accepts the hair clip accordingly. His whole interior is flooded with gratitude to Hanuman for his committed, triumphant performance. He ennobles the accomplishment by simply embracing Hanuman and commingling His full Self with his self out rightly pronouncing that He has nothing else to reward him with.

Hanuman is ecstatically blissful, as he has received accolades, more resounding, and a reward beyond price, the fortunate embrace from Raman, which is unobtainable by even the aspirants, the sages and the Gods.

Part - VI
Yutha Kandham

Chapter - I

Raman's Preparation for Restoration of Sita

Since Hanuman's visit to and return from Lanka, the unknown placement of Sita is no longer a cause for concern at Raman's camp. Raman expresses His happiness to Sugrivan that Hanuman, who bears the palm, has helped salvage the image and glory of the Raghu Dynasty and the honour of Himself, Lakshman and Sugrivan. He is full of praise for Hanuman whose bravura in accomplishing the most onerous task, one that no one else on earth or in heaven would have even dreamt of, deserves the highest distinction.

Raman is hopeful that Hanuman's visit has opened a new window of opportunity for finding imposing solutions to the existing problem and for making concentrated preparations for going to Lanka to war with Ravanan and retrieve Sita. Practically, He is dubious whether He would skillfully cross the horrific seas abounding with crocodiles, whales and ferocious aquatic animals and eventually vanquish the daunting enemies.

Cap In hand, Sugrivan alleviates Rama'ns phobia and incertitude, and eases His mind by assuring Him of the doggedness of the monkeys to go through thick and thin for His sake. He adds there should be no cause for anxiety as anxiety is the cause of failure and explicitly states they would right on reach Lanka and decimate Ravanan and all other demons. Further, Sugrivan emphatically announces that there is no other person in all the three worlds qualified enough to stand up and fight against Raman, when He shall hold His grand bow and infallible arrows in His sacred hands. Conclusively Sugrivan exhilarates Raman declaring that victory is inexorably theirs, for just as things go, He, Raman, has the ball at his feet, and sees felicitous signs all around them.

Nevertheless, Raman announcing to get started for crossing the sea by any means peps them up, enlivening the spirits of the monkeys. He calls for an authoritative statement from Hanuman who pioneered the search mission, to quote precisely the situation of Lanka so that they may draw out strategic sequels for formalizing aggression and defense in attacking the fort.

Hanuman gives a meticulous record of the celestial city nestled on the three peaks of a hill with palatial houses and sprawling mansions and chateaus looking splendid and beautiful, their windows, doors, pillars and gates constructed of fine gold and crystal. He draws a word picture of luxurious parks, beautiful gardens and tanks of unadulterated water. He describes the city being safe-guarded by a very strong fence surrounding it. Millions and millions of infantry, chasseurs and elephants, equipped with all kinds of arms and ammunition and canons constitute the sentry guarding the gates of the city very vigilantly. Hence, Hanuman asserts there is no room for doubt that if His Lordship Raman enters Lanka, He can beat them hollow reducing them to ashes in no time.

Raman delightfully acknowledges the throbbing of his right eye as an indication which spells victory and, it, being the most auspicious time for the troops to march towards Lanka. He chooses to ride on Hanuman's shoulders and suggests Lakshman to do so on Anghadan's. As they embark on the mission, Sugrivan, in the company of Raman and Lakshman the two brothers looking like the Sun and the moon at the head of the armies that follow them, is beside himself with joy leading millions and millions of monkeys who are raised to a state of excitement, exhibiting undaunted spirits. Frenetically marching day and night, they forge ahead and are able to pass Mandarachal, Sahadri hills with excellent and splendours forests. They are rapidly on the move crossing smaller hills and dales until they halt to confront the vast ocean. Soon Raman becomes disconcerted and a forlorn hope sets in at the sight of the vast ocean, which has to be crossed in order to reach Lanka. Moreover, finding the indomitable assemblage becoming dispirited and deeply depressed, Raman is on His beam-ends. Also, as he is playing a human personality, He is timorously anxious about Sita.

Indisputably Raman is no mediocre being, yet, acting the role of an ordinary human bereft of all sentiment and feeling of grief and tribulation, unlike the common man, for He is Supreme Lord Vishnu Omnipotent, Omniscient and Omnipresent. It is translucent that, viewing through the transparent veil of ignorance, base persons would never be able to cognize His quintessential and veritable entity, but drag Him down to their plane of nescience and know Him to be a stereotype of themselves.

Chapter - II

Ravanan's Expulsion of Vibhishanan

Ravanan, subsequent to the departure of Hanuman is greatly rattled at the imminent threat of Raman's army landing on Lanka's soil. So, the highly strung Ravanan convenes a meeting with his ministers and advisors who carry his banner, and ignominiously declares Hanuman's audacious venture of meeting Sita, the havoc he has generated levelling to dust his son Akshaya Kumar as well as millions of soldiers, reducing the city to ashes and returning to his destination unhurt. He inflames a fanatical appeal to the councillors to deliberate on promoting immediate and long term constructive and unfailing measures for their safety and well-being.

In unison, the ministers and councillors refuse to entertain anxiety and apprehension of any sort, and maintain it is pointless to do so. They openly confess their inadvertency and negligence to misconstrue the monkey to be an insignificant, puckish, impotent ape whom they could have trapped and killed easily, but allowed-him to give them the slip. Further, they tout Ravanan's ego articulating he is the most valiant conqueror of all the three worlds, Yaman, Kuberan and The Gods, and so, it is groundless to be apprehensive of ordinary men and monkeys, and in a chorus bragg the siren song that the enemy can be effortlessly wiped out.

They are all in readiness to go from one end of the world to the other and devour all men and monkeys for putting a stop to their menacing threat of destroying the whole demon tribe. They await his Lordship Ravanan to give them the go ahead or to kindly assign to each one of them the task to be performed outrightly.

At this juncture, Kumbakarnan, the brother of Ravanan, admonishes Ravanan for needlessly inviting death like a man rashly swallowing poison pills, for bringing sin and woe upon the entire demon tribe by his outrageous act of abducting Sita. He zeroes in on the truth that Sita is Lakshmi and Raman Lord Vishnu's manifestation and focuses on the impending destruction at His hands, which is a constantly nagging fear. Nevertheless he prates of setting right matters, thereby inducing solace and support and arresting their fears.

Immediately Indrajit obstructs defiantly promising to annihilate Raman, Lakhsman and all the monkeys, in due course of time, if only Ravanan his father permits him to do so.

But Ravanan's brother Vibhishanan, a lone votary of virtue and good conduct, prompted by devotion to truth tries every method to turn Ravanan away from the path of self destruction, convince him of the foolishness and triviality in thinking that Sri Raman could be vanquished, and impress upon him that restoration of Sri Sita to Sri Raman is the only course to save the entire Rakshasa race from extinction. As blood is thicken than water, Vibhishanan, out of brotherly love sounds a note of caution about the invisible calamity hanging over the whole race of demons because of his blatant stealth of Sita Devi. He brings home the naked truth that coveting others' wives brings infamy and adulterates the senses. Furthermore, he warns that the magnitude of Hanuman's flight across the sea and the harm that he had wrought in Lanka cannot be belittled. Neither his son Indrajit nor Kumbakarnan nor his mighty warriors can resist Raman. Thereupon, he intercedes with Ravanan to send Sita back to Raman with honour, in time, to evade the ire of the monkeys who will raze them and demolish the city in quick time. He entreats him to beg forgiveness of Raman and take refuge in Him. He upbraids Ravanan that he can neither live safely nor in peace, even if he implores the succour of the Gods - Indhran, Yaman and others to befriend him, or even goes into hiding underneath the earth.

Ravanan who has lost the grip over his mind is becoming a victim of his doom, always rejecting sane counsel, for it may be unpalatable And now, the last bits of wisdom offered by Vibhishanan makes his gorge rise making him rail at him, naming him a calamitous and mendacious imbecile who warrants death at his hands. The iron has entered Ravanan's soul; he indicts Vibhishanan for opposing him his immediate and closest blood relation. Ravanan nails his colours to the mast, but sends out an edict to Vibhishanan to quit the place and follow his own path. He also swears he would never set eyes on him again, as he, vibhishanan, his fond brother, has changed horses in mid-stream and joined hands with his enemy, a shocking sense of betrayal.

Vibhishanan, who is as different as chalk is from cheese, articulates very remorsefully that Ravanan has now misunderstood him, for he has always looked upon him as his revered father since he is his eldest brother.

Further he hauls Ravanan over the coals for his violation of ethical codes - his abduction and retention of Sita still - which is the antecedent for their ruination and specifically, his inevitable death at the hands of invincible Raman who is doubtlessly the Supreme God. He Inculpates Ravanan for being caught in the trammels of blind passion and becoming impervious to his sound counsel to abandon Sita, and, in the same breath unravels that Raman's incarnation on earth is for the sole purpose of annihilating him as well as all evil doers at the personal solicitation of Brahman the creator. He highlights Raman's phenomenal traits as being beyond and above nature, as being immanent in and outside the whole Universe and appearing in varied forms, though formless as the blazing fire which has neither size nor shape, but apparently shapes itself to different sizes when blazing the trees of different sizes.

Vibhishanan emphatically announces his decision to part ways with Ravanan and leave Lanka presently, so as to seek Raman who is His haven of eternal peace and bliss, and hopes his exodus would make him comfortable and happy and content, and gratified to follow his own egoistic ways. But reflectively he confesses that he cannot help feel sorry to know and see the catastrophe and tragedy that are always following him closely on his heels. Vibhishanan lays bare before Ravanan the fact that it is he who will be held responsible for any disaster that results, blame that imputes and vengeance that falls on him and the whole demon race Instantly Vibhishanan makes a huge leap above into the sky and flies leaving Lanka with all his establishments but filled with aspirations to devote his time and services to Raman alone, pleasurably.

Chapter - III

Vibhishnan Joins Raman's Camp
Or
Vibhishanan Surrenders to Raman.

Exalted Vibhishanan, accompanied by his four councillors makes the translation from Lanka by air to Raman's camp very safely. He introduces himself as Vibhishanan, the brother of Ravanan, and makes a vibrant appeal to Raman so that he may have recourse to His benign shelter the prime reason of his coming there. He does not camouflage the disagreeable truth that it is his brother Ravanan who stealthily carried away his beloved consort Sita, and to whom all his advocacy and injunctions for his own well - being proved null and void.

Sugrivan, at this instant, alerts His Lordship Raman about the grotesquely irrational appeal for asylum by Vibhishanan, a demon, thereby impugning his credibility, and cautions that demons are by and large treacherous and untrustworthy and urges Raman to issue a decree to the monkeys to slay him right away.

Instead, Sugrivan's exhortation is effectively countered by Raman with an amicable smile which legitimizes Vibhishanan's appeal and declares that, if He so chooses He can create and destroy the whole universe in a flash; but pronounces that He is bound to extend protection to anyone, even to a foe, if he unreservedly seeks it from Him. Therefore He embraces Vibhishanan into the fold.

Vibhishanan's reverential vision of Raman suffuses him with boundless joy propelling him to prostrate flat upon the ground and pay homage to Raman. He considers it providential to be permitted to even stand before this Extravagance of Light which invigorates and sublimates him to praise Him as Lord who shines as the light of Sita's heart, the holder of the mighty bow, the patron of the postulants, the comrade of Sugrivan and the chief of the Raghu race; he acknowledges Him as the creator, the sustainer and the annihilator of the Universe, the Supreme Soul, the Almighty soul immanent in all animate and inanimate objects, the unparalleled Lord to whom he vows to offer his respects ceaselessly.

Vibhishanan's underlying emotion of devotion and the longing and pining for Lord Raman, lurking in him, are fully exposed as his decisive mind acknowledges the paramountcy of Raman's presence in an individual's life, so as to break free the fetters of the cyclic births and deaths with His assistance. Also, he emphasizes that if the individual is unable to envision Raman through the medium of meditation and steadfast love, he is indisposed to renounce the besetting vices such as greed, temptation, bondage, licentiousness and repugnance. Individuals being strongly overshadowed by ignorance and materialism cannot cognize Him analogous to persons who cannot ascertain the silver in the white oyster, so too, worldly individuals shall not possess the power of discrimination between conscious soul and gross matter. He is the greatest of the great and the smallest of the small, embodying all the deities' Lord Brahman and Sivan too. He has no breach of time; nor does He have a beginning nor an end, as He is imperishable and eternal. Lord Raman by His illusory power projects a fleshy frame which individuals due to their nescience identify Him as a human person. In truth, He has no body and limbs, yet, acts and moves everywhere and everything. His aspirants and devotees know Him to be 'Nirguna', the Universal soul, formless and without attributes.

Vibhishanan supplicates Raman for liberation from bondage and the ostensible miseries of lordliness, in as much as he yearns to doggedly pursue the highway to salvation by dedicating himself thoroughly to Him, constantly. Raman is extremely delighted with Vibhishanan and grants the boon his heart craves for.

Vibhishanan radiantly vocalizes that there can be no one luckier than himself for the reason that his accelerated quest and his life long aspiration are actualized unreservedly by his mere acquaintance with Raman. He realizes that his attachment to worldly bondage is wholly cut asunder, and disregards the desire for further accumulation of any mundane pleasure and affluence, because he has attained his priceless treasure-Raman. He repeatedly entreats Raman to further bless him with His sustained intimacy and patronage exclusively, so that he may never lose sight of the goal of salvation, lest, he may become oblivious of his service to Him alone. Raman, readily accommodates Vibhishanan's request. He assures that He abides in unison with Sita within impeccable hearts of equanimous aspirants and devotees who have abnegated temporal pleasures solely for His sake besides practicing yoga with steadfast and unblinking faith in him. Raman discloses that even mediocre aspirants are eligible to attain salvation, so much as, if they peruse or write down or listen to His hymns. And so, since the time of aspiring to become a sincere devotee, Raman sees no apology why Vibhishanan should not attain salvation.

Wherefore Raman is progressively convinced of crowning Vibhishanan the King of Lanka. Consequently, He enjoins Lakshman to befittingly perform the ceremonial rites with the sacred water from the sea and coronate Vibhishanan instantly, as He chooses to bestow on him the sovereign crown of Lanka.

The coronation of Vibhishanan meets with extensive vocal support and felicitous ovation from the monkeys. They hail him as blessed Vibhishanan. Moreover they are deliriously joyful that Vibhishanan has warmed the cockles of Raman's heart and so, is in Raman's good favour.

Surging with healthy emotion, Sugrivan, despite his earlier stand enfolds Vibhishanan in a delightful embrace and the two quickly strike up an easy rapport. Significantly, Sugrivan vocalizes that they are after all only vassals of Raman, and is committed to assist Him in rescuing Sita. It is a fair expectation of Sugrivan that Vibhishanan would discharge his duties faithfully, to which Vibhishanan responds that they whirl like marionettes on a string, acting or dancing only according to the Almighty Raman's wishes.

Vibhishanan's modest speech pregnant with devotion and confidence, relieves Sugrivan and gladdens his heart.

In the meanwhile, an espionage agent named Sukan, deputed by Ravanan sneaks into Raman's camp. He meets Sugrivan and cajoles him into believing that Ravanan nurtures fraternal feelings, like that of a blood brother, for him. To boot, Sukan negotiates with Sugrivan to forswear his involvement in the fight between Raman and Ravanan, the special request sent by Ravanan, and primarily, conveys yet another valuable suggestion to him to return to Kishkintha on the grounds that every effort of his to vanquish Lanka would beat the air, as it is insurmountable for him, Sugrivan to do so.

The monkeys listening to such hogwash pounced upon Sukan and thrashed him with severe blows, which unnerved him making him vociferate a loud plea to Lord Raman to rescue him. Raman restrains the monkeys from doing further harm to him.

Fear for Ravanan and his anticipation for some kind of information from Raman's camp, urges Sukan to question Sugrivan of the rejoinder to be conveyed to Ravanan. But Sugrivan retorts angrily that he looks upon Ravanan as an enemy similar to Vali, who has abducted Sita and so, deserves the inevitable death punishment, inescapable at Raman's hands.

Prior to this incident, an intelligence report regarding Raman's prowess and his military force was smuggled out from Raman's camp by a demon spy, Sardula, and intimated to Ravanan who has, since then, become overwrought, restive and perturbed.

Raman, on the other hand, enunciates in a heavy voice to Lakshman, communicating escalating indignation and insinuating the sea God's disregard for Him, His disposition to dehydrate the ocean by shooting an arrow on account of the callousness shown to Him by the God of Ocean. Thus, Raman heaves his bow, strings a fierce and dreadful shaft brilliant like gold, and raises it to release the arrow when, simultaneously, Raman's blazing wrath hums violently in the air sending a terrible shock throughout, rattling the earth, forest, hills and the sky, with darkness descending on every place and direction forcing the aquatic beasts to scurry to and fro in fear under the water, and when the sea God appears before Raman bearing a variety of invaluable gems as souvenir to Raman and honours Him with a respectful bow.

The Sea God beseeches Raman, Lord of the Universe and Redeemer of the three worlds, to condone his nonchalance and protect him. He acknowledges his own ignorance, ludicrousness and proclivity to err because of his gross nature and banausic life. He confesses that on account of his materialistic obsession he cannot visualize Raman's Supreme form of God, and can only know that He, infact, has no form and attributes, but is omnipresent, omniscient and omnipotent. He hails Raman as the Trinity, union of Vishnu, Rudran and Brahman the creator, whose omnifice power none can cognize in the form of delusive actions necessitating the well-being and prosperity of all creatures of the three worlds.

Eventually the Sea God resigns himself to Raman's wishes to accord the path across the sea which is his body, as he originates from Raman, so as to make the transition fairly easily.

But Raman's shaft is still awaiting a target. Hence, Raman intones that his arrow never goes in vain once it is strung, and so queries for a destination to fling his shaft. The Sea God points to a location on the north side named Drumkulya where iniquitous people torment him persistingly.

Raman releases his shaft towards the northern region and after having killed the wicked and vicious beings of that area it returns to Raman's quiver in tact. The Sea God then discloses that the sea will be tapered, if a plan for construction of a bridge is hammered out and humbly suggests to direct Vishwakarma's son Nala to carry out the assignment. So saying the sea God vanishes into the depths of the sea.

At the behest of Lord Raman and Lakshman, the architect Nala sets in motion an army of emergency workers, the monkeys, exuding great alacrity, diligence and agility, to the committed task of constructing the exhaustive and enormous bridge at the earliest.

Chapter - IV

Sukan Counsels Ravanan

A temple commanding heights of excellence to Lord Shivan is constructed on the sea shore, at the very same place where the bridge is laid, and a glorious Shiva Lingam, proclaiming it as Rameshwaram (of Raman) is installed therein by Raman for attainment of blessings and spiritual and pietistic betterment of the world at large Since then, Rameshwaram has emerged as a sacrosanct locus (for) of pilgrimage and worship, where Raman Himself venerates Lord Shivan ceremonially. Raman also consecrates the sacred Lingam with the potential of absolving one of all his sins by the benign grace of Shivan, if he would merely offer holy water of the Ganges to Shivan's icon.

Regarding the construction of the bridge, meticulous Nala with the assistance of the army of monkeys who are pressed into service, is fiercely focused on the daring task, and completes it within a span of just five days.

Raman's dauntless spirit steels the crew of monkeys, millions and millions by the number, that they traverse the sea with Him and reach Lanka safely, Once there, they accommodate themselves on the mountain Subala that commands a view of the whole of Lanka. Atop the mountain, Raman has a bird's eye view of the entire city, where in, He espies Ravanan' who inorder to keep his finger on the pulse, is positioned with his ministers on top of his palace, with his anxiety soaring, an ironic testament to his eloquently professed invincibility, casting desperate glances in His direction of the sweet display of the armies of monkeys under His command.

Not suprisingly, Sukan, in a frantic attempt to survive the deadly attack of the monkeys, flees post-haste from Raman's camp, makes good his escape and reaches Ravanan's palace in hot haste. He very plaintively pays his respects to Ravanan while Ravanan is enquiring about his health and comfort and the headway he has made in ferreting out information about Raman.

He also expresses anxiety and concern about Sukan's harassment and torture at the hands of the monkeys.

Sukan vocalizes that had he not begged Raman to save his life, the monkeys would have decimated him, and so, has successfully escaped with his life to be there so as to inform him, Ravanan, about Sugrivan's knee-jerk reaction and that he, Ravanan, would have to meet the same fate as Vali had.

Sukan severely deprecates Ravanan of running his head against a stone wall in trying to entangle himself in war against Raman. By doing so, he is putting his head in the lion's mouth, and from the information collected and the happenings seen at Raman's camp, Sukan dissuades Ravanan for his own betterment in life, from perusing his hostility with Raman whom no living organism can stand against and whom no animate being can conquer as He is unconquerable. He scrupulously remonstrates that though millions of brave warriors are in preparedness for demolishing Lanka, Raman, unassisted by anyone is visibly accomplished to wipe out the city of Lanka in a trice. Talking in this fashion, Suka, from the terrace of the palace overlooking the mountain where Raman and his troops are stationed, pointingly briefs Ravanan of the chief warrior monkeys with their names and estimates the number of warriors to be at least twenty-one multi- billions.

Further, Sukan edifies Ravanan about Raman and Sita being the incarnations of Lord Vishnu and Goddess Lakshmi, who is the creator, sustainer and destroyer of the Universe. So, accordingly, he forewarns him to decisively desist from waging war against them.

Furthermore, Sukan proceeds to unearth lofty truths, instructing Ravanan on the fugacious nature of the organic body which will be, without recourse, levelled to dust some day. He especially designates the soul to be divine, interminable and synonymous with God. Sukan imputes Ravanan for perpetrating innumerable sins through out his life only to gratify his fleshy concerns and warns that as long as he does not realize his soul, the real self, he is bound to be enmeshed in the unrealistic worldly asymmetries of life; and the trammels of exits and entrances to this terrestrial sphere will become an unending cycle with constrains becoming stronger at each birth.

Suka regrets that Ravanan being a Brahmin should be so perverse, oppugnant and antinomous so as to breed disease of the soul, and woe betide, ever indulging in an unbridled cult of carnal pleasures like beasts, drawing a parallel to dogs which also feel pleasure and pain in their lives.

He, therefore, offering counsel intended solely for his prosperity, beseeches Ravanan to restore Sita to Raman, to lay a claim for refuge at

His Lotus Feet, and to seize this as the most cherished opportunity of praise and devotion to Him alone strongly effectuating his emancipation purely by Raman's benediction. If otherwise he does not painstakingly mend his ways, rebuild himself and behave wisely, he is programming himself for self-destruction to descend headlong into hell. He entreats Ravanan to aspire to appease Raman with pure love and veneration and never lose consciousness of the coruscating countenance of Sri Raman with bows and arrows in the company of Goddess Sri Sita. Also he appeals to Ravanan to have the extraordinary and salubriously holy feet of Lord Raman, persistently worshipped by Sugrivan, Lakshman and Visbhishanan, etched on his heart and mind forever.

Chapter - V

Commencement of the War

Ravanan's emotions get the better of sage counsel; hence, he criticizes Sukan's evangelic attitude. Driven by malignant energy fuelled by an over production of bile, he bawls at Sukan being an ignoble and ungrateful creature and accuses him of being a villain who has the audacity to shamefacedly catechize him in the manner he has done. He threatens him with death punishment, but pardons him on the grounds of the merits of his past good services. So he acquits him but screams at him to vanish from his sight. And Sukan quivering at Ravanan's explosive temper quits the place as it suits his Lordship Ravanan.

Sukan is an erudite Brahmin who by realization of his soul is one with Brahman. Consequently, his emancipatory impulse has renounced the mundane obligations of life indulging in performing yagnas and sacrifices for the betterment of the Gods and the upliftment of the citizens and the annihilation of the demons. Accordingly, he is now living the life of a saint, in solitude.

By the strange quirk of fate, Sukan's serene life is thrown out of gear. A demon named Bajradanstra has always been on the prowl seeking an opportunity for wreaking vengeance on Sukan. Such a chance has mellowed now, when Sage Agasthiyar nas arrived at Sukan's hermitage. He solicits the sage to favour him by acceding to his hospitality for that day to which the sage readily consents.

During the time, when the sage wends his way to the river for a bath, the demon Bajradanstra uses a subterfuge to materialize his plan and achieve his end; he plays Sukan false by disguising himself as Sage Agasthiyar He enters Sukan's cottage and discloses his long cherished appetite for meat, requesting him to cook the flesh of animal as food for that day's meal. Duly Sukan is painstakingly preparing the dishes.

Bajradanstra on his way back from the cottage descries Sukan's wife. He casts a spell on her that she falls senseless to the ground. Instantly he transforms himself into Sukan's wife, enters the hermitage again, cooks human flesh instead and serves it to sage Agasthiyar when he returns from his bath to the cottage. The sage on seeing human flesh being served is stoutly alarmed and gets into a state of violent emotion of anger, and in a ghastly tone pronounces a harsh imprecation that he, Sukan be turned into a demon.

Sukan, having no compunctions about the fauxpas, explains to the sage that it was only at his request his wife had conceded to cook and serve him meat. But then the game is up; for Agasthiyar by the process of meditation cognizes the precise authorship of this conspiracy and charade. He comprehends the fake posture and the clever handiwork of the atrocious Bajradanstra and acknowledges Sukan's inculpabliity. Nevertheless his imprecation still stands as words once split out cannot be collected and taken back. Invariably, Sukan would have to duplicate a demon form, but would repossess his Brahmin symmetry later when he would offer sage counsel to Ravanan for restoring Sita to Raman, and would have to be in the service of Ravanan till Raman proceeds to Lanka for killing ornery Ravanan, the ominous demons and other evil doers. He would then compass his previous structure of Brahmin through Raman's blessing and retreat to the forests to live in tranquillity as in the past.

In the meanwhile, Ravanan's maternal grandfather named Malyavantha approaches Ravanan and laments the destruction, the difficulties and the criticism the city of Lanka is confronted with ever since Sita has been held hostage there. He is spelling out the anomalistic signs that presage evil. He is recounting the many omens verbally, that, a number of malicious spirits have and are gravitating towards the city; dreadful thunderous clouds prestidigitate hot blood over Lanka; all the icons of the presiding deities are weeping and sweating and unseating themselves due to fear and diffidence. Even Goddess Kali ostends her hideous yellow teeth and laughs mockingly at the demons; asses are being born to cows; cats and mongooses are being tormented by mere rats and the vultures, and the Garudas, Lord of birds, are afflicted by serpents, The dreadful God of Death, bearing a monstrous ugly body of black and yellow hues, sneaks about visiting houses of demons at regular intervals, and many more such heinous prognostications connoting deleterious effects are still in the offing.

In view of these facts, Malyavanthan initiates this shot at a peace process with Raman, pleadingly, urging Ravanan to offer Sita back together with a huge amount of wealth to Raman, and establish sustaining peace for the welfare of his race. He requests Ravanan to cognize Raman as really God Narayanan and put an end to this long-festering hostility and repugnance for Him which undermines the security and prosperity of the empire of the demons. Again, he accentuates that Raman is no ordinary human person, but Omnipresent God. He unravels the truth that aspirants, devotees, Sages, Seers and Saints purge their mind by their exclusive inveterate faith, ardent devotion and sustained intimacy with Raman and anchor at His feet by which they effortlessly cross the ocean of mundane obligations of life.

Malyavanthan underlines Ravanan's obliquity and unfolds his uncharacteristic attributes such as cultural sterility and spiritual illiteracy. Inorder to bring him around, he addresses him as the king of kings and therefore supplicates him to yield to his wholesome wisdom for the welfare of the demon race. In addition, he points that his moral character not being sound, he could by devotional worship to Raman chasten and redeem himself.

When one's fate to be doomed is predestined, at such times, to grasp at the straws of wisdom always just floats out of reach. So is Ravanan's doom sealed; he is confronted by his own mortality. Every cell of his is so incompatible in lifestyle that he cannot be swayed from the path of unrighteousness, not even by Malyavanthan's strong dose of conventional wisdom.

Ravanan in turn lambasts Malyavanthan for his brashness of boasting about Raman's eminence, chivalry and dynamism. He essays to delimit Raman's renown and prominence to only within the circle of men who have taken to a life of asceticism, and living in the forests. He derogates Raman for having been banished by His own father, and for associating with and dwelling amidst monkeys. Ravanan insinuates whether Raman Himself had sent him to negotiate His cause and further, reprehends Malyavanthan for his acrimonious gibberish, which is biting his ears. He explodes that he has been enduring his nonsensical blabber for so long only because he is a decrepit relative of his. He instructs Malyavanthan to get lost from his sight because, if he hangs around and persists in exhorting him further it would only incinerate his ears.

Aggravated, Ravanan ascends to the top most floor of his palace overlooking the mountain and has a grand view of the armies of monkeys garrisoned there. He is affected with an itching to strike with unprecedented ferocity; so he begins deputing warriors for assaulting the monkeys.

Later, Ravanan who is luxuriating on his gorgeous throne with his queen Mandothari at his side, attended by demon warriors of his palace, is discomposed by Raman's arrow which comes charging in first cutting asunder thousands of royal ensigns of white fixed in all places, next toppling and crushing into pieces the crowns on his ten heads and then dislocating and breaking the glittering ear-rings worn by Queen Mandothari.

The rattled Ravanan is highly flabbergasted at Raman's astounding tour de force. The feat being a severe blow to his vanity, he lapses into distress and delusion after his short respite of basking in pleasure with Mandothari and retires to his room very much chagrined.

The increasing evidence of Raman's bravura confounds him. Concurrently he galvanizes into action ordering Prahastha and other chief officers to attack the monkeys instantly.

Armed with a motley of weapons such as swords, axes, spikes, bows, nooses and rods, alI the demons press into action hastening out of the city amidst sounds of trumpets and other musical Instruments. They charge at the monkeys who are put on hold with huge stones, uprooted trees and hillocks in their powerful hands. Under the leadership of Lakshman who in league with Sugrivan escorts a supernumerary army of monkeys cheering, applauding and exclaiming the rallying cry of victory for Raman. Being filled with expansive fury, they all surround the city. The gates are encircled on all sides by the chief warriors - Hanuman, Anghadan, Kumundan, Nila, Nala, Sharab, Kesaryi, Maindha, Dwinbidhya, Jambavan, Dashimukh, Tara and all the other champions. Exhibiting heavy bias, the monkeys are beginning to bludgeon the demons, having a go at them by biting and tearing them with their strong claws, teeth and nails and thrashing them by hurting stones upon them doing away with them in a trice.

The preponderate army of demons mobilizes into action running wildly towards the monkeys and begins to exchange blows. So there is a formidable combat and the death toll on both sides is horrendously high. For the battlefield is thickly spread with corpses, shattered chariots and carcasses of horses, elephants and mules.

The monkeys with added rapaciousness continue to slaughter and eliminate the demons quite easily. Forthright, as Ravanan is corrupted by the grave sin of abducting Sita, it has a telling effect on the demons who evidently become powerless and unstrung with an appalling inability to execute an effective retaliation on the enemies. Consequently, the loss to the demon army is well high astronomical; it is reduced to one fourth of its size. On the other hand, the set back in the monkey troops does nothing to dampen their enthusiasm and power as the fortune of Raman's grace is incessantly used to prime the monkeys pump. Hence they are protected and sustained by Raman, Sri Vishnu, with His nectarous food.

The demons' army incur a heavy loss, which is visibly noticeable by Meghnath who becoming avowedly strategic takes an invisible form. In this invisible mode of being, he is flinging from the air deadly weapons and a supercharged Brahmasthra on the monkeys, which is striking down a very large number of monkeys on the battlefield in quick time. Large-scale violence is being predicated upon them by this seasoned and barbaric demon warrior.

In as much as the Brahmasthra being the divine armament of Indrajit, Raman, as a mark of respect is forced to suspend his counter attack for the nonce. Moments later, Raman's intense anger surfaces that he exhorts Lakshman to bring His bow and arrows to showcase His intrepidity. Now He aims at negotiating the Brahmastrha uncompromisingly and rigorously by annihilating the callous demon Indrajit, its possessor, by his own weapon. Meghanath eaves dropping on this intriguing strategy plays it safe by inscrutably escaping to his residence.

Raman verbally requisitions Hanuman to flee to Dronachal abounding in divine herbs and bring herbs at once to resuscitate and revitalize the dead monkeys. Raman assures Hanuman that the performance of this extraordinary feat would explicitly endorse his charisma and renown throughout the world and also in all the three worlds. Hanuman soldiers on and only by his blinking dedication to Raman alone, as a standing example, is able to traverse the ocean swiftly, soon unhinge a portion of the mighty hill of herbs and bring it to revive the monkeys instantaneously, and also, to replace the hill on the same spot.

Ravanan, on hearing that all the dead monkeys are brought back to life, is driven to despair and relapses into consternation and fear. Nonetheless, he selects his prime and most valiant soldiers, equips them with the deadliest weapons for attacking the monkeys, yet cautions them against the well-honed attack of Raman's army of monkeys, for he is heedful that Raman is appropriated to be his greatest adversary with the mission to annihilate Him and hence has manifested Himself in tangible form. The furious demons try to dominate with their relentless attack on the monkeys killing them with numerous lethal weapons such as pikes, tomor, bows, bhindipal etc. It is a disturbing and distressing trend now for the demons that are being obliterated heavily by the rampageous monkeys led by Sugrivan, Angadan and Hanuman because of the divine intervention of Lord Raman's animated puissance, a silent force, favouring and invigorating them. And this animated puissance impossible to the demons who fight against God Himself are easily vanquished.

By fighting in this manner, Raman, God of all Gods, Omnipotent, Omniscient and Omnipresent, is showcasing His sportiveness and play-acting in a human fashion.

Chapter - VI

Lakshman Falls Unconscious

Losing is a hardship no warrior king like Ravanan would like to face. Ravanan is provoked to an explosion of anger by the news of the obliteration of his mighty warriors Athikayan and others. Moreover he hears of the colossal destruction of his army, and adrenaline pours through him. Ravanan prone to violence, armed with enormous conceit, himself sets out to counter the attack of his enemies leaving Indrajit in the citadel to protect the city.

Ravanan's anger is of such intensity that he quickly mounts a divine chariot which is well equipped and charges at Raman, While rushing headlong towards Raman' inparticular, using his serpent-like shafts which are very sharp, he wounds Sugrivan and other brave monkeys in the bargain. He espies Vibhishanan also who stands face to face with him at the fore of Raman's front-line warriors. At such a moment he aims a divinely potent arrow in Vibhishanan's direction. The moment he releases the arrow, meaning to kill Vibhishanan, concurrently, Lakshman shields Vibhishanan by standing infront of him so that the arrow may not strike him, for Vibhishanan is entitled to insurance and needs to be jealously defended by Raman who has espoused to stand by him guaranting his life, And instead, Lakshman is pierced by the greatest infallible arrow.

And Lakshman's counter intuitive strategy is to effectively employ a sham syncope; because no arrow however serpentine and perilous can wreck havoc on Lakshman who is the incarnation of Lord Seshan, verily the fountain head of all the energies of the Universe. So he falls senseless to the ground only to play-act the part as a human being.

Ravanan alights from his chariot with the strong motion of raising Lakshman from the ground inorder to carry him away with him. His embarrassment is greatly palpable as he is unable to lift him up from the ground.

Hanuman, discerns Ravanan's futile gesture of trying to haul Lakshman from the ground and carry him away, when he wrecks this very objective, working havoc by dealing him a savage blow which makes him stagger and fall upon his knees thereby loosening his grip on his lusty bow which falls to the earth from his mighty hands. Simultaneously Raman projects a clever strategy to rein in Ravanan by capitalizing on his crescent shaped shaft, which is profoundly potent, and fells his monarchical helmets at first.

Raman's healing power of divine compassion far outweighs any corrosive power of evil. Beholding Ravanan, the corrosive power of evil, being critically wounded this day by His full blown attack, Raman exhorts him to return to Lanka for the day, take rest, compose himself and come back the following day for witnessing how He, Raman, is going to play fair towards him. Consequently, Ravanan's psyche is highly tilted. His mega egotism, the prime vice, suffers a cruel blow. He feels disparaged and hangs his head down in humiliation for being so gravely wounded in this manner. With heavy steps Ravanan ambulates tracing his way to the palace.

Raman play-acting the role of an enfleshed being is also despondent, painfully aware of Lakshman lying unconscious on the ground. He bewails Lakshman's critical condition and enjoins Hanuman to repeat the act of resuscitation, as he did the monkeys, by fetching the divine drug to revive Lakshman.

Performing, for Hanuman, the incandescent devotee of Raman, is the touchstone of his quality of life. Hence he starts instantly for Dronachala hills. This news when carried to Ravanan by his spies makes him worried sick and apprehensive that he pressingly hastens to Kalnemy's residence. Kalnemy's face telegraphs consternation at Ravanan's unforeseen visit to his plebeian lodgings. Hailing Ravanan as the king of kings, kalnemy pays his respects to him in a fitting manner with folded arms and enquires about the purpose of his visit to his humble residence, but pledges readiness to be invariably at his service.

Ravanan apprising Kalnemy, his cherished and sagacious confident, of Lakshman's unconscious state - the sequence of the venomous shot of his powerful shaft and Hanuman's departure to the Dronachala hills to fetch the divine stimulant he cajoles him to develop a strategy by which Hanuman may be rendered confused, reckless and unperceiving in locating the divine portion. Ravanan's, vicious verve presses Kalnemy to deceive Hanuman by his illusion so that he may return unsuccessful in his aspiration of bringing the celestial herb.

Initially, Kalnemy pleadingly advocates that he, Ravanan, should give ear to his sound counsel and act wisely. Then, he commits himself to execute his orders, doing good adequately, even at the cost of his life, though he is painfully cognizant of Mareeson's fate in the form of a gold deer which he too, doubtlessly, will have to face. Kalnemy primarily, enlightens Ravanan on the bitter harvest he is currently reaping-his relatives, friends, sons and innumerable demons having been killed already. He also makes him realize he cannot make good the loss of his kith and kin and the meaninglessness of existing still with all the pleasures after their annihilation and, therefore, the unproductivity and invalidity of having kidnapped Sri Sita. Hence Kalnemy entreats Ravanan to restore Sri Sita to Sri Raman and his imperial state to brother Vibhishanan and retreat to an isolated unworldly habitation.

Further, Kalnemy exhorts Ravanan to abnegate a self centered existence by gradually constraining mind from having a sway over materialistic pleasures and to enhance it to hold communion with his soul internally; mind should be trained to cognize that the external world, the universe and all the objects seen and enjoyed outside his self, even his supposedly animated body are just matter and so subjected to perish in time.

He educates Ravanan about the immortality of the soul which is indigenously and authentically beatific, pure and real. It is only God's illusive power of Maya which fabricates all the objects and the creatures incorporated in the Universe, which from Brahman to the tiniest insects are doomed to perish. On this fertile soil of illusion sprout the seeds of materialism and worldliness with its three attributes, Sathwik (Quiscent), Rajas (Material) Tamas (Predatory) its functions being creation, sustenance and obliteration of all creatures as well as the Universe. The vices like greed, anger, prejudice, slaughter etc., are the offsprings of illusion and these operative vices conquer their master-soul which is immaculate, faultless and pervasive. All operations of deeds and exertions are superimposed solely on the individual by illusion and thus the individual is inflated with egoism and subsequently, involuntarily, falls into the labyrinth of worldly attachment, getting himself entangled in the short-sighted mundane bindings. The individual oblivious of his real self, his soul and his inherent bliss lying dormant in him, gets steeped in the sea of worldly existence, experiencing pain and pleasure, heat and cold and misery and mirth. Birth reclaims the erring individual, he is again born into the cycle of births and deaths and not until he encounters a genuine, bonafide Spiritual Preceptor to shepherd him onto the right path, can he realize his soul and know god. Since then, he cuts asunder the trammels of dark nescience and instantly attains salvation even while living in the fleshy frame in the present life.

Kalnemy heavily emphasizes on Ravanan to adhere to the righteous path, have holistic knowledge of his soul being purely distinct from his physical sheath and to one-pointedly concentrate on the interest of realizing, finally, the soul which is God. If Ravanan is adverse to adhering to the path of deliverance and realisation of his soul in the procedure he has described, Kalnemy, pressurizes him to meditate on the form of Sri Raman with immaculate attributes and cognize His charismatic and most handsome manifestation, adorned with a high crown and bejewelled with spectacular ornaments coruscating as the rising sun. Kalnemy convincingly assures Ravanan that his sins would be wholly incinerated, if, by his fire of devotion, analogous to cotton burnt by fire, he is faithful to Sri Raman and Sri Sita, befittingly attended by Lakshman bow in hand, dwelling in the depths of one's unconscious. He supplicates Ravanan to abandon his enmity with Raman who is Immaculate, Immortal, Omnipresent, Omnipotent, Omniscient and infact has no name or even form, and to adore Him ardently with commitment.

Chapter - VII

Hanuman Obliterates Kalnemy and Lakhman Regains Consciousness

Kalnemy's Cajaling in honeyed words only escalates Ravanan's choler and impatience like the fire heated butter that is affected when water is sprinkled on it. Ravanan marks Kalnemy as a slave who is believed to have received some kind of allurement or lucreative favours from Raman to become his slave, inorder to propagate devotion to him in turn, as he has done forthwith, to persuade Ravanan to worship Raman with fervent devotion. Incited with this foolish notion, Ravanan swears to slay him if he does not execute his ordinance.

Kalnemy who shudders to incur Ravanan's wrath and dislpleasure professes to perpetrate his ordinances promptly. In order to focus on his assigned task, he leaves for the Himalayas. There at the foot of the Great Himalays, he conjures up a hocus - pocus hermitage by which Hanuman is anticipated to pass, so as to hamper his design of reaching for the divine herbs from the Dronachal hills. Assuming the false colours of a saga, he seats himself in the cottage.

When Hanuman arrives there in high time, he is astonished to see an elegant hemitage, which he had not hitherto seen on his first visit. He carries his memory back to the previous sojourn to the Himalayas and quizzically reflects whether he has now taken an erroneous path or if his mind has gone insane. Nonetheless, he composes his mind decisively to look in on the sage, and for the pressing reason to quench his thirst.

Within the cottage, Hanuman finds the ambience very tranquil and beatific and also, he sees trees laden with exceptional fruits. The giant Kalnem's clever deception as a sage beckons Hanuman irresistibly to dialogue with him. The ambience and Kalmemy's clever deception lend colour to Hanuman's innocent announcement of his identity and also his principal mission of crossing the mountain for Raman's sake. In the same breath, He requests the sage to guide him to a waterscape so as to drink and gratify his thirst.

The deceitful Kalnemy in the garb of a sage instructs Hanuman to drink the water of his bowl and further spurs him to tarry his expedition recommending some rest and sleep for a while. He goes on to dupe Hanuman, asserting that by reason of his prescience and transcendental knowledge, his cognizance of the past, the future and the present of events is possible for him, and so relates by painting in bright colours the on-going condition of Lakshman way back in Lanka regaining consciousness and being administered to by Raman Himself.

Hanuman, expressing his displeasure at being unable to slake his thirst with the bowl's mearger water, requests the sage to direct him to a tank or fountain if there be any. Kalnemy's never ending duplicity summons up a sham boy-attendant who escorts Hanuman to the tank. And woe-betide Hanuman, when a huge crocodile assails him, charging forth voraciously to devour him as he bends to drink water from the tank. Oddly enough, Hanuman beholds a surprisingly beautiful damsel emerging from the body of the crocodile as he catches hold of it and tears it into two pieces.

Initially, a resurgence of gratitude wells up from her being. She acknowledges to be a fairy named Dhanyamala. She thanks Hanuman bountifully for emancipating her from a sage's imprecation of long ago, which had transformed her into a crocodile. She is convinced to be obliged to him for sanctify her this day by the generous touch of his mere hands. So, as to reciprocate his generosity, she unveils the ferocious demon Kalnemy's duplications, mask of a sage and his evil intention of designing a phony hermitage by his magical powers only to barricade his expedition to the Dronachal hills. Hanuman is provoked by her to eliminate the demon and forge ahead to accomplish his mission. And she exchanging a farewell with him chooses to ascend to Heaven by his blessings.

On Hanuman's return, Kalnemy eggs him on to seize that moment as the opportunity for making haste in accomplishing his errand to the Dronachal hills, for he sees in it a fortunate chance for the lucrative disposal of a secret manthra sacred advice, which he forces upon Hanuman.

Kalnemy's bashfulness is palpable, as Hanuman exposes his true colours of demon from and nature. Piqued by his insidious nature. Hanuman rewards him with a heavy blow, the remuneration for the disposal of his manthra. But the blow also makes him repossess his indigenous demon from facilitating him to retaliate with inordinate violence using his illusory techniques, making him very potent and unconquerable too. But, ere long, Kalnemy's head is shattered by Hanuman's powerful blow that eliminates him in the end.

Within a brief moment, Hanuman reaches the Dronachala hills and to his utter astonishment finds no herb there, but judiciously unearths the whole hill, carrying it on the palm of his hand he reaches Lanka in no time. The promise of bringing the hill itself pleases Raman as Hanuman implores Lord Raman to expeditiously administer the divine medicine and do the needful to alleviate Lakshman's condition.

Raman ordains Sushena to ferret out the divine drug and competently treat Lakshman, promptly regaining consciousness and being rejuvenated by the divine portion, Lakshman provocatively yells a loud warning note of caution to Ravanan, wherever he is. Raman articulates his indebtedness to Hanuman for his phenomenal valour, because of which, He acknowledges that Lakshman is back to life. The monkeys too axpress their happiness and are revitalized with greater zeal to fight.

As precisely as the snakes are tortured by the vultures Garuda, and the elephants by lions, so rightly is Ravanan very much afflicted by the wounds sustained in the fight against Raman by His arrows. He now showcases an expansive remorse for his actions. He grieves to his ministers about the presentation that is given to one's preceptor. He further regrets that his death has been entrusted to the hands of a thoroughbred invincible human being, predesigned by Grandfather Brahman the creator. Also, he is retrospective of Sage Aranya's invocation of a terrific imprecation upon him, that he as well as his lineage would be completely extirpated by a man, who, on earth, is acceptably meritorious, invincible and lion hearted to kill him. Therefore, he undeniably recognizes Raman, at whose hand his death has been sealed, as the incarnation of Lord Vishnu.

But, still, to mitigate his growing apprehensions even after it has become evident that Raman is the inimitable man to say him Ravanan is decisive in evading His deadly attack and his ubiquitous infirrnity of unprincipled deliberations enginers the plan of delegating Kumbhakarnan to spearhead the counter-attack against Raman. Evidently, vexed at Kumhakarnan's affectation of somnolence all day and night, uninterruptedly, for a lengthy period of time, Ravanan despatches soldiers to arouse the imbecile from his deep slumber so that he may send him to fight Rama.

After their weary efforts to stir him from his hibernation, the soldiers deliver him up to Ravanan who tutors him about Raman's arrival in Lanka, the calamitous ongoing war against him and the confounding task of outmaneuvering him, as, on the other hand, He, Raman is unrestrictedly unnevingly, demolishing his armies and deracinating the very demon dynastry.

Hence capitalizing on Kumbakarnan's warfare knowledge and potentialities, unparalleled by any other warrior, he has cause to awaken him from his deep slumber to fiercely wage a full blown attack on Raman and conquer Him.

Kumbhakarnan cynically emanates a booming laughter and downplays Ravanan's words, rebuking him for unheeding his forewarning against the inescapable consequences that would befall him. Likewise, he reviles him for his shocking string of crimes by which he has not only invited his own death but has also illegitimately inherited the unfortunate extinction of the demon race and, furthermore, is predisposed in prolonging the war as is his wont.

At his juncture, Kumbhakarnan, in addition' discloses Sage Narathar's stunning revelations to him long ago. It was informed to him by Narathar that all the Gods in unison had prayed to Lord Vishnu to incarnate Himself in the physical sheath for annihilating them both. In addition, he reveals that the creator, Brahman had constituted Ravanan's death only at the hands of a human being, a man, and, that Raman is the enfleshed form of Lord Vishnu on earth, who would effectuate His commitment in a righteous manner. Therefore he verbally deliberates that it is unwise to press forward his vicious malignancy and incur the wrath of Raman who is the Supreme God, now borm into the race of the Raghus. He emphatically states that his death is predeterminedly inevitable. With extravagant solicitude, Kumbhakarnan essays to influence Ravanan's mind towards the attainment of salvation by his utter devotion to God, which is the best and most fruitful means. Otherwise, all the deeds of an individual who has no faith and love in God are of no use. He further proceeds to illustrate that all the previous incarnations of Lord Vishnu had acted upon the earth in various ways to fulfill the different purposes. But the incarnation of Raman with Shivan at the basis is the greatest and the most perfect of all incarnations of Lord Vishnu.

Moreover he endeavours to make Ravanan cognize that Raman is infinitely compassionate too and can be propitiated by unalloyed love and ardent devotion to him, beyond question. He advocates that those who cherish single-minded devotion to Raman can effortlessly conceptualize. Him and can thus cross the turbulent sea of worldliness. It is stipulated that those who read the life saga of Raman and Sita are undeniably sanctified and are made worthy of achieving liberation with everlasting bliss.

Chapter - VIII

Raman Kills Kumbhakarnan

Ravanan's muscles clench, involuntarily, as Kumbhakarnan sermonizes at length though, moral superiority belongs to neither of them. Disdaining the thought of listening to the impertinent homily aimed at advising him on matters irrelevant at this crucial hour of crisis, Ravanan, fuming with rage castigates him for touting his wisdom, uncalled for. His worst fear is that Kumbhakarnan would weasel out and not buttress him in his struggle against Raman; hence being overpowered only by sleep, he bawls at him to go into hibernation.

As things stand, Kumbhakarnan senses that no argument or counsel can move Ravanan from his consuming determination to go all out and destroy Raman. It is transparent to him that his hot headedness is soaring and he reeks of desperation. Since the situation warrants, he prepares, despite his expansive bout of somnolence to engage himself in the battle against Raman. So, he vehemently escalates over the walls of the city and instantly rushes to the battlefield.

Kumbhakanan, the soaring monster heralds his advent by detonating a loud bellow that startes and petrifies all the monkeys. He dominates all the lands and the seas which reverberate with his loud bellow. Looking very hideously ruthless and as voluminous as a hill, he commences to ensnare the monkeys and devour them. The outlandish monster's unbridled violence terrorizes the monkeys to the core of their being impelling them to flee pell-mell from the battlefield to save themselves just as would all the beings run away at the apparition of the God of death.

On beholding Kumbhakarnan, the sapient Vibhishanan finds himself in an emotional crisis. Nonetheless, he approximates and pays homage to him, renewing kindred ties as siblings, beseeching him to be gracious to him. Thereafter Vibhishanan confesses to him about his persuasion in dissuading Ravanan to renounce his smouldering rancour for Raman, and his own palpable fear that he had felt imagining the outcome of the war which made him adduce several reasons for averting the battle. He verbalizes Ravanan's hard-nosed refusal to recognize and accommodate wholesome counsel and his ignoble act of dictating his expulsion. He laments Ravanan's folly of being influenced by sinful and imprudent courtiers who feast him with sordid reflections and deliberations, as a result of which he had denounced and kicked him out of the kingdom. Ravanan's negative posturing had turned on the heat for Vibhishanan to repudiate his unwise counsel, flee the kingdom and find anchor and security at the feet of noble Raman. kumbhakarnan's mental status, refreshed with pleasant vibes at the moment, engages him in a warm embrace of his sibling Vibhishanan expressing an affectionate benediction that he may live long and salvage their dynasty as he has secured Raman's favour and sanctuary. He communicates the sage Naradhar's expose of Vibhishanan being a telltale sign of pure devotion to Lord Vishnu. His mental status steeped in emotional sentiment melts in a trice, now, leaving him emotionally drained. The building tension in the air, evidently palpable, fiercely focuses Kumbhakarnan's attention on the task at hand. And apprehensively nonplussed at his own fury which blinds him, inhibiting him from telling apart a friend from a foe he respectfully entreats Vibhishanan to leave the place instantly Despondent about their bond as siblings being dissevered, Vibhishanan with heavy steps retreats to his camp after making a deferent bow very sorrowfully to his elder brother. On the other hand, a collective groan rises from the terror-stricken monkeys when a huge tide of freaked violence streams from the inimical Kumbhakaman flaying and lacerating a large number of them, and creating chaos and destruction all around.

At this instant, Raman, seeing Kumbhakarnan in the throes of a full blown temper and destruction is extensively piqued, and is provoked into using the Bayabasthar - the divine stormy shaft which he shoots at Kumbhakarnan sundering his right arm in a flash. The fall of his monstrous arm crushes many a monkey to death by its heavy weight. The grisly combat that ensues between Raman and Kumbhakarnan instills awe and panic in the monkeys who watch it. Kumbhakarnan goaded on by his unbridled vandalism uproots a huge sal tree with his left hand and charges towards Raman. But Raman mangles his left hand too in the earlier fashion Kumbhakarnan's mind is shattered; unable to contain his surging wrath he perforce rushes forward to ingurgitate Raman. Now, Raman's powerful shaft lacerating both his legs grotesquely rag rolls them, hurling them at the gates of Lanka. Kumbhakarnan's dismembered torso buckles to the ground. But, notwithstanding, he, looking so dreadful as if the planet 'Raghu' was eclipsing the full moon, relentlessly copes with moving his dismembered torso to rout Raman.

In no time, with a single shot called 'Aindhra' Raman decapitates Kumbhakarnan's head from his body making it fall heavily beyond the gates of Lanka, and his titanic body is tossed upon the sea pulverizing many aquatic creatures by the fall. This visible out come - the tragic end of Kumbhakarnan sends the Gods into an ecstatic joy; they rain flowers upon Raman from the heavens and begin to pray and sing His praises.

Concurrently at this time of jubilation, the divine sage Naradhar is drawn towards the radiantly happy Raman coruscating like the blooming blue hued lotuses. Beholding Raman being mercifully disposed towards the monkeys wounded by Kumbhakarnan's arrows, Naradhar pays his obeisance to Raman, hailing Him as God of all Gods, the Supreme Soul, the Eternal Entity, as Narayanan the support of the Universe and the witness of all the worlds. He eulogizes Him as the immutable, self - enlightened symbol of transcendental knowledge as well as worldly knowledge. He paints a word picture of Raman's manifestation of personality traits of happiness or sadness when assuming human form by his illusive power which apparently shields Him, also when He dwells in the mind of every individual.

Granted that Raman is indigenously self-enlightened He can be conceptualized only by His own devotees who are pure-hearted. He is not merely the cause of the world but the very ground of its being and becoming. All the three worlds are created when He opens His eyes and they at once disappear when He closes them. He is Brahman from whom existence of all other objects originate and beyond which there can be no substance, as He is the terminus of existence- beings exist in Him. He is the very manifestation of the Universe itself, and the realized souls cognize that it is His self that is apparently conscious in nature, soul, time and even objects that have no visible or tangible form.

The Vedas declare that He is the absolute Spiritual Principle, which is the ultimate ground and explanation of all else here; hence, He is pervading every object in the whole Universe. The Vedas also clearly state that He only acts by the power of His own illusion. Again, the Vedas validate that He is the Pure Knowledge and enlightenment which cannot be transmuted. So it is mandatory to attain His grace inorder to realize the genuine truth; it will be antithetical otherwise. Further, similar to the sun's rays that are seen in the water is His creation and its object of the world that are seen upon His existence. He is the Lord who is eternal and perpetual with limitless spiritual wealth, which is His possession. There is none who can see Him as He has no form; as He is invisible as He is formless; there can be none who can worship or even meditate on Him. The illation is that it is only the wise by worshipping His tangible form from in an incarnation, in the way of the knower as well as the known, who strive to attain pure knowledge and salvation.

The individual categorically meets with obstacles like illusion, lust, anger, greed etc., during worship and meditation that hamper his mind and concentration and terrify him just as cats that terrify the rats. But the devotees who cherish and nurture unalloyed love for Him can vanquish, very effortlessly, their egoism and traverse the sea of worldliness as if they are crossing the footprints of a cow by chanting His names, singing His praises, meditating on His holy form, listening to the nectar-like sagas of His life, and associating with like-minded aspirants and devotees.

The sage Naradhar divulges that he meditates constantly on the incarnate, enfleshed form Raman. He acknowledges that in his status as a realized soul he saunters along all over the worlds, and has thus earned the deference of all the Gods. Hailing Raman as the Lord he accredits Him with the success of annihilating the mighty and vicious Kumbhakarnan for the welfare of the Gods. He verbalizes his foresight of Lakshman subjugating Indrajit the next day and Raman Himself exterminating Ravanan the following day thus, thoroughly wiping out the demon clan thereby redeeming the afflicted world from sinking into the quicksand of sin. Promising to witness all the events from heaven, Naradhar postulates Raman for consent to take leave of Him. Thus by Raman's benign grace, Naradhar, highly lauded and ushered in by the heavenly Gods, ascends to pure Brahmaloka - the abode of the creator.

The diffidence engendered by the tragic news of his brother Kumbhakarnan's death Shatters the executive head of the demon race Ravanan's mental equipoise. His son Meganath now acts as an anodyne with soothing words pacifying his revered father, the wise king, not to grieve. He takes a savage resolution to extirpate all the enemies by propitiating the God of Fire for procuring a divine chariot and other potent and foolproof weapons for the purpose. He is confident of being triumphant. Instantaneously, he starts for the impenetrable Nikumbhala caves, attired in red robes and adorned with red garlands, and taking with him various additives for worship aplenty. Once there, he sets up a sacrificial altar and commences the long-drawn-out worship of the God of fire by offering oblations to the fire.

The vigilant Vibhishanan is all agog that he replenishes Raman about Meganath's performance of sacrifice to propitiate the God of Fire, and if he does placate him, he would inevitably become invulnerable and unconquerable. He evolves a strategy and entreats Raman for permission to balk Meganath's sacrificial worship by taking Lakshman who is the most appropriate person to kill him. But Raman himself chooses to go out there and kill Meganath with his Agnya shaft - the fire-emitting arrow. Vibhishanan realizing his gross error apologizes to Raman for his impertinence in opting for Lakshman and begs to speak his mind as his intention is of a different cast; because Meganath cannot be killed by any other person other than the one who has totally abstained from food and sleep consecutively for twelve years. By reason of doing so for the last twelve years, inorder to keep incessant vigil over Him, Lakshman has refrained from eating and sleeping; Visbhishanan persists it is he alone who is the better choice to slay Meganath.

Furthermore, Lakshman is the sole person on earth who can proficiently annihilate Meganath as he is the incarnation of Seshanag, the Serpent God. Additionally, Vibhishanan reveals his humble knowledge of their incarnations, that both of them have condescended to manifest themselves on earth in enfleshed forms, just to enact the worldly drama for relieving the earth from the quagmire of sins. He emphasizes that Raman is Lord Narayanan and Lakshman is decidedly the tangible form of Sesha assigned to protect this banal world.

Chapter - IX

Lakshman slays Meghanath

Raman who knows all in an everlasting present, articulates to Vibhishanan that He is cognizant of the formidable monster Meganath's mettle, illusive nature and competence in battle. He adds that He is also knowledgeable about Lakshman's abstinence for twelve years, a celebrated fast to be wholeheartedly and unconditionally dedicated to his onerous vocation of serving Him.

Raman expresses His laxity in acknowledging Lakshman's standing example of servitude, a remarkable commitment to his vocation in His service, for the reason that he has yet to kill Indrajit. Thus He instructs Lakshman to spearhead the attack against Meghanath by escorting massive army with Vibhishanan, Hanuman and other valiant combatants following him.

Lakshman after paying his humble obeisance to Raman, touching His holy feet in great reverence and showcasing his stupendous bow, articulates that his bow and irresistible arrows will announce to the world today the death of Indrajit, piercing and puncturing his body, after which, they will plunge into the Bhagavathi river in the under world inorder to slake their thirst.

Penetrating dense forests, Lakshman reaches the Nikumbhila cave which is under tight security and surveillance, guarded by millions of ruthless demons looking like dark and opaque bundles of black clouds. Coming up behind are Hanuman, Angadhan and Vibhishanan with a huge retinue. Vibhishanan meanwhile espies smoke emitting from the cave and boosts Lakshman not to tarry in discharging his indomitable arrows towards the Nikumbhila cave. Sensing the mounting pressure Lakshman, devastates Meghanath's worship and his oblations to the God of fire, by releasing a powerful shaft and forcing Indrajit out of the cave. Indrajit when out, rushes immediately and confines himself voluntarily to the seat of a weighty chariot establishing his superiority in the equipment of heterogeneous singular weapons. He instantly commences a complete assault on Lakshman; further the attacks and counter attacks develop into a really dreadful battle from both sides.

Armed with conceit, Meghanath acknowledging Vibhishanan as his paternal uncle, swaggers that he is confounded as to why he, Vibhishanan, who was born and raised along with them should accept the captivity and servitude of their antagonists. Moreover, he cannot comprehend why Vibhishanan whom he denunciates as unrighteous, egocentric and abject should preposterously and unfairly nurture envy towards his own nephew.

Lakshman adjudges that Meghanath's bloated egoism needs radical surgery. Ergo, he fastens an arrow upon his bow and exhaling like an incited serpent fires it at indrajit who is simultaneously inflamed with excessive rage. Meghanath is an example in point to evince that celebrity and fame can devastate some people when he syncopes for an infinite moment as the arrow which is as mighty as Indhran's thunder bolt strikes him.

Precisely after regaining consciousness, Meghanath, charging forward with extravagant petulance, bawls out at Lakshman to stay in his position and witness his heroism if he had not perceived it earlier in the past. He penetrates Lakshman with seven acrimonious shafts and Hanuman with ten shafts. Lakshman being subjected to a battery of a hundred arrows, augmenting his duress and passion, releases in retaliation numerous shafts which shatter and reduce indrajit's armour of gold to ashes. In a related development Meghanath viciously releases one thousand arrows, hardly a mean attack against Lakshrnan's well honed attack, piercing Lakshman badly. Thus in this mode of exact retribution, alternating attacks successively from both the sides, mastery over arrows in the air is established and the two invigorated warriors fighting very menacingly, exchanging deadly shafts preponderantly, sustain grave wounds by the shots from each other. Arrows sing through the air that none can hypothesize the definite duration of the battle, how long it would last and who would gain dominance.

Essentially, to substantiate his manual skill, the dauntless Lakshman shoots five lethal shafts killing not only Meghanath's charioteer and horses but also snapping off his bow and crushing the chariot in which Inrdrajit is seated. Instantly Indrajit grapples another bow which Lakshman, yet again, fractures by shooting three arrows. Now, at the moment when Indrajit is divested of his bow from his hands, Lakshman wounds Meghanath seriously by firing numerous shafts simultaneously predicting that he is now in the shadow of an early death. Firmly refusing to chicken out, the highly valourous Meghanath again snatches yet another weighty bow and retaliates by firing innumerable bright and sharp arrows concurrently, wounding Lakshman together with the army of monkeys.

The battle between Lakshman and Indrajit, invariably, turns out to be very menacing and uncontrollable, prolonging for three days and nights, uninterruptedly. With each move, Lakshman realizes a better strategy and eventually fixes 'Aindra', his phenomenal arrow upon his bow. With a great flourish he draws the strings very energetically, as far as it would stretch up to his ears, and for the nonce, reflecting on Raman's lotus Feet invokes His grace and releases the tightly strung arrow supremely confident that if Sri Raman is the most sacred and unparalleled warrior in warfare, then, this shaft would doubtlessly annihilate Indrajit. The arrow moving at astonishing speed darts directly severing Meghanath's head and flinging it sadly upon the ground.

Exalted joy is visible in the heavens when the gods sing Lakshman's praise in sweet melody and stream down flowers upon him from above. Their joy is boundless when they descry Indrajit lying inanimate on the ground. Indhran and all other saints bask happily in the ocean of delight. The celestials with a rush of pleasure sound various musical instruments, drums and trumpets. There is rejoicing everywhere in heaven and on earth. They applaud Sri Raman in solemn prayers and soulful hymns. Peace and Light prevail upon the earth and also in heaven.

As a mark of his superlative victory, Lakshman blows his marvellous conch with relish and gusto, after the fatigue of the war has drained out of him. Again, heralding his superlative victory, he twangs his mighty bow which enlivens the spirits of the monkeys in the battle field. Garnering all his troops he wends his way to Raman's camp and reverentially pays his respects to Him. He recognizes His brother Raman's hand in his triumph, and announces that it was purely by His grace that he had killed Indrajit. Raman who is beside Himself with joy enfolds Lakshman in a warm embrace. To commemorate his wonderful achievement, He proffers His hearty thanks and showers His blessing on him.

Lakshman's tour de force is ennobled by Raman. The achievement of the most onerous assignment, the gusty triumph and the amazing performance in annihilating Indrajit, consuming three days and three nights of incessant fighting makes him the point man. Raman vouches it will be very feasible now for Him to obliterate Ravanan, as He is able to assess Ravanan's present plight of being drained of all punch in the event of his son's death.

Whereas Ravanan is afflicted with unsupressed agony at his son's death for which he moans greatly. He desperately seeks many a channel to expend his shoreless grief at the irreplaceable loss of his precious son. All he receives is cold comfort from well-wishers who though, contribute their deeply felt sentiments. Necessitating a fresh evaluation, Ravanan invites his warmly supportive ministers to deliberate anon, on ending the grim situation.

Suddenly building on the passion of his anger which fuels his resolve for vengeance, Ravanan becomes belligerent again, and so, with a steely intensity of duress runs berserk to do away with Sita outright. But his wise counsellor Suparshva intervenes and voices concern laying heavy emphasis on the ignoble deed of killing a woman which is most unbecoming of him, for he is Kuberan's brother and the respected son of Vishravan. And to reinforce his stand, he opines that he so learned, well grounded, diligent and generous should not be overpowered by feeling of injustice. Suprashva generates a deep-rooted conviction in him saying that the gloomy cloud of defeat has a silver lining, he shall regain his past glories and he shall unequivocally establish victory by killing Raman and Lakshman on his won strength.

Ravanan accedes and relishes the wholesome and beneficial invigoration of his well-wisher. In line with this he holds a meeting the next day, wherein, the crux of the deliberations is to orient their plans for evolving a fool-proof strategy to slay Raman.

Chapter - X

Ravanan Prepares the Ground for War

After his near brush with death in the previous encounter with Raman, Ravanan now presses forward his vicious verve for recommencing the combat along with the remaining counsellors and military forces. But alas, he gets seriously wounded. His morale hits rock bottom. Congruous to the locusts that rush forth towards the burning fire never to return, so too, all the demons who come out to do battle against Raman never returned alive. Ravanan fathoms and marvels at the phenomenal valiance and brawn of Raman and Hanuman. Since the heavy loss of his demon forces he is overwrought and is continuously living in the grip of insecurity. So he calls on his preceptor Sukra for hatching revenge scenarios to defeat Raman.

He questions the authority of Sukra for the untold adversities that have befallen him when he, Sukra' is his divine preceptor and protector. He has a rude moral awakening that it is unwise to think one could succeed against the unalterable course of destiny. Yet, he incriminates and ascribes the death of his brother, sons and a majority of his forces as the handiwork of Raman.

The seductive proposition offered by Sukra takes the form of a sacred manthra for performing sacrifices which shall make him inexpugnable, accompanied by a stringent stricture that his worship should be performed single-mindedly without it being stymied in anyway by anyone; the promise of a rich harvest is also assured; he will be proffered with a heavy, very heavy chariot with divine horses and an enormously potent bow with a quiver fraught with divine arrows by the fire of his worship.

Committed to his task, Ravanan with the necessary trappings and paraphernalia covertly commences his worship single-mindedly, concealing himself in the innermost recesses of a very secret cave underground. He has all the doors of the cave carefully and tightly fastened, and all the gates of his palace too are cunningly fastened.

Interestingly, the plausible surmise Vibhishanan makes when he perceives smoke ascending the sky is communicated to Raman; he speculates that Ravanan is perhaps commencing his sacrifice and worship, the pure motive being the achievement of the quality of invincibility at its consummation. Thereupon, Vibhishanan appeals to Raman to depute the monkeys to discompose Ravanan and tamper and fracture his worship instantly. Raman assigns the onus of derangement to Hanuman, Anghadan and other mighty leaders with a hundred million monkeys for assistance, who at once bounce up and enter the compound of Ravanan's palace.

Raman's forces, launching a sudden invasion attacking violently, extending into the night and easily eliminating horses, elephants and countless soldiers who were guarding the entire territory. The next morning, after the night's fight, Shurabha, Vibhishanan's wife, makes a break through in finding Ravanan's place of worship. She beckons them secretly towards the place. Thereupon the mighty warrior Angadhan invades the cave by disintegrating its gates with a forceful kick. All at once pandemonium breaks out inside the cave as the monkeys who enter clamour about rampaging the sacrifice, scattering the additives and fracturing Ravanan's worship; they strike him with hard blows, bite him with their sharp teeth and accost him in his meditation and worship. But amazingly Ravanan does not violate the words of the sage. Instead, unabated, he stays faithful, very quietly and calmly with closed eyes hangs on like grim death to his one-pointed meditation.

To add fuel to the fire, Angadhan expeditiously enters the palace, yanks Ravanan's wife Mandhothari and drags her away from the palace bringing her into the presence of Ravanan, while the other monkeys also bring all the other wives of Ravanan to the cave in the same fashion.

Mandhothari feels nothing but a cold knot of despair as Angadhan holding tufts of her hair drags her out of the palace and into the cave. She is in bad shape; her dignified beauty is flowed, her garments and robes are shredded and her ornaments broken and scattered all over the place. The ambience inside the cave has gone haywire. She is flooded with a mixture of dread and fear at how close disaster has come now. She cries out woefully calling Ravanan a presumptuous being still engrossed in meditation only for accomplishing his egocentric ends.

She rants that he is a scoundrel of the deepest dye for he is showing a flagrant disregard for the sentiments expressed by his wives when they are being persecuted and beaten by the monkeys in his very presence. Further she bawls that it is only his vested interest and his own safety that have lulled him into complacency and silence. She craves him better dead than alive to permit his better halves being harassed, humiliated and slandered by the monkeys. She swears she would not have been pressed to bear such calamities had her son Indrajit been alive.

Ravanan is in the cast of the male as the protection of the female, so on hearing the most afflictive, denigrating and contumely language of his consort Mandhothari, and unable to put up any longer with the brutality of the monkeys, he unseats himself, and striking a hard blow upon Angadhans waist with his sword yells out to untangle his hold on the lady and to get out from the place. Gleefully satisfied that they have got through with their cunning stratagem of putting a spoke in Ravanan's wheel of worship and making his objective and anticipation fall through, Angadhan and all other monkeys without further harassment retreat to Raman's camp.

The prospect of death wonderfully concentrates Ravanan's mind on transcendental philosophy. He lulls Mandhothari's fears and anxiety by eloquently defending his own philosophical reflections and enlightening her on the alternate circuits of happiness and misery coursing through man's life as it is the sine qua non or will of providence that monopolizes his life. He articulates that it is quite insignificant to attempt to access how long a man lives. The acquisition of lofty knowledge is the only approach to steer clear of sorrow, for sorrow is inexorably and undeniably the outcome of nescience. The flesh is heir to the recurrent cycle of births and death because the individual is egoistic. Thus the fountainhead of all suffering in the life of man is due to ignorance, egoism and undue bondage to kith and kin and other materialistic objects. The fleshy bag is clearly distinct from the soul which is pure and blemishless, and is the eternal reality which is free and aloof. It is devoid of earthy feelings and is ever blissful and self illumined. The soul is indestructible; Ravanan tempts the lady to realize her soul, the real self, so that she may not feel misery's sting. Ravanan, forcefully and explicitly, pronounces his last chance to again wage the decisive battle against Raman. He vocalizes that in case he gets killed he shall unequivocally be united with Raman, the Universal Soul. Also, he directs her to effectively kill Sita and subsequently immolate herself in the funeral fire along with his corpse.

Mandhothari very dejectedly pleads with her Lord Ravanan to heed her verbiage, do some valuable soul searching and comport himself prudently. She accentuates the fact that it is out of one's depth to identify ways and means to conquer Raman as He cannot be defeated by him or any one else. She proclaims Raman the Lord of all Gods and the Universe.

Further; more, she enumerates the various incarnations of the Lord featuring his omnipotence, omniscience and omnipresence. On the eve of creation he, Baivas and Manu, had placed the massive Someru Mountain on his back at the time of churning the nectar from the ocean in the form of a tortoise as big and boundless as hundreds of miles, had riddled the mighty demon Hiranyaksha by impersonating Himself as a grand boar and had salvaged the earth from plummeting into the sea, and also incarnated Himself as Sri Narasimhan who jumped out of a pillar and had torn Hiranyakashipu's bowels. He had bestowed all the three worlds upon Indhran by taking them away from the possession of Bali whom He deceived by growing from the size of a dwarf to a gigantic proportion pervading the entire universe when He assumed the form of Trivikran and measured the heavens, the earth and the underworld with just three of His paces. Inorder to weed out the martinet monarchs and to put an end to their imperviousness and global terrorism, He had incarnated Himself as Parasuraman. Thus He had conquered the whole world and handed it over to Kashyap. And this time, He has incarnated Himself in human fleshy sheath as Lord Raman and has presented Himself here to annihilate him.

By her own rhetoric, Mandhothari re-examines Ravanan's modus operandi of having brought disaster upon them vilifying him for his abduction of Devi Sita, which is a flagrant violation of the principles of ethical and moral codes of conduct and the root cause of wiping out their whole race. Her desperate attempt is to beseech Ravanan to effectuate peace in their lives and lead a life of asceticism in the forest. So she begs him to restore Sita to Raman and to apologetically supplicate His forgiveness and mercy to spare his life. She enthuses him to also give back the Kingdom to Vibhishanan.

Ravanan starts to thaw a bit towards Mandhothari's rhetorical peroration, as now there is a transition in his stand from focusing on killing Raman to being killed by Raman. He is explicitly presumptuous that he shall be, absolutely, killed by Raman. Moreover, he opines that there cannot be even a shred of justification in going to the forest only to save his life, when his siblings, sons and countless other demons have already been exterminated by Raman. He is so uncomfortable with his own vulnerability that he closes himself off to a compromise on retreating to the forest to live in strict asceticism.

Ravanan's percipience acquaints him of his own certain death only at the hands of Sri Raman for, only He can challenge his sceptre of power and authority. He is filled with a presentiment that he shall secure the celestial abode with all his followers, though he shall have to be killed along with his near and dear ones. He articulates that should be he killed by Raman, he would at once be freed from false attachment to relations, the entanglement with terrestrial affairs, and free from all sorts of miseries and misunderstandings.

Chapter - XI

Raman Kills Ravanan in Fierce Battle

Ravanan is positively determined to fight the battle against Raman with his back to the wall. He has decided to have a go at Him hammer and tongs. So he needs to fortify himself at length when embarking on the indefensible and alarming task. He gears himself with assorted weapons which are promiscuous and formidable. Thereafter, he mounts a very sturdy chariot of sixteen wheels well built and sheilded with miscellaneous equipment cast in ferrous meatal and drawn by fiendish and inexorable mules and reaches the battlefield assertively. The awesome apparition of Ravanan filled with wrath, passion and destructiveness evokes fear in the armies of monkeys at the battlefield. As Ravanan moves forward hurriedly to fight, Hanuman with the same rapidity strikes an arrow whereby Ravanan phlebotomizes excessively, he is made to eat humble pie when he, Hanuman, taking priority in forestalling his movements, dominates by striking him first and wounding him severely in the bargain. So, inevitably, he professes meekly and apologetically, that Hanuman is very mighty.

Immediately Hanuman retorts with outraged propriety disapproving his own might as he finds Ravanan still alive, that he had not killed him yet, but has kept him alive for root long.

Remarkably, Hanuman commands yet another opportunity to prove his might and together challenges Ravanan to test his own might too by striking him with all the strength he possesses. With the objective of facilitating Ravanan to strike him, Hanuman stands motionless and calm, while Ravanan mustering all his power delivers a violent blow with the maximum strength and force. It is a futile exercise which does not jar Hanuman's equilibrium, but making Hanuman quiver slightly for just a tiny fraction of a second. Now, when it is Hanuman's turn to strike back, Ravanan gives Hanuman a wide berth, likely, to obviate further conflict with him as he deeply fathoms Hanuman to be mightier than he is.

Thus a crucial war is triggered off and in the ensuing fracas the demons - Agnivana, Saparome, Khadaroma, Brishchika who are very menacing and unrestrained, with their out- spread hair looking like blazing fire swords, serpents, scorpions and the like, are thrashed to death quite effortlessly by Hanuman, Angadhan, Nila and Nala and some brave monkeys. Bursting with pride and raising loud cheers of victory at their initial triumph the monkeys return to Raman. At this, fear and panic rise like bile in Ravanan's throat; he is piqued and becomes febrile. Trading on his raw prowess, massive puissance, numerous forces and impressive weapons he stages a come back, steeped deeper in arrogance and ruthlessness, charging extra savageously in his chariot towards Raman and begins pelting a volley of powerful shafts at him. Raman retaliates by shooting stronger powered arrows, in the affray several monkeys are wounded and killed by Ravanan.

The king of Gods, Indharan, is obligated to help when he beholds Raman, a stunning variety and scope of human goodness, placed on the ground, thus, countering Ravanan's attack, whereas, Ravanan has hoisted himself on a high pedestal which is dangerous, for a lot of noise is made when you fall to the deepest depths from such a great height, on his imposing chariot fighting hard against Raman. Indharan sends his chariot with Matali, the divine charioteer, who hastens to Raman, humbly pays his obeisance to Him and beseeches Him to mount the chariot sent by Indharan for vanquishing Ravanan absolutely.

Appropriately, Raman happily takes His position on the comprehensively equipped chariot and unleashes His prowess, shooting equally divine arrows in large numbers with the precision of a synchronized team, which begin, to wreck havoc, smashing Ravanan's Agnviana, Devastra and the most dreadful Rakshastra which glitters like gold. Mutual shooting of arrows is escalated generating a very fierce battle between the great warriors, Raman and Ravanan. Ravanan fires black with greater fury; the incredible bombardment of arrows however powerful that pelts so incessantly at Raman is easily challenged with deadlier shafts as bright as fire or is thwarted by Raman the Supreme Archer whose skill in archery is non pareil and unrivalled. Soon the battlefield is covered all over with the broken pieces of the divine and mighty shafts shot from both sides.

In another move, the Garudasthra, which begets vultures to destroy the vicious serpents discharged by Ravanan's arrows is fired by Raman. At this, Ravanan's fury begins spewing again; with virtual impunity, striking lethal arrows and pulling down to pieces the chariot's banners and flags of gold he kills two of Raman's horses.

All the celestials, gandharvas, siddhars, and the spirits in heaven and the sages on earth are racked with consternation, angst and insecurity at the prospect of finding Raman being overwhelmed when entangled in this terrible fight against malevolent and dreadful Ravanan.

An ugly ferocity builds up in Raman too that He very seriously lashes Ravanan and crushes his shafts which are like death fire, wounding him critically. Raman's ferocity that accompanies the attack rocks the earth shaking its very foundation, petrifying all the creatures as if He were going to annihilate the Universe itself.

Ravanan is on his beam-ends, following which he has a massive anxiety attack as Raman's supernatural gallantry and savior faire precisely appals, daunts and intimidates him. Raman commands His Indhrastra which fells the numerous heads of Ravanan, and as they souse in blood the others begin to fall one by one from his body similar to fruits that fall from the Tal tree. With astonishing speed the heads of Ravanan mushroom again and again as Raman keeps felling them incessantly and, in quick time, numerous heads are severed by Raman that they strew the length and breath of the battle field, and in no time they engulf the sky too.

Raman is struck with awe to find that every time He cuts a head synchronizingly new heads grow afresh. A surplus of more than one hundred heads are cut off purely to be supplanted by fresh ones. Alas! Raman's lengthy effort is exhausting His command of all the dreadful weapons in His possession which flounder to annihilate Ravanan; He is helpless in evolving a strategy to fulfill His mission.

Vibhishanan beholding Raman now at the end of His tether, apprises Raman of a sportive boon bestowed upon Ravanan by Lord Brahman the creator, by which capacity his heads are multiplying speedily and repeatedly. It is the secret placement of the nectarous fluids, which he divulges to Raman, filling a square tube bellow Ravanan's naval and which, he instructs, should be wholly dried for the purpose of killing him.

Resurgent Raman, aiming at the vulnerable feature of Ravanan in high spirits, instantly shoots an arrow which emits fire, scorching Ravanan's naval and facilitating Him to decapitate his heads and severe his arms too with the next arrow. Only a head and two arms hang back but Raman is incinerating his naval. Evil is always angry and hurtful; Ravanan's anger multiplies at a prodigious rate as he learns of Vibhishanan's shocking sense of betrayal, disclosing his secret boon to Raman, and so, fires a dreadful shaft towards Vibhishanan to kill him instantly, but Raman, such goodness, putting evil into perspective, deflects it wrecking Ravanan's very objective with His gold edged arrow.

Though looking very gawky and hideous, Ravanan is still stoked up with determination and mettle, and prolonging his fight, he, very bravely and insolently fires a fusillade of shafts. The unprecedented combat between the two mighty warriors gathers momentum, growing out of all proportions and causing great panic to everyone.

The charioteer Matali ultimately intimates Lord Raman about Death virtually casting his spell on Ravanan, his death-knell being sounded determining the precise time of his death. As the moment of Ravanan's doom is at hand, Matali persuades the Lord to pierce his heart with a powerful shaft because it is unsatisfactory and inadequate that his heads alone are severed, for that is insubstantial to obliterate him.

Raman affixes a superlatively heavy shaft powered with the potentialities of the elements, the sun and the gods of directions and, evidently, as monumental as the mountains, Sumeru and Manderachal, and as voluminous as the sky, on his bow and triggers it towards Ravanan. The profound impact of the arrow rocks the earth itself terrifying all terrestrial life. The great demonic evil is met with by a wave of heroism that dwarfs it. Forthwith the arrow straightaway enters the bosom and pierces the heart which is shattered into fragments by the blow and Ravanan with an inertia to resist, is weakened to the limit and all his machismo evaporated thunders down upon the earth. With his death, Ravanan's soldiers, followers and ministers beat a hasty retreat, while loud trumpeting of conch shells, the harbinger of Raman's victory, proclaims His singular triumph.

From the heavens to the earth, the air throbs with vibrant sounds of drums and trumpets, and every kind of musical instrument is played sonorously and sounded lustily by the celestials and the gods thus manifesting their joy and celebrations. Their jubilation knows no bounds; they rain flowers upon Raman and the sages chant manthras and the fairies are intoxicated with divine frenzied dances.

A radiant light emanates from Ravanan's inanimate body and saturates with Lord Sri Raman's Self. At this juncture, all the saints, sages and gods, who pronounce that they still nurture a yen for terrestrial pleasures and objects, however, eat their heart out at Ravanan who is very providentially blessed. Despite Ravanan being the most sinful and desecrated demon, cumulatively accountable for super numerous crimes, and the enemy of the

Gods and the saints, he has straight away attained emancipation which is tantalizing and yet unachievable to the celestials.

Sage Naradhar at this moment gives a fitting reply to the Gods whose envy he effaces by elucidating Ravanan's incessant reflections on and of Raman, even in enmity, always reminiscing about Him, day in and day out and never forgetting Him in his sleep and dreams. Ravanan was never oblivious to the truth that his death lay at Raman's hands and hence he was always solicitous of and cognizant of Raman's activities. Thus he is enfranchised, indisputably, the highest place in Elysium only because Sri Raman has obliterated him.

Further the sage promulgates that it is mandatory for every individual at the moment of his death to atone for his sins and remember Lord Raman with love and devotion so that he can assuredly attain salvation though he may have perpetrated a number of sins during his life span. He pronounces positively that chanting the holy name Raman with sincerity and devotion creates an ambience of divinity and bliss thus leading to an expansion of the consciousness of the presence of divinity in even the great sinners and unfailingly securing for him the great passage to be anchored in His heart. He invokes glorious Raman, whose upright posture and poise bearing the gorgeous bow and arrow in His two hands and, who, is a luxurious extravagance of Light, looking more radiant than a thousand suns together, to be benign to him.

Chapter - XII

Vibhishanan's Enthronement and Sita's Return

Raman and others in His camp are basking joyfully in a wave of euphoria that His superlative victory has brought in its train. He eloquently acknowledges the visible contribution of succour, valour and bravura of Hanuman, Angadhan, Sugrivan, Jambavan and other leaders who were on the band wagon to help Him triumphantly fulfil His mission in killing Ravanan. He declares resoundingly that this glorious tour de force and its complementary eminence shall be perennially inexpugnable as long as the Sun and the Moon shall shed their light upon this earth. Raman explicitly promises the highest status in Elylsium to those who will read or even listen to His inspirational story in confederation with all His associates and devotees.

Confronted with the dire tidings of Ravanan's tragic death, Mandhothari and all the other wives of Ravanan afflicted with profound grief, arrive at the locus where his sad corpse, all passion spent, is lying dead. They wail and weep inconsolably. Vibhishanan too is affected and laments dejectedly.

Raman enjoins Lakshman to comfort Vibhishanan and Ravanan's wives. In addition. He asserts that Vibhishanan should be instructed to perform the funeral rites of his brother Ravanan with no further delay and the body cremated soon after.

Vibhishanan who is gone so far out of his comfort zone is filled with overwhelming grief when Lakshman amiably entreats him to reflect deeply on the consanguineous relationship between himself and Ravanan. Further he urges him to perceive who Ravanan is for whom he is exhibiting such profound anguish at his passing away, and what appellation to affix for this affiliation of his to Ravanan after his death, and who he was to him in his foregone birth. This volley of questions has put the issue of the pseudo ties of familial consanguinity on the boil setting in motion Vibhishanan's thinking mechanism.

With this, Lakshman takes the lead to expound the unknown truths, the crux of it being the pseudo kindredship, which, under the monopoly of time and death the individuals are influenced to congregate, meet and interact by coincidence, and then depart from one another, to be as transitory as the sands accumulating on one corner of the river and being washed away by every ebb and flow of the river water each moment. It is by the illusory power of providence that a creature is born of the other analogous to a seed sprouting from another just to die away. This illusion also having a bearing on the individual is simply due to the individual's nescience. But this egoism to procreate the diversity of worldly things vanishes when he is in deep sleep. Hence there is no distinction of a separate, different world to the individual who has realized his self which is one with all creation and has attained transcendental knowledge.

Enlightening Vibhishanan on the pseudo congeneric ties, Lakshman expands his focus on encompassing the transitoriness of life too. Vocalizing that as long as the individuals are immersed in illusion, the same fate befalls himself including Vibhishanan and all living creatures and consequently they are bound to annihilation with transmigration of the cycles of life and death, intertwined according to the established natural law of karma. And if so destined by the same fate an individual shall be certainly killed by another. The apparent creation of all creatures, and again, the seeming annihilation of them all by the unborn Almighty Infinite God with no appurtenance to them is akin to a child's play. The immortal soul which is a distinct entity is always aloof, but, evidently, seems to be an enfleshed being so long as it is in a fleshy sheath which is perceptible, tangible and also perishable. The alliance between the soul and the body is consonant with that of wood with fire which is immanent in the wood latently.

The soul is unvarying and immutable, a vibrant spirit, but is conjectured to be associated and identified with materialistic objects, worldly actions and earthly shapes. So the illusion of death, birth, degeneration, development, animation and passivity are speciously perceived, similar to fire which assumes different shapes, forms and proportions in respect to the dimensions and quality of wood that burns.

Moreover, Lakshman instructs Vibhishanan to meditate concentratedly, and eventually come to realize the soul to be the only eternal reality and the body a separate entity, delusive, destructible and transient. The individual does not hanker after workaday objects when he peaks the state of realizing his egoistic disposition. As the individual enjoys repose and respite in deep sleep, he luxuriates on the plane of perennial peace and bliss. Lakshman asserts that he, Vibhishanan, renounce all perfidious mundane rapaciousness and cravings, impound his mental interior and exterior avocations, make a detour towards Lord Raman and saturate himself only in Him who is omnipotent and reigns supreme in the core of every creature's heart. Bewitched by the evanescent desires, the individuals conceive a nexus between the different things and persons as parents, sons, wives and near and dear ones. If the individual is wholly cognizant of his own soul then he would repudiate all such bondage and possessiveness. It is exclusively nescience that deprives the individual of establishing the veracity of the soul, making him falsely deduce that women, affluence, prosperity, custodians, power, kingdoms, earth and other phenomena are all authentic, enduring and permanent.

Lakshman adjures vibhishanan to go forth and accommodate himself as the Monarch of his Kingdom so long as divine providence has ordained him, ever mindful and implicitly devoted to Lord Raman. However he enhances his verbalization by making it essential for him to bury the past, not be remorseful and regretful about it and also not to be anxious and preoccupied about he future; but to acclimatize himself and draw strength from the present as time is a precious vibrant commodity. Also, he accentuates that he, Vibhishanan should be a stickler for propriety, always righteous and honest acting with rectitude and piety as then he would not have to grapple with and experience the constraints and adversities from the external world that have a natural sway over him. He pronounces Raman's directive for performing the funeral rites of his dead brother, Ravanan, without further skepticism and procrastination. Lakshman amicably advises prudent Vibhishanan to cheer himself up and also to comfort the ladies as well and send them back to the palace in good time.

Lakshman's calming influence on lofty spiritual natters mitigates Vibhishanan's grief consoling him perfectly, thereafter, prompting him to meet Raman instantly. Vibhishanan in the presence of Raman humbly yet judiciously unclogs his doubt about the appropriateness of executing the funeral rites of his brother Ravanan who was cumulatively sinful and massively callous. As with the love of a brother, Raman unveils that with Ravanan dead there is no longer any more enmity with the body that is lying lifeless. All relations, all passions pertain to and culminate with the body. So it is befitting that in the capacity as his younger brother he treats it in the right manner According to vedic injunctions, and in the presence of all other relatives, chiefs, ministers and retinues Vibhishanan agreeably executes Raman's decree by duly performing the funeral rites, consoling Mandhothri, the docile wife of Ravanan, and sending all the queens back to the palace. Therefore Vibhishanan then wends his way to pay obeisance to Raman who is cheerful as Indhran has been on exterminating his horrendous enemy Birtrasura. The charioteer Matali receiving Raman's benevolent blessings and His consent too, pays his due respects to Raman and ascends to heaven.

Then Raman instructs Laksnman to chaperon Vibhishanan to Lanka and there to establish him statutority on the throne as the monarch with all pomp and ritualistic solemnity. Thereupon, Vibhishanan is escorted by Lakshman, the retinue of monkeys, and Brahmin priests who bring to fruition the coronation ritual with great celebrations, pomp and circumstances.

It is a great moment of delight for Vibhishanan. His healthy loyalty directly leads him straight away to meet Raman taking with him an expansive amount of luxurious articles to offer Raman as a mark of his respectful homage to Him. Raman is all the more delighted to ascertain the perfect realization of His promise of designating Vibhishanan as the crowned head of the state of Lanka.

Raman showers his gratitude on Sugrivan by way of repeated embraces for his help rendered in vanquishing Mighty Ravanan. Raman, captivated by Hanuman's bulletproof faith and unwavering loyalty again picks him as His emissary to Sita. His task is to brief Sita with all the up-to-date happenings and to bring back some message from her back to Raman.

Intellectual Hanuman is given a warm reception by the demons this time when he enters sLanka. He is mirthful about the celebrated encounter which is to take place with Sita, but is saddened to find her debilitated to the limit, gaunt and emaciated, safely guarded by the demonesses. Sita is exuding a high voltage of piety; with the totality of her organic being she is absorbed in prayer to and meditation on Raman. Solemnly hailing Goddess Sita, Hanuman reverentially pays his obeisance to her and thereupon, fills her in on the developments-the extirpation of monstrous Ravanan with all kith and kin, the restoration of the kingdom to Vibhishanan and his subsequential coronation as monarch of Lanka. He conveys Raman's happy disposition in the company of Vibhishanan, Sugrivan, Angadhan, all the monkeys and the other leaders. He apprises her of Raman's fond enquiries about her physical and mental wellness. This rendezvous with Hanuman, the faithful envoy of Raman, whom she had met earlier is a healing interlude, at this juncture, for Sita who is extremely delighted to see him once again. She is wonder struck at the sight of Hanuman and is at a loss for words to eulogize his goodwill. She disregards as worthless the wealth of all the three worlds when juxtaposed with the honeyed words brought from Sri Raman.

At this moment, Hanuman proffers his respects to Mother Sita proclaiming his spotless servitude and appraising Raman's nectar-like words to be more invaluable than all the riches, even the kingdom of heaven, because the effulgent grace of victorious Raman is so effusive, protecting him and keeping him well all the while, and to whom he pays his obeisance every moment. Sita commending Hanuman's indigenous exemplary virtues and excellent caliber acclaims him as a divinely blessed person. Eventually she verbalizes her express desire to envision Raman and solicits him persuasively to conduct her to Him at the earliest.

Thereupon he bids adieu to Sita and blasts off to meet Raman to whom he faithfully acquaints of what transpired between himself and Sita; additionally he tenders a personal supplication to Him. Hanuman eloquently phrases his supplication to Raman to exhibit His graceful generosity for visiting Sita to whose advantage and honour all their expansive, laborious endeavours have been rewarded with eclat. He also conveys Sita's express desire and anxiety to behold His brilliant self.

This time Raman entrusts Vibhishanan with the assignment of going to Lanka and bringing Sita attired elegantly and adorned with exquisite jewels. Meanwhile Lord Raman deliberates on forsaking the fabricated illusory form of herself on this earth and bringing the real Sita back which had been commended to the God of Fire and so lives concealed in fire.

In accordance with Raman's intention, he Vibhishanan shepherds Sita's ground palanquin in which she, so gorgeously dressed, looking radiantly beautiful, is carried by a retinue of demons. All the monkeys filled with zest and longing, rushing forward converge on the palanquin to catch a glimpse of the celebrity, Sita. The huge multitude of monkeys create a great flutter and flurry all around inorder to see her, impeding the progress of the palanquin, when the attendants thrash the monkeys away so that they proceed unhampered. Raman seeing the harsh treatment being meted out to the monkeys inhibits the attendants issuing a decree that Sita should relinquish the palanquin and go on foot, so that all the monkeys may behold their celebrated Mother without any hitch. Dutifully Sita alights from the palanquin and traces her steps, gracefully and graciously, towards the exalted presence of Raman. Sadly enough, Sita is cut to the quick at Raman's seemingly, uncaring attitude and caustic words which pull at her heart strings that she requests Lakshman to blaze a fire into which she so wishes to enter for proclaiming to Raman and all the world that she is chaste, pure and pietistic.

Raman concedes to Lakshman's prayer of igniting a fire. Immediately after, a large fire is blazed with a huge pile of wood collected by him. It is an unwritten code of conduct that wives pay deep respects to their husbands on every auspicious occasion. Before embarking on her fire immersion ordeal, Sita with hands folded, in great reverence makes a circuit round Raman and then prays the God of Fire to salvage her if she is pietistic, immaculate, innocent and ceaselessly and interminably devoted to Raman alone.

Therefore, making a circuit round the blazing fire, paying obeisance to the God of Fire, Sita, ascending to the plane of composure, tranquillity and stoicism enters the blazing fire unflinchingly. She disappears and becomes invisible to all eyes witnessing the painful ordeal' in the heavens, all the deities, sages and saints and on the earth, the citizens and the monkeys are disillusioned at this awesome spectacle. They are perplexed as to why Raman should permit Sita to endure such a perilous ordeal. The multitudes begin to murmur; whimper and debate on why Raman, the erudite scholar and Lord, should abandon Sita, the incarnation of Goddess Lakshmi, in this fashion, solely for whose sake He had in her absence battled against such tremendous odds and great hardships to retrieve her.

Chapter - XIII

Agni and Indhran Pray Raman

Gods Indhran, Yaman, Varunan, Kuberan, Shivan, Brahman, the saints, the sages, the gandharvas, the fairies and all other deities, who are all in perpetual thought of Sri Raman, descend upon the earth to pay obeisance in great reverence to Him at His camp. They reckon this as the most cherished and felicitous opportunity for praising their Lord. All of them in consonance panegyrize Raman as the architect and prime mover of the entire Universe, the one who exists alone as the deponent of all the creatures. They offer rich plaudits, hailing Him as veritably the Holy Self, the enlightened Supreme Soul. He is the chief Basu. He is the Lord Shivan and the Creator Brahman. Ashwini Kumar is His smelling energy, His eyes project as the Sun and the Moon. He is the consummate soul in whom all the worlds have their final resort since they originate from Him, the prime source of all births. He is the everlasting, deathless, independent, unparalleled Supreme Soul. An enlightened soul realizes him to be none other but the Supreme God while those who are invisibly clouded by ignorance due to their illusion figure Him to be but and ordinary being sheathed with a mortal coil. They applaud Raman by offering their gratitude for having retrieved, by His benevolent grace, their kingdoms which Ravanan had seized by his duress and force.

Brahman the creator salutes Raman as the benignant Lord and bows to Him, the veritable manifestation of Supreme God Vishnu. He is the Omnificience of the Universe and life. The saints and sages in meditation journey from the unknown to the known, Raman the prime object and sublime culmination of all meditation. He continues to articulate that Raman is an enigmatic, unfathomable being, Omnipresent, Omniscient and Omnipotent. He is personally unrestrained and has no attachment, hatred or love. Further, he elucidates Raman to be the gravitational force which draws everything to its source, as He is the single existence vibrating beyond nature though he appears to be Omniform. Brahman offers his salutations to Raman whom the sages who observe austerity and practise samadhi hold communion with His veritable spotless Self. He cognizes Raman in the enfleshed form as the consort of Sita, the incarnation of Goddess Lakshmi, the prime substantive energy, the very substructure of the Universe and the prevailing entity.

An endless string of accolades is strung by Brahman hailing Raman as the mystical glow suffusing the sounds creating the sense of cosmic oneness and reverberating as Ornkara, the cardinal Divine Word; He is the preeminent Preceptor of Yoga; He is the pure essence of happiness of all beings. He transcends the limitless bounds of births and deaths. He is the only One who is the first and the greatest of all-beings, who is worshipped by Lord Shivan the principal illustrious Yogi. He is everlasting; sacred; absolute; the annihilator of vicious demons and offensive beings. He claims Raman as his own philosophical Master and dispenser of all his petitions; He is Narayanan transcending time and space; He is beyond the ken of tangible, plausible inference and proof. He is the sustainer of the world. The reading of abstruse dharma texts is but a sterile gathering of information which barely succeeds in cognizing Him; only pure love, unblinking devotion, expansive sincerity and inveterate faith are the attributes to envision Him. He is the destroyer of the fetters that bind one to attachments and worldliness and He is the sheer bliss of a yogi's mind.

Brahman kudizes Lord Raman as the Almighty among all Gods; hence He gives birth to the Universe, so beautiful and sublime, and then demolishes it to His sweet will. He is inaccessible; anyone stands powerless to capture Him, bewitch Him,, allure Him through mundane phenomena or even mental analysis. But Brahman endorses that He unsheathes Himself only to His beloved aspirants and devotees. He features Raman's handsomeness to be so arresting as blue lotuses. He repeatedly bows paying homage to the Lord of Lakshmi. Brahman declares that He, Raman is obscure to minds which are irreligious and always mired in worldly affairs and objects. Brahman unravels His esoteric singularity of transfiguration, when, once, He transformed Himself from Raman's to Krishnan's in Brindhavan, in accordance with the yearning of His devotees and sages when they supplicated Him. Hence no line of distinction can be drawn between Raman and the Lord of Mathura, Sri Krishnan as He and Krishnan are one and the same Universal Self. He visualises Raman to be as bright as blue emeralds. Brahman acknowledges the extravagantly handsome, eternally joyous and self enlightened soul Raman to have incarnated himself for the only purpose of accomplishing His mission and bolstering the welfare of the world in all aspects.

Agni, the God of Fire, gloriously manifests himself visibly; amidst cheers, acclamations and chanting of mantras, from the effulgent fire Sita emerges so immaculately and beatifically attired, and humbly entreats Lord Raman to delightedly receive the celestial damsel Sita who He had entrusted with him at Tapovan in Dandaka Forest. He now unravels Lord Hari's mystical attribute of fabricating an illusory Sita with Him all along for His own purpose. And now that He has triumphed in effacing Ravanan and his posterity from the face of the earth, He has thus emancipated it from the malevolent sway of the vicious demons.

Raman gleefully welcomes Sita and pays His respects to Agni the God of Fire in a felicitous manner. In turn, the God of Fire is himself enormously appeased to have accomplished the assigned task dutifully, bids adieu to Lord Raman and takes leave with His permission. Then. Indhran very happily, with rectitude and impeccability, worships and prays to Lord Raman and Sri Sita Devi who are together.

Taking the cue from Brahman, Indhran too eulogizes Lord Raman with a rhapsodical portrait in mellifluous verbiage, hailing His lustrous blue appearance to be like the lotus, whose very name suffices to incinerate the bushes of worldliness, whose euphoric form is always vivid in the memory of Goddess Parvathi, who is the annihilator of the cycle of transmigration altogether and who is the sanctuary for all the deities including Lord Vishnu. He consecrates himself to the surpassingly revered Lord Raman who disencumbers the Gods of their desolation and afflictions. He is the sole redeemer of the Gods, and He is now in tangible form of human incarnation, though, in reality He is formless. Indhran repeatedly bows to Him who keeps His devotees and aspirants ever jubilant in every way And His name is constantly chanted by saints and Sages as they have and axe to grind, solely for enlightenment with divine knowledge and salvation and for scorching away their dark nescience and despair. The sages despite their exalted yoga and austere penances cannot easily even conceptualize Him or visualize Him.

Indhran pledges perpetual alliance to the holy feet of Lord Raman who is ever ecstatic, enlightened, the most steadfast comrade of Sugrivan and other monkeys, the most affectionate consort of Sita and who is obscure and unobtainable to those who are consumed with concupiscence, but is easily attainable because He is in close proximity holy etc. aspirants and devotees of pure hearts and acts, who step out of their narrow individuality relinquishing their stout egoism and love His holy name. It is only through His own inscrutable power, identified as illusion or Maya that He manifests

Himself as man and plays the part of a human person. Those who are predisposed and those who simply hear the exposition of His attributes, glories, exploits in His incarnations shall undoubtedly achieve liberation. Indhran confesses his abstraction always carousing, so luxuriously obsessed with celestial inebirates, and his pride in sovereignty, all which now. have been extinguished by Raman's benignity. Again, he prays to Him who is adorned with dazzling and coruscating garlands and amulets studded with precious gems. He lauds Raman, as being radiant as burning fire, who has extirpated all the demons. He extols Him as Divine Lord whose countenance is attractively graceful as the moon of Autumn, and His benign eyes being very congenial and sparkling like lotuses. He commends Raman to have neither a beginning nor an end nor even a form, yet, His venerable physique in this human incarnation is wholly resplendent as blue emeralds. Further he praises and endorses the installation of peace on earth by benevolent Raman after having destroyed Ravanan, Bradhan and all other nefarious demons. He glorifies Raman's divinely captivating looks, attired in exquisite and delicate habiliment, crowns and ornaments authorizing Himself as Lord of the Raghu dynasty and being the most cherised convivial prized possession of Lord Shivan. Once again, he offers his humble salutations and prayer to the efficacious, dynamic Raman who with Sita on His lap is visualized as being vibrantly gorgeous and scintillating like shimmering gold, flashing like lightening in the sky.

Lord Shivan too seated with Devi Parvathi in the airborne chariot in the azure sky blithely makes his contribution of adulation to Raman, extolling Him as Raghunandan and in the passing, amicably suggesting that he would make his presence at His coronation ceremony at Ayodhya, Meanwhile, he requests Raman to perceive visibly the soul of His father; and Raman with Sita and Lakshman espies the departed soul of His father king Dasarathar, together paying their respectful homage to the king. Instantly, king Dasarathar embracing his son Raman, indebtedly acknowledges Him as his saviour who has sundered all his worldly desires and has salvaged him from drowning in the ocean of terrestrial miseries, materialistic thinking and bondage.

Indhran is sedulous in heeding the decree issued by Raman to sprinkle divine nectar upon all the monkeys lying dead on the battlefield for invigorating them. Subsequently, by virtue of the divine nectar sprinkled upon them the sheer volume of dead monkeys bounces back to animation, gets up cheerfully and pays obeisance to Lord Raman. Nonetheless, the nectar falls upon the dead demons too, but still, they are not revived because the souls of dead demons have incorporated with Raman's Supreme Self.

This authenticates Raman's divine force, actions and powers are transcendentally superior to the impact or result of the divine nectar.

Vibhishanan complaisantly acquaints Raman of the fourteen years of life in the forest as a Hermit that have just lapsed, and so humbly persuades Him in conceding to take a bath, disrobe Himself of His hermit's garb and to attire Himself in royal robes. But Raman is uncompromisingly determined not to disrobe His garb as hermit for He is knowledgeable about His affectionate brother Bharathan's angst, anticipating His return in the garb of a hermit at Nandhigram, which all weigh heavily upon his mind. His query as to how He alone can disrobe His attire is an unwelcomed proposition to Him. He expresses an alternative wish of taking immense comfort if, he, Vibhishanan entertains Sugrivan and all other monkeys. Vibhishanan deems it a privileged opportunity in presenting the monkeys with innumerable luxurious articles, jewellery and raiments. Raman solicits the monkeys to return to their habitations. He proposes to Sugrivan and all other chiefs to return to Kishkindha with their forces of monkeys immediately. He instructs Vibhishanan to rule over Lanka, and, more importantly, educates him to eternalize Him in his memory. He assures him of His constant protection and guidance and guarantees that no harm in any form can approach him from any quarter, especially from the Gods in the heavens or even Indhran himself, Consequently he acquaints Vibhishanan of His departure from the place, to Ayodhya. Taking Sita lovingly in His arms along with Lakshman, they all board the Pushpaka air chariot generously presented by Vibhishanan.

Instantly, all of them with no heart and mind to take leave of Raman, in one harmonious note, with folded hands entreat Raman their Lord, even against His wish, to permit them in witnessing his imminent coronation ceremony and adore mother Kausalya as they so desire, Raman kindly subscribes to their request and permits them to accompany Him on the grand Vimana. Thus Sugrivan, Vibhishanan, Hanuman together with the other mighty chiefs board the Pushpaka and merrily seat themselves when the airborne chariot takes flight towards Ayodhya.

Chapter - XIV

Raman Reaches Ayodhya

Raman and His entire entourage are airborne in a glory of sunlit gaiety by the exceptionally exquisite Pushpaka, While traversing long stretches they have a sweeping view of the whole terrain; as Raman enlightens Sita on all the places pointing to her the battlefield where He had trounced the enemies, killing Ravanan, Kumbhakarnan and several other mighty warriors, and, advancing further, points out to her the impressive and imposing bridge, the exalted temple of Rameshwaram where He had worshipped Shivan, the city of Kishkindha and the Rishyamugha hills. Sitha's overwhelming choice of taking Tara and other women from Kishkintha with them is met with appreciation from Raman. So Tara and other women of Kishkintha join the entourage by boarding the Pushpaka with Raman's acquiescence. They fly over the Dandaka Forest where Raman meets the sages Agasthiyar, Suthikshanan and others. Enroute to Ayodhya via Chitrakutha Raman halts on the outskirts of Ayodhya at the hermitage of sage Bharadhwaj who offers Him and His retinue accommodation for the night.

Raman acknowledges the hospitality of the Lordly sage, pays His respects to Him and queries about the well-being of Bharathan, the salubrity of His queen mothers and the prosperity of Ayodhya. Sage Bharadhwaj perspicuously elucidates that all is well with Bharathan. He pronounces Bharathan's unrelenting perfection in the garb of a hermit abiding in Nadhigram, and concurrently governing the kingdom of Ayodhya by having placed His pair of gem studded sandals on the throne to represent Him in His absence. Thus, he has spent fourteen long years consuming merely fruits and roots and now, at the lapse of the scheduled time he is anticipating His home coming at any time. The perspicacious Bharathwaj verbally recognizes Raman's tour de force in the Dandahka forest, also how Ravanan had kidnapped Sita and extols Raman's victory, valour and intrepidity in killing Ravanan, Kumbakarnan and destroying his clan, thereby rescuing the earth from the acquisitive and the aggrandizing power of the vicious demons, and how He has, thereupon, brought Lanka under His governance.

The sage eulogizes Raman as Supreme Brahman over whom the manacles of birth and death cannot hold sway. He hails Raman as also the source of all the creatures of the Universe; he verbally picturizes Raman as reclining constantly on the surface of the water of the expansive ocean which He Himself had created at the very genesis of creation. He praises Raman as Narayanan the soul of the Universe, the nucleus of the Universal Soul, the Universal dweller in the hearts of every creature. He declares Raman as the most cherished, paramount Preceptor of the whole Universe, from whose navel even grandfather Brahman the creator has had his birth, He perceives Raman to be, veritably, Lord Vishnu and Sita His consort Lakshmi His illusory power called Maya, and Lakshman to be Seshanag the God of Serpents. He explicitly states that Raman is pervasive and there is nothing above or beyond His limits as He creates the Universe with His indigenous vital dynamic energy. Though all creatures spring from His intrinsic vital dynamic power, He has no bond or attachment to any of His creation, but stands as mere witness to everything which originate from him. Though He is the in-dweller, still, He abides within and without all the creatures as He perennially permeates all places. Ordinary individuals totally hogged down by dark ignorance perceive Him only as a circumscribed and ineffectual human being. He is the invisible exhibitor of the manifest Universe, who is its prime cause too. He is the preserver, collaborator, the genial entertainer as well as the object of entertainment and enjoyment. There is no other phenomenon other than Himself for whatever is apprehended, experienced, heard and cognized is nothing but His manifest Self. Though Raman is formless yet He proliferates the Universe by His illusive primordial potential hence, He is called Birat- the grand bodied Self, because He is Omniscient, Omnipresent and Omnipotent. By virtue of His inconspicuous ethereal form and substratum, attributable to the genuine pristine and sentient energy, which is pertinent to give life and birth to all creation. He, Raman is proclaimed as 'Hiranyagarbha', So an incalculable number of creatures originate from His indecipherable and Infinite form and they eventually amalgamate with Him when once the purpose is served,

'He outrightly enunciates that individuals who piously read or even harken to the chronicle of Raman's life shall be warranted salvation of the highest order. The sage recalls Brahman's austere penances undertaken by Him as a request to Raman for appeasing Him, for the sole reason that He might redeem the earth from the evil influence and afflictions caused by the incompassionate persecution and mordacities of Ravanan and his innumerable forces of savage demons. He comprehends that Raman has readily complied with Brahman's request and has incarnated Himself in the dynasty of Raghus, and also, has fulfilled the onerous task for the welfare of the world. He recognizes Raman's aura and renown reverberating in all the three worlds and they shall remain vibrant on the earth perennially; further he envisages Raman, thereupon, executing His duties punctiliously and performing abundant disparate altruistic and chivalrous deeds, leaving behind for posterity a quintessential paradigm to be decorously and heartily emulated by humans and god-drunk souls as well.

Sage Bharadhwaj extends an implicit invitation to Raman to sanctify His hermitage by his propitious halt there for the night that day. He assures Him that He shall reach Ayodhya the next day. With immense pleasure Raman with His entire retinue sojourn at the hermitage for the night. With a welcome touch of hospitality the sage entertains Raman, Sita, Lakshman, Sugrivan and the rest of the company.

Meanwhile Raman's focal point is to send an emissary to Ayodhya and Shringaberpur so as to illumine the denizens there of His arrival and to meet and appraise Bharathan and Guhan of His accomplished mission. Once again He picks Hanuman, who, unpronounced, proclaims spotless servitude to Raman, on this errand and exhorts him to return to Him soon after. No sooner said than Hanuman races like the winds in the guise of a man. At first he conveys the news of Raman's safe arrival to Guhan and thereafter rushes to Nadhigram to astonishingly find Bharathan emaciated and thin as rail, leading life as an ascetic in a hermitage, clad inbarks and deer skin, his lean body smeared with holy ashes, partaking only fruits and roots and ceaselessly chanting the sacred name Raman. Hanuman sees, conspicuously, Raman's pair of gem-studded sandals placed on the throne by which Bharathan lords over the state.

Hanuman together with Sita and Lakshman, deferentially heralds the good tidings of Raman's advent to his Lordship Bharathan, for whom he is yearning every moment each day. He conveys he has been sent by Raman as His messenger. Bharathan's unspoken unbounded joy appended- with maximum amazement sends him into a trance that he falls unconscious for a while. When he comes back to his own again, he very excitedly with overwhelming joy end eyes flowing with fond tears enfolds Hanuman in his arms. He sighs like a furnace. He is spelling out his astonishment in a query, wishing to know whether he, Hanuman is some celestial being or an ordinary human who has been so gracious to convey the good tidings. His passionate emotions prompt him to reward the harbinger in return with one-lakh cows, one hundred hamlets and sixteen beautiful damsels extensively decorated with jewels. However, he unbottles his long accumulated sentiments and vearninas and articulates that many years have transpired since Raman had left him, and he has been missing Him increasingly as the years went by He truly asserts that prosperity and exuberance will undoubtedly accrue to an individual, if he can wait and live for more than a century despite the fact that he has to journey through the different formidable fluctuations of life.

Most illustrious Bharathan who is all agog to know the complete saga about Raman's feats, achievements and victory, requests Hanuman to relate the whole spectrum of events, happenings and occurrences He had endured in the forest. Hanuman replenishes Bharathan of the whole gamut of phenomena commencing with the abduction of Sita and ultimately concluding with the annihilation of Ravanan and his ilk.

Having heard everything eagerly, Bharathan, becoming exuberantly excited hustles Raghunandhan, that is, Sathrughan, to send out an order to all the erudite priests to offer worship to the Gods according to, conventions, ritualistically and piously in very temple in Ayodhya; again, to send out a directive to the cream of the best musicians, dancers, rhapsodists, flutists and female dancers forming three different groups to start anon in a stately procession from the city for presenting a sweeping ceremonial reception to welcome Raman, He is desirous of a regal delegation comprised of the Queen mothers, other members of the royal family, ministers, feudatory chiefs, a vast array of the army, civil officers and all the citizens to be present at the grand occasion.

Sathrughnan makes all arrangements in the plenitude of power as commended by Bharathan, The entire city looking ethereal is exquisitely embellished with festoons, colourful flags, banners and streamers of bright hues, with skillful artisans burnishing and artistically decorating the city gates, with all the roads of the city looking elegant festooned with flags and banners of varied patterns and hues hanging all the way and with the galleries and pillars of the palace and gates studded with precious and dazzling jewels. With an excitement tempered with joy, the denizens begin to set out of the city at wee hours of the early morning. The magnificence and dignified royalty that the occasion commands is heightened by the parading of one lakh splendidly saddled horses, ten thousand attractively decorated elephants and ten thousand chariots drawn by ostentatiously bridled stalwart stallions. The citizens too take with them fascinating gift articles for presenting them to Raman The queens in handsome palanquins and the associates of the royalty follow the glamorous procession. Inorder to receive Raman, the punctilious Bharathan bearing, very reverentially, the sacred gem-studded sandals of Raman on the crown of his head goes on foot in all meekness, accompanied by his attendants, to meet Him.

Instantly distinct is the Pushpaka plane bathed in the glittering brightness in the sky, which they all espy, making them to enthusiastically announce the presence of Raman, Sita and Lakshman along with the chiefs and the monkeys seated in the plane. As the plane is descending towards the ground, the multitudes detonate into loud cheers hilariously crying that their beloved Raman is coming; He receives a highly tremendous ovation; their zestful cries rent the air reverberating thoughout the heavens Raman looking gloriously radiant as the effulgent moon in the heavens alights from the divine Puspaka plane to the delight of all hearts gathered to receive and greet Him. Bharathan prostrates at the feet of Raman and very deferentially pays his humble salutations and respectful veneration to Him. At this moment, Raman voices concern for his queen mothers and queries about their well-being from Bharathan and Sathrughnan. As becoming of Bharathan, he offers his felicitous obeisance to Sugrivan, Jambavan, Yuvaraj, Angadhan, Maindan, Dwividan, Milan, Nalan, Rishav, Sushen, Gorakshya, Gandhamadan, Sarva and Panash by embracing them one by one.

Simultaneously he felicitates and applauds Sugrivan for the benevolence offered to Raman in helping to kill Ravanan and his demon race and annexing Lanka. Again he postulates that by his benevolence and assistance he has created a bond of kinship among them, and so, acknowledges Sugrivan as indeed his fifth brother. Sathrughnan also offers his respectful homage to Raman, Sita and Lakshman in the same manner.

Raman while bowing to His mother Kausalya to offer His homage to her scans her unspoken yearning and anxiety which have made here very thin and woe begone. He also pays His deference to Kaikeyi and Sumithra.

As a significance of the healthy consummation of his peaceful rule in Ayodhya. Bharathan, devoutly prompted offers the pair of gem-studded sandals, which he had vowed to wait upon, revere and worship, keeping it on the throne to rule Ayodhya until His home coming, to Raman.

He solemnly enunciates to his Lord Raman that he is surrendering the throne and also handing over to Him the reins of the kingdom entrusted to him. He is doubly happy as first he finds his Lord Raman in Ayodhya precisely, to his hearts content, and that his mission in life has culminated successfully. He adds joyfully that he had multiplied the stock of grains, the nation's coffers and the strength of the army ten-fold. He takes immense comfront in acknowledging Raman as the Lord of the Universe, who is the Lord over this expansive country which is all His.

All the monkeys relapse into quantitative joy and vivacity that they praise Bharathan to the skies. In the meantime it is Raman's compelling need to visit Nandhigram. He boards the divine Pushpaka and alights at the hermitage of Bharathan with unconfined mirth.

Raman, by virtue of His noble gesture, with abundant gratitude for his service, sends the divine air chariot Pushpaka back to Kuberan as it belongs to him. Then, immediate emphasis of priority and prominence is focused on to Sage Vashisthar whom Raman meets and bows to, paying deference very reverentially and offering him the exalted seat and Himself very modestly sitting below him.

Chapter - XV

Raman's Coronation as King of Ayodhya

The glorious day of Raman's coronation dawns with great pomp, pageantry and fanfare. The quintessential preparations for His coronation still being carried on goes on preposterously right. Bharathan's resolute persuasion in the character of ardent and solemn requests does mellow Raman's mind and also tenderize His heart to accept the throne of Ayodhya.

Veritably, Raman, who is Supreme God, who transcends all bounds of materialistic pleasures and pains, this ostensible globe over which He reigns supreme is but an insignificant toy to Hhm. His munificent grace bestows prosperity to lord Indhran too. Raman by His delusive power can shape and also demolish the whole Universe by simply the twinkle of His eyelid. The sublime truth is that His human plays, deeds and acts, an unwritten pact with humanity, have ethical depth, exalting everyday life and the living past, destined to be eternally valid, catechizing and enlightening all humanity.

As preparation for the coronation ritual, Raman and siblings take a holy bath and restyle themselves in royal robes. Raman is held hostage to monarchical etiquette, when Lakshman, Bharathan and Sathrughnan themselves bedight Raman with aristocratic garments, gorgeously and elegantly made of satins and silk. They bedeck Him with precious ornaments, necklaces and amulets. Together they fashion and enhance the handsome personality of Raman. Sita who exercises a charming grace is being beautified by the royal maids while Queen Kausalya embellishes the wives of the monkeys.

Sathrughnan orchestrates affairs ordering Sumanthan to bring the extravagantly embellished chariot, lustrous as the rising sun for Raman and other special chariots used for the occasion for Sugrivan, Vibhishanan and Angadhan. The other monkeys and their wives are accommodated on horses, elephants and decorated palanquins.

The royal procession commences with Raman seated solely unparalleled on His chariot proceeding towards the city of Ayodhya, bearing resemblance to Indhran going on his charriot. drawn by green hued horses.

The ebullient Bharathan dons the mantel of servility and stations himself as Raman's charioteer. Sathrughnan is pleased to carry the royal ensigns. So also is Lakshman delighted to sway the royal fans and of course, Vibhishanan is enthused to bear the shining chamar (a kind of fan made of Yaktesils). While Bharathan propels the chariot at an unhurried pace, the others synchronizing their movements in measured motion amble beside it, with Raman the cynosure of all eyes seated unsurpassed on it as it moves along amidst cheers, greetings, prayers, frenzied dancing and enchanting music which redoubles through the streets and rings in the air.

Raman on His migratory path, accompanied by an aura of royal splendour and aristocracy, adorned with necklaces armlets, varied ornaments and sporting the most coruscating diadem on His head, His countenance like the 'Durbagrass' once again explodes into public consciousness with a volcanic impact. All the citizens breathless with delight throng the streets with crowds spilling onto the roads, trying to settle themselves on either side of the roads, waiting to have a glimpse of their Lord Raman. The whole city feels transformed to another world of celestial ecstasy. His imperial robes of gold glitter. When Raman casts benign glances at the crowds of people with His beautiful pink hued eyes like the cute buds of lotuses, He reflects grace, elegance and cheer, which send them into raptures. He is also sporting a garland of sacred blossoms, which glows like the moon. He has His countenance daintily glossed with a coating of cosmetic dyes, conventionally prepared from sandal, saffron and perfumes, emanating a golden glow akin to the visible radiance of the rising sun from the eastern horizon.

Remarkably, the multitudes go insane with joy as Raman in pompous and majestic procession has access to the city. The conventional yet disquistive women with a heady rush of excitement race to their windows to espy Raman and have His glance fall upon them. They are so awed and charmed by Him that they worship and praise Him in their hearts and rain blossoms upon Him.

Upon arrival, Raman enters the threshold of His father's palace which has been fashioned analogous to Indhran's for the occasion. At once He acknowledges and greets all the dignitaries and citizens who with an all pervading sense of holiness, deference, devotion and affection have congregated to welcome and receive Him. After the exchanging of the opening pleasantries,

Raman, once again offers His respects to his mother Kausalya and other queen mothers with love and cheer. Yet again, he enjoins Bharathan to provide accommodation for Sugrivan and the other monkeys in His sprawling, adequately equipped palace and to administer to their every need.

Bharathan thanks Sugrivan, in large part, at whose behest the fantastic exertions of a zealous workforce of expeditious monkeys-Hanuman, Angadhan and other leaders, at supersonic speed in the air, conduct water from the sea in ceremonial pots of gold for the coronation ritual of Raman.

The exalted delegation comprises Sage Vashisthar the chief of the sages, Bamadeva, Javali, Vishwamithrar, Gautham and several other saints, savants, eminent priests and erudite pundits who are duly present to witness the ceremony.

The long-awaited coronation ceremony is in progress. Amidst the chorus chanting of Veda manthras, Raman and Sita who grace the magnificent throne are ritually sprinkled with holy water and Tulasi flowers observing all liturgy and tradition; the celestial beings proffer 'Tilak' to Raman. Sathrughnan hoists a glorious white ensign over Raman's head and Vibhishanan sways the white chamars and fans from both sides. The magnificence and grandeur of Raman's coronation scale expansive heights of excellence, rivalling that of Indhran's whom the Basus had coronated on the sacred throne.

At this juncture, gift articles keep heaping up. The God of Winds proffers a celestial gold necklace and Indhran offers Raman an invaluable garland embedded with lustrous precious stones and glowing pearls; all the while, choirs of gandharvas and deities, melodists and vocalists keep vocalizing, psalms and anthems synchronizing with the varied musicians who render tuneful resonance which is euphonious par excellence' with divine musical instruments. Incessantly, soft and tender flowers are being showered on Raman and Sita from all sides in the heavens.

Inevitably, Lord Shivan takes his relatively privileged position at Raman's coronation ceremony. With him the other deities, gandharvas saints and sages pray Raman with immense joy and deference. Evidently x-evincing exceptional sublimity and renown, congruent as the Sun, Raman, with Sita graces the majestic throne. Their robes, crowns, ornaments and jewelry put those of even cupid in the shade.

Lord Shivan bowing to Raman respectfully' showers resounding accolades on Him. He verbalizes that Raman, gracing the majestic throne with Devi Sita is looking adorably statuesque. He articulates that Raman knows neither Alpha nor Omega for He is ever. As He is the very breath of the Universe, He neither knows birth nor death. He is the eternal reality, the Supreme Soul who creates and sustains the whole Universe with both inanimate and animate beings incorporated in Him and also annihilates them in due course of time. He is without mutation, is self-complacent and lacks predilection for anything.

In His manifold incarnations, He plays human roles on earth, which warrants special mention for His role play serves as a beacon to educate humanity for its multifaceted welfare. He recognizes Raman being mutable to transmute Himself into Sashanag inorder to underprop the earth, and to bestow animation and dynamism to all creatures by emblazing himself as the Sun and the Moon with attributes of lighting and medication and further more falling down as the rains from above.

He is the one who operates as the invisible energy which digests and assimilates the food thus sustaining the lives of all creatures.

Though panspohists and savants plausibly visualize different Gods as Indhran, Vishnu, Shivan, the sun and the moon, the God of Death, the God of Wealth and such others, yet Shivan endorses Lord Raman alone as the Supreme Soul who is the provenance from whom these motley forms of Gods manifest.

Lord Shivan substantiates Raman as being corporeal as well as spiritual, delusive and yet so intrinsically tangible. The Vedas advocate that He is the Supreme Soul; they ascribe His incarnations such that of fish, tortoise, lion, bear and other beings as being His own credible forms and from whom alone these incarnations are definitely expedient. These incarnations in every context are resolved to serve explicit rationale behind their fulfillment. So it is transparent that all existence, animate or inanimate, is His own manifestation, from His own energy since these are incorporated in Him alone. He transcends nature and exists outside matter He asserts that cognizance of even an iota of Raman or a minuscule aspect of Raman is denied to individuals caught in the web of His illusion which deludes them. It is only those whose hearts and minds have been elevated to the plane of sanctity by His lovely grace that can envision them and comprehend who and what He really is. Notwithstanding, the Gods including Brahman seem to have not fathomed Him wholly and completely, then mention of other creatures is futile. The most influential and amenable highway for discerning and perceiving Him and attaining salvation is unalloyed- love, single-minded worship and earnest devotion to His tangible form of Sir Raman with Sri Sita. At this juncture, Lord Shivan professes that personally he is ever delighted and content with assiduously chanting and singing His name "Rama" ceaselessly. He reaffirms that he abides with Devi Parvathi at Kashi (Varanasi) where he bestows his name, 'Rama' to persons at death's door for their own redemption. Repeatedly, Lord Shivan entreats Raman enticingly to bestow a boon on those who most devotedly listen to, learn and also recite this invocation that they may scale the heights of prosperity, harvest sublime knowledge and attain salvation as well.

Felicitous Indhran establishes Raman's prowess by vocalizing Raman's wonderful benevolence alone by which he has retrieved and also repossessed his kingdom and all his properties, respectively, which Ravanan had coercively expropriated, All the celestials in an incredible shower of words applaud Lord Vishnu, the killer of Moor, the demon, for paving the way, thencefore, for uninterrupted access to the shares of offerings which Ravanan had begrudged them for so long. In the same vein, the departed souls (spirits) too exhale a sigh of relief as they, hereafter by His grace will be able to feast on the 'Pindas' offered by their relatives in Gaya, which Ravanan used to devour till then. Again, Yakshaya is also inspired to laud Raghunandan for His clemency which has unburdened their hardships unleashed on them by Ravanan who constrained them to toil hard that they had to bear his heavy palanquins and heavy loads without any kind of remuneration The gandharvas no less, put forward their grievance and resentment against Ravanan's obstinate compulsion for them to sing only his name and praise, when they were in the main, customarily, glorifying His names and singing His praises.

Eventually, however, all the other beings like Prajapathi, Brahman's son, the Serpent God, Sages, Cows, subordinate and debased spirits, birds and fairies consecrate their humble veneration to Lord Raman in keeping with their echelon. Sri Raman reciprocates enthralling all His guests including Lord Shivan, Brahman and Indhran by entertaining them with His cordial reception and gracious hospitality, after which they return to their respective abodes quite delighted.

Hallowed Raman with Sita and His brothers Vibhishanan and Sugrivan were spectacular, dazzling like a thousand suns at the time of His glorious coronation.

Chapter - XVI

Raman's farewell to His Monkey Friends

Prosperity reigns supreme equably as and when Righteous Raman, the provenance and universal bestower of prosperity and good fortune, ascends the throne. This leads naturally to the plenteousness of opulence, good fortune and sustenance throughout the realm. All the trees everywhere are laden with fruits; ever since, the fields yield a sustained succession of abounding harvests; and even the trees and bushes bearing inodorous flowers inherit luscious fragrance and thenceforth bear odoriferous flowers with beauty harbouring in them imperceivable secrets of medication and alleviation from man's ills.

The magnitude of Raman's munificence finds expression in His gifting away with great delectation lakhs of lacteous cows, thirty crore gold coins, hundreds of bullocks, numerous priceless jewels and expensive clothing to Brahmins. He lavishes a fabulous diamond necklace, as brilliant the sun, on Sugrivan: He presents marvellous divine armlets to Angadhan and another diamond necklace of incredible value to Sita, who in turn presents it to Hanuman.

Hanuman a non pareil incandescent devotee of Raman has ascended the pinnacle of Raman's praise and favour which, now, Raman translates with immeasurable pleasure into admiration and satisfaction for his professed spotless servitude. He motivates Hanuman to make the choice of a boon from Him, closest to his heart. He coaxingly vocalises that He is enthusiastically inclined to bestow any such thing which may even be, enviously, out of the reach of the Gods of the three worlds.

Initially, the incredibly soulful Hanuman enunciates that he is wholeheartedly content with the oral experience of integrating himself with His names only which he chants incessantly.

But then, in devoted response he most meekly prays Lord Raman to empower him to live on this earth in full animation and dynamism as long as His name is vibrant and is commemorated here.

The Lord bestows this divine dispensation asserting that he, Hanuman, shall live on this earth happily, yet independently till the delusion of the Universe when he shall saturate with His own Supreme Self and enjoy a sustained intimacy with Him perennially. Synchronously Devi Sita too affirms her Lord's benedictions pronouncing that aliment of all variety and prosperity shall favour him till he lives. Hanuman has risen to the stature of being praised by both the Lord and the Divine Mother.

Through Raman's power and grace of gratitude, Hanuman is satiated at this good fortune that has been bestowed on him, Very reverentially he pays his utmost deference to Raman and Sita, but very reluctantly takes leave of them to return to the Himalayas. Raman cheerfully blesses His friend Guhan with enjoyment of every kind of pleasure and prosperity during his lifetime and then to attain His form after death. With this He doles out numerable jewels, ornaments and riches to Guhan and all other monkeys who have come to Ayodhya. Radiating an underlying emotion of devotion, Guhan, Vibhishanan and all the monkeys including Sugrivan bid adieu to Sri Raman and Sri Sita to return to their respective habitations.

Raman grants Jamabavan with life on this earth till the Dwapra yuga when He shall again come into being as Krishnan and meet him so as to entangle him in a fight with Him for a specific cause.

Inevitably Raman's breath-taking goverance enhances the quality of human life, though the values are instrumental in subserving the deeper elements of the human spirit, which leads the kingdom onto the path of peace and prosperity such that, peace, happiness and prosperity dominate in every family throughout the land. There is no crying and gnashing of teeeth; no woman is a widow and the young never die prematurely. The citizens love and worship their Lord Raman. They lead honest and pious lives with absolute self-control, adhering to scriptural injunctions and observing fast agreeably and promptly. Consequently the cyclic seasons occur in uninterrupted concatenation; the monsoons never fail to be punctual; invariably so every business of the people goes on congenially and compatibly.

Raman annoints Lakshman as His heir apparent Yuvaraj, despite Lakshman's enthusiastic reluctance to accept the office. Lakshman dancing attendance on Raman and Sita is ever in their service administering to their every need. Regular yajnas and sacrifices are performed by the Supreme Lord Raman following which He distributes enormous wealth and gifts to Brahmins. The people experience the universal feeling of oneness because Sri Raman respects and values His subjects as His own sons and daughters. Raman's magnificent humanitarian rule extends over an expansive epoch of eleven thousand years during which He demonstrates universal love and righteousness and establishes religion, discipline, morality ethics, traditions and everlasting fame all over the globe.

The 'Adhyathma Ramayanam' is held in high esteem by the greatest authority Lord shivan who had found it to be the only truth and the essence of religion, has condescended to enlighten his consort Parvathi Devi on it. Such a laudable chronicle, if chanced upon or listened to or read by the individual, he can lay a claim to cumulative prosperity, longevity, health, bliss, good fortune and well-being.

Part - VII
Uthara Kandham

Chapter - I

Agasthiyar Narrates Demon's History

Lord Shivan pays felicitous extolment to the victory of the Lotus - eyed Raman, designating Him as the cynosure of the Raghu race, acknowledging Him as the prize and joy of Kausalya's heart and eulogizing Him as the pride of Dasarathar in the form of a son.

The interlocution between Lord Shivan and Devi Parvathi is in continuance. Devi Parvathi's mind is racing with abounding questions. Her unbounded enthusiasm goads her on to interject questions broadly aimed at knowing the desirous consequences of Raman's phenomenal victory. Her appetite to learn about the aftermath of Raman's victory is excited. So, in the course of their parley, She wheedles Lord Shivan her beatific beloved to enlighten her on Raman's course of action taken after obliterating ferocious Ravanan and other mighty demons; also, she is all wishful of knowing how long the all-abiding God, Raman, lived in His human incarnation after His enthronement in the kingdom of Ayodhya with Sita Devi, the finale of His reign and conclusively His exit from the sublunary world.

Devi Parvathi grows increasingly avid in comprehending the ambrosial saga of Raman. She expresses her longing to Lord Shivan to kindly reveal his story precisely yet comprehensively.

Inorder to respond to her queries and to satiate her yearning, Lord Shivan elucidates the solidarity fostered by the sages to call upon Raman at Ayodhya to felicitate him on his spectacular achievement. He commences with Raman's triumphant return to the kingdom of Ayodhya after vanquishing all the heinous demons and the confederation of sages coming to Ayodhya to compliment Him. Vishwamithrar, Asit, Durvasa, Bhrigu, Angira, Kashyap, Vamadeva, Atri, the seven divine sages called Saptharishis and Agasthiyar the principal sage, together with many disciples arrive at the gates of Raman's palace and petition the guards to convey the message of their arrival to Raman for the purpose of proposing their tribute and benedictions in recognition of His extra ordinary feats.

Forthwith, the guards expeditiously convey to Lord Raman the tidings of Agasthiyar's entourage of sages and disciples waiting at the gates of the palace to have an audience with 'Him. At Raman's behest, the whole retinue is escorted into the palace where Raman receives them and ushers them into divine seats rightfully entitled to each of them. With folded hands He pays His cordial respects to them. He entertains them very reverentially adhering to all formalities, conventions and suavities. He extends a hearty hospitality by offering them varieties of foodstuffs. While lavishing the gift of numerous cows on the different guests, He and the sages reciprocate pleasant vibes and enquiries about their salubrity and the prosperity of their respective kingdoms.

The sages basking in a sunshine of gaiety at Raman's congenial reception and hospitality, happen to glorify Him as their Lord whom they are very fortunate to behold. Raman receives wide appreciation and acclaim from the sages for having extirpated, scrupulously and meritoriously, the accursed and powerful demons — Ravanan and Kumbhakarnan and many others. They accentuate that when He holds the bow doggedly in His hand, He is able to obliterate the three worlds in a trice and so, it was credibly feasible for His Supreme Self to annihilate the mighty demons. An observation about Raman's seeming ineptitude to kill Indrajit the son of Ravanan is made in the passing by the sages. Nevertheless they are overcome by a shoreless joy as Raman has relieved them from the phobia of cruel demons, effaced all dangers threatening them and has also given them shelter by easily killing demons with His puissant arrows.

The sages being inordinately ecstatic that Raman has accomplished His mission befittingly, deserving all praise, perceive that He is abiding happily in Ayodhya now. The sages' baffling observations about His non success in slaying Indrajlt which comes like a bolt from the blue has caught Raman's attention. He is propelled to modestly question why so much ado is made in speaking immoderately about Ravanan's son, despite having killed the chief of the demon clan Ravanan and Kumbhakaranan as well and all other mighty demons who had overpowered the three worlds. It behooves the most erudite sage Agasthiyar to enlighten them on Raman's query. He slips his memory into the shadows of the Sathya Yuga and delightfully engages everyone's attention in a riveting yet brief narration about the birth of the demons, their deeds and the boons they had procured. First he regales them with Brahman the creator's son, highly illustrious and prudent, who had made a spirited excursion to the Mountain Meru for practising severe austerities. He had dwelt there in the herrnitage of Tribindu. He was inordinately sunk in his vocation, preoccupying himself with erudition and worship and undertaking astringent penances too.

It was habitual for all the damsels, deficient in principled demeanour, of Gandharvas, Gods and Kinnaras to congregate there and bedevil the sage with their noisy gracelessness, garrulity, laughter and yodel. The sage was extensively irked by such disgracious behaviour that he had, one day, spat out a malediction that whoever came into his sight shall be pregnant. All the maidens never ventured again to molest him for fear of the bane. But a lone damsel the daughter of the royal sage, Tribindu, assertively strutted in front of him, ignorant of the malediction. The aftermath was she conceived and soon symptoms of gestation ensued. Her father the sagacious Tribindu by his percipience cognized the facts when she approached him and accordingly offered his daughter to Pulatsya.

The sage Pulatsya authenticating the calibre of her character and services accepted her promising that he would give life and protection to her biological offspring who would prolong their dynasty. And desirously enough, she begot a propitious male child named Vishravan who had by and by established renown all over the world by virtue of his erudite stature. His renown and erudition were a trumpet blast to sage Bharadhwaj who gave his daughter's hand in marriage to Vishravan who begot a very promising son, whose genetic legacies were as illustrious as his own. He was called Kuberan, the God of Wealth, for he had aspired to obtain, cumulatively, boons of inexhaustible wealth from Brahman by his earnest and unrelenting penances. He was desirous of fostering all the wealth with progressive prosperity in an advisable, tranquil and exclusive place exempt from all malice. The most appropriate locus suggested by his father Vishravan when asked, was the city of Lanka built by Viswakarma as the habitation for demons because they were necessitated to go to the nether world for fear of Lord Vishnu.

The city of Lanka sat on an island well girdled by the sea and therefore it was inexpugnable, diminished expectation, even by the most potent enemies. Kuberan the God of Wealth flourished there luxuriating merrily for a lengthy period of time.

It so happened that, once, a demon named Sumali visited the earth with his beautiful daughter who looked like a goddess and chanced to lay eyes on Kuberan, the God of Wealth, living in Lanka. The sage instilled in her the desire for marriage and impressed upon her mind that she so young and beautiful should marry the sage born into Brahmin family and should then bear children undifferentiated from Kuberan, the God of Wealth and the son of Vishravan, immediately after, nurturing the prospect of marriage to Vishravan, she had access to his hermitage and planted herself at its doorstep. Though the perspicacious sage had perceived her transparent desire while in meditation still, he enquired of the damsel's identity and purpose of calling on him. She visibly acknowledged and hailed his omniscience, the knower of all things. At this, the sage unravelled her innermost desire of begetting sons through him. More shockingly he utters an impious statement that she shall beget dreadful and ferocious demons as she had arrived there at a star-crossed moment. She humbly negotiated with the Lordly Sage that it wouldn't augur well if she gave birth to such vicious sons from such a pious person as himself. The sage seconded his own former statement with a benign blessing that she shall beget another son who would be very holy, pious, intellectual and a faithful and ardent devotee of Lord Raman.

Precisely enough, Kakasi the maiden, Sumali's daughter, begot absurd Ravanan with ten heads and twenty arms. Ravanan's birth at a very unpropitious moment heralded the extensive evil that was to be unleashed, later, by him, threatening the very existence of the three worlds, because foreboding omens were visibly abounding all around, concurrently, shaking the very foundation of the earth at that inauspicious moment. These ill omens presaged grave danger to the people. of the earth. She next begot Kumbhakaranan who was as monstrous as a hill. Then Surpanakai who was as fiendish as her brothers was born to her. And lastly she begot the handsome Vibhishanan who was noble. He was passionately covetous of entering the portals of learning to acquire knowledge. From the very beginning he had tailored himself to become a staunch and genuine devotee of Sri Raman.

Regarding Kumbhakarnan whose mind was bent maliciously was a globe trotter; circumnavigated the whole earth devouring Brahmins, sages as well as human beings, brutally. As for the mighty Ravanan, he had tormented and intimidated all the three worlds with extinction by his limitless ruthlessness and callousness. The atrocities unleashed mercilessly by him, like an epidemic disease knew no bounds and had spread far and wide infecting even the innocent and the good, enough to dry up their inspiration and faith.

With this, sage Agasthiyar hails Raman as the immanent one who dwells in the hearts of every creature and witnesses every action, as He, the holy one, is the omniscient and omnipotent Supreme God. Further, he not only perceives but also proclaims Raman's choice of playacting the role of an enfleshed being is feasible only by His illusory power, yet, He is never attached to the human plausible activities. The all-knowing Raman pretends to be ignorant, when in fact He knows everything in an everlasting present and, seemingly, requests the sage to replenish Him with the history of the demons. The sage advocates that Raman is the One Absolute Truth. He announces Raman's power to be mind-boggling. He recognises Raman as one who is unborn and is imperishable. He endorses Him as the very the essence and the ultimate source of bliss. He surrenders himself to the holy feet of Lord Raman, which he desires to be his perennial shelter, for he reveals that it is only by His grace he is living happily.

Raman who happily revels in the eulogy of the sage, verbalizes that the Universe though it appears to be concrete and real, it is but His Illusion which superimposes such impressions on the ignorant mind. Also, the Universe is in no way wholly separate from Him. He guarantees salvation and atonement of one's sins by simply praying and chanting His various names.

Chapter - II

Ravanan's Penances for Bravery

Sage Agasthiyar resumes his narration of the history of the demons. He proceeds to brief Raman about Kuberan, the God of Wealth, who once visited his father Vishravan. At such a time, Kekari espying him, influenced the attention of Ravanan to an interesting observation of Kuberan being an epitome of eminence and enlightenment. She instructed him to emulate his ways and be like him so very prosperous and happy. At this Ravanan's adrenaline shot up and he retorted instantly pledging that he would do better and be even greater, mightier and all the more prosperous than Kuberan. Thus he extinguished her fears.

Ravanan and his siblings, Kumbhakarnan and Vibhishanan got started for the said task of improving and strengthening their station in life. They had geared themselves up with the armour of dauntless perseverance and probity, so much so, that their severe austerities and penances had the qualities of burning all the three worlds. Kumbhakarnan undertook strict austerities for ten years; Vibhishanan when he under took penances he had passed five thousand years standing on one foot and Ravanan undertook abstinence from food and water for one thousand divine years and at the termination of every hundred years he sacrificed each of his ten heads. And with the momentum that his years of severe austerities had provided, continuing them was halted by Brahman's apparition before him expressing his satiety and pleasure at his rigorous penances. He provided Ravanan the opportunity for wishing his heart's desired boons which he was ready to bestow upon him. instantly Ravanan beseeched Brahman for superlative power that may, perpetually, have immense privilege over the Gods, Garuda, Serpents, Kinnaras, Yakshas and gandharvas. Man whom he regarded as picayune figured not in his list of the awesome, and daunting. In addition, Brahman granted the restoration of his heads and their indestructive affirmation hereafter.

Next in turn, Brahman requested Kumbhakarnan to state his desired boons. Kumbhakarnan simply pronounced his desire for uninterrupted slumber for six months and appeasement with the food consumed only once half yearly. Lastly Brahman interviewed Vibhishanan and enjoined him to lay claim to his aspired boons. Vibhishanan meekly solicited Lord Brahman that he should ever spend his life peacefully and piously, and further entreated that under no circumstance he should entertain immoral and rancorous deeds Brahman was propitiated and delighted with Vibhishanan that he complemented his aspiration by yet another advantage the privilege of immortality, albeit, unbidden by him. The ruthless and crude Kumbhakarnan was later remorseful and reproached himself for the unintelligent and ridiculous boons claimed by him.

Sumali having discerned that his grandsons had procured favours from Lord Brahman, emerged from the netherlands accompanied by Prahastu and many other demons. While the demons hailed and felicitated Ravanan, Sumali impudently opined it was just their good fortune which had favoured them in securing the desired boons. He exhorted that they all go to Lanka, a Kingdom for their habitation built by Vishwakarma, to flourish there in prosperity. He deprecated that they were prevailed upon to dwell in the underworld only for fear of Lord Vishnu. He added that from then on they were being extricated from every kind of phobia, threat and danger emanating from all quarters. He brazenly admonished Ravanan to overthrow Kuberan and capture Lanka either by force or blandishments. Ravanan artfully made a trenchant rejoinder that it did not behove Sumali to dish out such an erroneous and felonious piece of advice.

But Prahastu intruded upon their confabulation, persuading dear Ravanan to be judicious politically. Moreover he pointed out that his trenchant rejoinder was blurted out, inappropriately, merely from the point of view of his kindred relation to Kuberan. He impressed upon him that there can be no such bondage to be cherished or reckoned with by the mighty like him, and quoted an example in point about the sons of Kashyap who were both gods and demons, but forgetting their brotherhood, wrangled with one another for the supremacy of power. Complimenting Ravanan's matchless puissance, Prahastu polluted his mind to disaffillate such kindred relations which are not propitious. Inorder to distort his mind further, he revealed the long enmity between the gods and the demons that existed from even primeval times, Ravanan was enticed by Prahastu's edifying enunciation. On the strength of it Prahastu was delegated as an envoy to Kuberan, and consequently, by deploying coercive measures, Kuberan was driven out of Lanka, whereby, Ravanan became the execlusive possessor of the dominion. The genial Kuberan stripped of kingdom, but with piety as his saving grace retreated to the Himalayas and engaged himself in penances to gladden Lord Shivan who had counselled him to reside in Alkapuri designed by Vishwakarma for his habitation.

Ravanan the usurper had become the self-appointed monarch of lanka. He reigned supreme wielding absolute power in all the three worlds, tyrannizing and terrorizing all the creatures, men and Gods. He gave his sister Surpanakhai in marriage to Brihat Jiva, the son of Kalkanja. His siblings, Kumbhakarnan, was married to Bairochan's daughter Brihatjwala, and Vibhishanan to Surabha, the daughter of sage Saibush. Ravanan himself married the most pulchritudinous of all damsels in the three worlds named Mandhothari. Her father was called 'The Maya', who was Diti's son, a great and skillfull engineer, had proffered an intimidating and overpowering weapon to Ravanan at the occasion of his marriage. Mandhothari begot a son, Meghanad, meaning the roar of clouds, because the intensity of his loud cry that he emitted at his birth was thunderous like the roaring of thunderclouds. Hence he got the appellation Meghanath. Kumbhakarnan did nothing more than hibernate in a solitary deep cave and Ravanan was persistently focused on his onslaught against Brahmins, sages, serpents, gandharvas and all other beings in the three worlds. He coercively and vehemently plundered the properties of the gods and ravaged even their royal residences.

Kuberan learning about Ravanan's atrocities sent him a proscription constraining him from further such loathsome deeds. But Ravanan had instead, his anger inflated, could brook no such prohibitions and defeating Kuberan in a combat, snatched his air chariot Pushpaka away by force, Ravanan's malcontentment had spurred him on to attempt an onslaught on the chief of the Gods, Indhran. Deplorably, he was defeated and taken captive. But his son Meghanath went up to heaven, subjugated Indhran and brought him a prisoner to Lanka. His notable valour procured the release of his father and also a motley of boons from Brahman, the creator who in reciprocity induced him to set free Indhran. Ravanan overpowered all the inhabitants and the kings of the three worlds - the heavens, the earth and the underworld. He rose to the status of the Supreme Ruler who regined over even the gods.

Ravanan was the personification of arrogance that he once sojourned to the Himalayas and ventured to dislocate the mountain Kailash - the abode of Shivan. But soon he was bound by an imprecation from Nandhi, the attendant of Shivan, that he, Ravanan would be annihilated by men and monkeys sooner or later. Despite the overwhelming odds and repeated defeats Ravanan had faced, still, he relentlessly pressed forward his arrogantly vicious deeds. Again, he went to Shathrarjunan with whom he clashed but was captured and confined in a horse stable. Later, Pulatsya released him from there. Nevertheless, he was over come by Bali who crushed him under his arms and hurled him into the sea some hundreds of miles away. Consequently, Ravanan by this incident had entered into a bond of friendship with him.

By and by he established sole authority and proprietorship of all the three worlds conquering gods and men as a result of the many boons he had obtained from Lord Brahman. His supremacy of power had its own repercussions' for rituals, religious rites, yajnas and worship to Lord Vishnu, Lord Shivan and other Gods came to a grinding halt, almost forgotten, as he had interdicted them, and preferably unleashed terrorism, coercion, peremptoriness and distress ubiquitously. Sage Agasthiyar digresses from his narration of the story of the demons and at this moment hails Raman as Supreme God Narayanan, the Creator of the Universe, who is Omnipresent and Omnipotent, for He, virtually together with Lakshman had effaced all these demons from the face of the earth, who were heinous, unnerving and towering.

The sage continues to enunciate that all the objects, animate and inanimate, manifest His different forms. Acknowledgingly, he celebrates every part of His body as being instrumental and purposive because Brahman, the Creator has come into being from His navel; that the God of Fire and the God of Speech from His mouth. He recognizes the sun and the moon as His eyes and the guards (Pillars) of all the worlds as His mighty arms. All directions and intersections are extended from His ears; and Ashwini Kumar from his nostrils. The different worlds (Lokhas) such as Bhu, Bhuva, Swa etc. have come into existence from His thighs, knees, buttocks, legs etc. He glorifies Him as Lord Hari from whose belly the vast oceans have taken shape. The god of winds and Indhran are born from His chest, whereas His semen has effectuated Bali and the other sages. Yaman, the God of Death has been Created from the lower part of His body, the pelvis. His wrath has generated the three-eyed Lord Rudran, the mountains from His bones. the rains from His hair, herbs from the tiny hairs of His body, insects and animals from His nails. Comprehensively, the sage cognizes the entire, pervasive Universe incorporating animate creatures and life as objects to be merely His revelations. Ergo, everything is, sui generis, one without a second. It is His Illusive power alone that sees ail the objects in its diverse forms. He is the custodian of the gods and favours them with even the nectar produced in the sacrifices (Yajnas), which is obtainable to them by dint of His potency and dynamism.

Sage Agasthiyar eulogizes Raman as being immanent in all the created objects of the Universe similar to butter that is inherent in milk, Nonetheless the sun and the moon shine because of Him alone, yet they cannot illumine or enlighten Him. He emphasizingly proclaims it is only those who possess an exalted clairvoyance can know and conceptualize Him who is omnipresent, infinite and absolute; but the decaying ignorant minds cannot comprehend even a wee bit of Him like the blind who cannot see the blazing sun. The sages and the seers consider the study of the doctrines of the highest ideals of religion, philosophy, dogmas and mores as a sterile gathering of information, for, though they yen after Him in themselves, pray to Him in their hearts day and night and meditate on Him incessantly, yet, they are bereft of perceiving Him, but they ultimately realize that the only way to please Him, find Him, is by love or devotion to Him alone.

Sage Agasthiyar knowing Lord Raman to be the Supreme God, further, invokes Him with greater devotion to befriend him always.

Chapter - III

Births of Vali and Sugrivan

Raman earnestly entreats sage Agasthiyar to be pleased to enlighten Him on the story connected with the births of Vali and Sugrivan who were the sons of Indhran and the Sun God correspondingly. Sage Agasthiyar began with a vivid description of the stately mountain Meru which aspired sky-high with its peak of gold dazzling like gems, and which was once the abode of Brahman the Creator. During that time while Brahman was immersed in intent contemplation in the impressive hall some hundred miles in length, he had shed tears when in a divine ecstasy of bliss. He consciously scooped up some drops of tears in his hands and casting a divine spell on them gently rolled them onto the ground. And behold a remarkably prodigious monkey egressed out of it. The monkey was very ingenious and Brahman named him Riksharaj. He also bestowed his benedictions on him and enjoined him to live there merrily.

One day Riksharaj espied a very beautiful divine waterscape. He saw his inevitable reflection upon the still waters and misconstrued it for another monkey ready to assail him; so he jumped into the lake to attack him first. But alas, he was transformed into a ravishing damsel when he emerged from the water. Indhran and the Sun God chanced to espy the damsel on their way to worship Brahman the creator, and allured by her beauty cohabited with her. In consequence Vali was born to Indhran and Sugrivan was born to the Sun God. Under the mysterious circumstances Riksharaj in the form of a lady had two sons born of him. He slept in the night as a woman but awoke the next morning transmuted into his own monkey form and taking his two sons went to have an audience with Brahman. On the other hand Brahman was delighted to see the two valiant and suave monkey lads. Effectively, Brahman ordained Riksharaj to go with his sons and live in Kishkintha which was a beautiful city built by Vishwakarma, and also sent a messenger to escort them there. The principal town Kishkintha was christened the capital city, as Bali, the executive chief held regal sway over it and all the countries where monkeys inhabited.

Further more, Agasthiyar deviating from the subject panegyrizes Raman as the Lord of all the creatures, who has now redeemed the earth from sinking into the quagmire of sin by incarnating Himself in human sheath individually at Brahman's venerable obsecration. The sage viewing the annihilation of the demon clan in the correct perspective acknowledges it as no fascinating deed to Raman personally. In truth He is the in-dweler in the heart of every being, the only energetic source of all life, assuming countless forms but is in reality only a singular infinite power. His humanistic deeds which cleanse and consecrate sinners and delight the animated beings are glorified by the saints, the seers and the aspirants. Agasthiyar enunciates that individuals shall be positively bestowed with piety if they will read or recite the celestial saga of the births of Vail and Sugrivan.

Raman is enthused by the sage's volitional narration of Ravanan's rationale and justification behind his abduction of Sita. Agasthiyar apprises Raman of how Ravanan once approached sage Sanath kumar whom he appraised to be very knowledgeable and ingenuous. He deferentially requested the sage Sanath Kumar to shed his ignorance of the one who was the most Supreme High to whom all the celestials adjure, and by whom they were blessed with exalted energy to vanquish their enemies and whom the holy beings and enlightened ones worshipped.

Sage Sanath Kumar was highly pleased to respond to Ravanan's queries. He was ecstatic to articulate the very name of Sri Hari Narayanan as the most Supreme Lord of the Universe. He epitomized the unfathomless power of Sri Hari Narayanan who is infinite, of spontaneous origin and everlasting. He is the pre-eminent cause of all the living beings and is the beloved of all the deities who worship Him, adore Him and sing His praises ceaselessly. Brahman himself the Creator has come into existence from His naval. The sublime function of creation is accomplished by Him, the Almighty God, for none else but Himself has created all the worlds, and the Universe, saints, deities and all living creatures. Men on earth implore Him and benefit themselves with great energy. He is formless though He assumes form from, age to age. He is invisibly immanent in lakes, rivers and in all animate and inanimate objects. He is the Omkara. the Supreme Logos-speech and is the eternal Truth. He projects Himself as Goddess Savithri; He is Sesh who is the buttress, the sustenance and preserver of the Universe and the Earth. His Multivarious forms such as deities, oceans, Yama, the sun, the moon, death, the sunrise, day, night, the winds, the fire, Indhran, the clouds, the rains, Basus, the Creator Brahman, Rudran and all the creatures of the Universe itself are all but His manifestations. He is the one without attributes, activities and yet He is immutable and inalterable. Inscrutable are the manifold ways in which He acts and plays. He coruscates in the design of lighting, blazes in the fashion of fire, preserves all beings as Vishnu, demolishes everything as Rudran because the whole Universe and all that it encompasses is established only within Him.

In this enfleshed symmetrical form, He appears as exotic as the blue lotuses; is adored in shining gold yellow Satin Pitambaram. Accompanying Him ever is His consort Shakthi who is visibly seen sitting on His lap embracing Him in great fondness which is an exposition of her vibrant coexistence with Him. His escort Lakshmi who manifests such lustrous radiance as gold is the unique one with whom He is integrally allocated.

None can have access to Him, not even the Gods or serpents, giants or men; it is unquestionable that only those who are patronized by Him can see Him, meet him and commune with Him. Even mindful practices such as sacrifices, yagnas, penances, charity, mortification and gathering of knowledge become purportless and unproductive and do not serve the purpose in finding Him. The ultimate qualification is the total surrender to His feet where refuge can be secured and intimacy established. Thus it is only by this tenacious inwardness and purely by the acquisition of transcendental philosophy, they can be purged of all sins, made immaculate and eventually made to realize Lord Vishnu in the recesses of their hearts.

The unrevealed privileged revelation - Lord Vishnu's incarnation in the appellation 'Raman' in the Thretha yuga was disclosed to Ravanan by sage Sanath Kumar. He replenished him with supplementary information about Raman to be born as the son of king Dasarathar of Ayodhya, His marriage to Sita and His expulsion from the Kingdom to live in exile in the forests at his father's behest. Ravanan, to His entire satisfaction, was apprised of all that he had desired to comprehend by the sage. In addition, he instructed Ravanan that if he also yearned to see and associate with Raman, he should please and propitiate Him in every way, when He descended on the earth to mitigate the miseries of the people and thereby, install peace, prosperity, solace and well-being on earth.

Sage Agasthiyar, coming now to the crux of the story, briefs Raman of the antecedents which preceded Ravanan's wandering around the three worlds, prerogatively wielding power and fighting against the mighty people there. The exclusive reasons for which Ravanan, the king of demons, had so perseveringly resolved to be His adversary were to have contact with

Him and then to execute the abduction of Sita, with the convincing intention of getting killed by Him, because he presumed he was bereft of good will in pleasing Raman.

Sage Agasthiyar expounds outrightly that opulence, longevity, perpetual bliss and all types of prosperity will accumulate to the individuals, and also their desired objectives achieved, if they, with devoted deference are kindled with interest to listen to this story.

Chapter - IV

The Banishment of Sita to the Forests

Sage Agasthiyar reopens his narration of Ravanan's exploits. He recounts to Raman how, once, Ravanan had chanced upon sage Naradhar and supplicated him to acquaint him with details of the locus where the rnightiest people inhabited. Ravanan's strength was the bloated vanity of constantly remarking to the world that he was all-powerful. Hence, the challenge to conquer the mightiest people was the driving force behind the supplication made to sage Naradhar.

Ravanan's long held arrogance was not thwarted by the sage. He had briefed him of a beautiful continent called 'Swetadvipa', where only the earnest devotees and steadfast aspirants of Lord Vishnu, and more significantly, where the providentially fortunate people who had happened to encounter death at the compassionate hand of Lord Vishnu Himself dwelt there. Those noble people were filled with impavid fortitude and insuperable powers. Ravanan was all set to confront even the worst to bring that continent under his sphere of influence. No sooner said than he flew in his Pushpaka, but was dismayed when he could not land there due to the high powered and fulgurant glaring lights of the ground. But this did not deter him, therefore harbouring his air chariot on some other safe ground, he reached the continent on foot.

However, his pursuit was fraught with its own dangers. The chance of flaunting his power and valour was cruelly denied to him even as the women too of that land were extraordinarily gigantic and stalwart that they had caught hold of his neck and hoisted him up as if he were a miniscule rag doll. He did not manage to extricate himself from their clutches without strenuous resistance. Their hyperactivity appalled him and his bravado melted momentarily, They inquired about his whereabouts, his business on their land and then tossed him up into the air. Forthwith, Ravanan had nurtured the tenacious resolution to fight against Lord Vishnu only with the cherished desire that he too shall be made happy and mighty if he were annihilated by Lord Vishnu himself, and subsequently was propelled to enact the elaborate ruse of the abduction of Sita, though he respected her as Mother. Sage Agasthiyar concluding his narrative informs Raman that in truth, Ravanan has had foreknowledge about Him, Raman' being Lord Vishnu.

Sage Agasthiyar with an ebullient enthusiasm endorses Raman as the Omnipresent Lord who cognizes the past, the present and the future. All actions of the individuals do not go unnoticed by Him, as He is simply a witness, though He doesn't have any concern or attachment with them.

He commends Raman as the living demonstration of exemplary human actions defining the paradigm of the optimal kinds of righteousness to be emulated by individuals for realising the genuine goals in life. Conclusively, the sage remarks on Raman's, seeming attentiveness to his narrations in the garb of a human being as just a play act.

Sage Agasthiyar hosts a hearty toast to Lord Raman and thus pleases Him by his salutations, adulation and invocations, eventually bidding adieu to Him.

The royal couple Raman and Sita, spend their days happily in the kingdom with Raman's rule escalating to the towering pinnacle of prosperity and happiness in the kingdom, His sovereignty over the dominion extending over thousands of years. Raman is placed on the highest pedestal of honour and reverence in the exclusive sphere of all time greats, and for this reason Hanuman, Sugrivan and other monkeys pay frequent devoirs, as a token of inarticulate deference for Him. Once Kuberan, to express, his regards for Raman dispatches the air chariot, Pushpaka, with the generous notion that it might be instrumental in the service of mobilization till His stay in Ayodhya. Raman duly acknowledging Kuberan's generosity with thanks sends back the Pushpaka because it does not serve the intended purpose but promises to use it occasionally when the indispensability arises.

Prosperity is in full bloom in His region and the health, the wealth and the moral disposition of humanity flourishes extensively that the earth is likened to Paradise. Raman's magnanimity and philanthropy in materializing many public welfare schemes and services for the well-being of His citizens to which He devotes Himself in right earnest only exhibits His good governance. His realm pulsates with life because spiritual values, religious fervour and piety permeate the entire tenor of life of its citizens. The shadow of dying young does not frame their lives. The young do not live in the shadow of premature death and nobody ever sees the death of his son or anyone younger than he. Inorder to obtain first hand knowledge of the prevailing status quo of His subjects, Raman frequently tours the whole realm on the Pushpaka.

On one occasion, a Brahmin bearing a large emotional burden comes to Raman. He has brought his son who died a premature death. As his heart craves for a miracle, he pleads Lord Raman to resurrect him. Brahma, the creator, finding this to be an incredible occurrence as nobody has so far died prematurely, at juvenescence, reprimands Raman for this sort of unnatural calamity. To the Omniscient Raman what appears as the consequence, therefore, is really the cause of what appears as the cause and so, He reanimates the Brahmin boy. Raman's clairvoyance cognizes the penances of Sudra as the cause of the premature death of the Brahmin, Being propitiated by Sudra's sincerity, Raman slays him so as to resurrect the Brahmin boy thus granting Sudra a berth in paradise.

Vital in keeping spiritualism, the religious faith, and the torch of knowledge ablaze, Raman installs crores of icons of and temples to Shivan, a popular outward medium, at numerous places for channelling the different areas of human energies physical, mental and spiritual, for securing order and harmony at different levels of the individual and for the betterment and benefit of mankind at large.

Raman, by virtually placing His country's highest priorities above Himself and by dint of His conscientious and virtuous governance, establishes Himself as the most righteous and celebrated sovereign that ever existed on earth. His glorious rule expanded over a lengthy period of eleven thousand years, Unquestionably, Sita too, by virtue of the noble qualities of a chaste woman that she has been endowed with, is celebrated as the most dutiful queen who whole heartedly pleases and adores Raman in every way.

The divine couple, Lord Raman and Devi Sita, comfortably cocooned in the interior of His room, enjoying an ambience of perfect bliss and peace, duly, Sita hitches her parley to a post of supplication. She sums up the requests of all the Gods as a proposition which she puts forward to His good self that they should now arrange to ascend to their celestial abode.

Raman has serious reason to wonder why such a request is being made by the Gods and Sita herself. His wonder wanes as Sita voices the desire of the Gods who have unreservedly consigned themselves to serve Him in Elysium for His mission on earth has culminated and moreover, He has nothing left to accomplish on earth. She acquaints Him of the suggestion of the Gods, that if she would go to heaven first, then, He Raman would naturally follow her and they would have their anticipated desire to serve Him effectuated. Hence she meekly resigns to Raman's choice of doing what He fancies best.

Raman responds to the dignity with which Sita conducts herself by acknowledging her proposition and at the same moment articulating His owns reflections on similar lines, ascending to heaven as His mission on earth has been accomplished. Raman, now in league with Sita hatches a strategic scenario to send her to the forest on the pretext of a banishment for her. This decision is taken in the context of the public opinion against Him to which He is so uncomfortably vulnerable, that it is a gross faux pas on His part in keeping Sita with Him even after Ravanan had forcibly kidnapped her to Lanka and she had lived in separation from Raman alone at another house, which pulsates as a loss of honour for Him throughout the kingdom and which He is cognizant of.

As Sita has conceived, Raman instructs her to spend the days of her parturiency at sage Valmiki's hermitage and prophesies she would give birth to two male children. Raman espouses to bring her back after some years and also preindicates it would be obligatory for Him to stipulate her to validate herself as a chaste lady, being widely perceived as a loss of honour, when she shall then ingress into the earth, after which He shall proceed to His celestial abode.

Inorder to iron out His anxiety and more specifically to feel the pulse of the prevailing public temperature, Raman convenes a meeting and under a reliance on secrecy, questions Vijay, one of his sleuths to brief Him, candidly on what the public opinion is about Him. Vijay not considering it an unfair attempt in tarnishing Raman's noble image, incorporating his own view together with the widespread opinion of the citizens, modestly reports that the people of the city are talking about his improper and fallacious action of keeping Sita with Him since she had been abducted by Ravanan. He adds it is true there is willingness by the subjects to break with convention and set new standards by being a prototype of their ruler. And they assert that righteousness will no longer be preserved in their families if they shall also have to bring back their wives who would be abducted by others.

The revelation is not horribly different from what Raman had conjectured. Hence, He resolves methodically to re-examine the moving and revealing statements. The next day, Raman exhorts Lakshman to escort

Sita from the city of Ayodhya and leave her in the forest near Valmiki's hermitage. Lakshman is peremptorily constrained to carry out Raman's injunction though reluctantly, and is ordained by Raman not to remonstrate or dispute or even utter a single word on the decision.

Chapter - V

Sri Rama Githai

Lakshman working serenely and faithfully towards a supremely sublime consummation, professes his unswerving attachment with steadfast devotion to Raman just as bees are drawn naturally to lotuses. Lakshman entrusts himself totally to Raman's holy feet which efface worldly bondage by sundering the manacles and which are the only source of inspiration for sages and saints who seek them by their constant meditation.

Lakshman entreats Raman to bestow on him such transcendental spiritual knowledge as may help him to traverse, fluently, the endless sea of dense nescience. The exalted sovereign Raman, who is the principal celebrity of kings, the resort of the devotees, is delightedly appreciative of Lakshman's invocation and in a very ecstatic disposition commences the elucidation of the highest esoteric doctrines of the scriptures, the panacea for all maladies and worldly ignorance.

At the outset, Raman pronounces that pre-eminently an individual should with a chaste mind perform all his religious and household commitments, and his own nature-born duties in all the different phases of life, for example, Brahmacharya - strict continence or abstinence in the aspirant stage, Grihastha - the stage of a householder and Vanaprasth - the stage of a recluse or hermit, conforming to the injunctions ordained by the Vedas.

When the oscillations of the mind cease to exist and the individual is content with regard to performance of his religious obligations, he should exercise continence on his external and internal sense and sense organs by the austere practice of Yamam, Niyamam, Dyanam, Dharanam and Samadhi and should with a sincere quest of the precepts of the 'Sathguru', the spiritual teacher, who has already realized God, realize his own soul.

According to one's variegated needs, actions invariably and helplessly drive the individual towards the labyrinths of pleasures, consequently resulting in entanglement of interminable cycles of births. The individual is embrangled with the fetters of recurrent births and deaths which are the aftermath of his self-perpetuating deeds accrued from his previous births. So long as the individual persists in active, result-oriented actions there is bound to be an endless concatenation of births and deaths since his actions alone give birth to the seed of life, which actions in reality sprout soley from nescience. Actions of every kind cannot be eradicated but the acquisition of transcendental knowledge alone can dispel dark ignorance.

Ignorance and actions are complementary and reciprocal; because the former begets the latter and every action is imperatively and indigenously interconnected with others, the impact being nothing else but rebirths.

Those who have their wisdom carried away by nescience contend that precisely as knowledge is indispensable for accomplishment of actions, so too religious actions are also supplements for the acquisition of knowledge. Equitably the Vedas advocate relative action to be the modus operandi for achieving Salvation analogous to articles required for performing sacrifices (yagnas). In addition, they argue it is erroneous for the postulant to disregard actions enjoined as basically fundamental duties by the Vedas for exculpation which is to be eventually achieved. But evidently the contentions are ungrounded for the reason that actions and knowledge cannot synchronize, each with the other, and the former is the harvest of the intrinsic egocentric active pursuits which are completely eradicated and rebuffed by the latter, knowledge Undoubtedly the ultimate parameter to realise the chaste self i.e., the pure soul, is knowledge. Immediately upon the waves of thought of an individual called 'Vrttis", are being totally dissolved in the consciousness of his soul, he inherits sublime knowledge- All mental activity and egoistic notions, which are consistently subjected to complete obliteration by knowledge, give birth to every type of action. Knowledge has its existence, and actions too never cease to be; but there can never be a consonance between actions and knowledge. Therefore, the individual should nullify actions. This supreme knowledge is immaculate and lustrous by virtue of it being the causatum of the righteously purified self. This knowledge is realisation of one's soul or God. Hence an individual should fittingly and equitably realise his soul. And this can he made possible by a spiritual restraint, which is a sure means, on his senses and sense organs and its wide variety of activities.

So long as the aspirant has not surpassed or uprooted his egoism with its earthy, rooty characteristics, which is the chief provenance for all attachment to the body, it is mandatory that he performs righteous actions in adherence to the law of Virtue. Discrimination is the detector by which the aspirant thoroughly distinguishes and relinquishes every object as clearly unreal and focuses his mind on realizing the real, the Supreme Soul, Paramathman. Hence the necessary sense of discernment is the prerogative of the individual. Eventually being illumined by the inner light of his innate consciousness the aspirant settles on the plane where every kind of nescience evaporates, simultaneously, realizing the distinction between his soul and God is non existent.

Subtle ignorance cannot persevere any further nor can it have its sway or hold, if the striving soul expunges it by the application of analytical and judicious reasoning based on the scriptures, whereupon, he becomes one with God. As nescience, egoism, worldliness etc., have been already eradicated, they cannot gallop back into the life of the aspirant if he is enlightened by completely realising the pure absolute holistically thereupon. It follows that the aforesaid reasons clearly indicate that knowledge or Vidya is autonomously self-reliant, not depending on any kind of agency or phenomena for its acquirement.

Renunciation of every kind which is mandatory is clearly expounded in the Upanishads and avabadi branch of Brihadranyak Upanishad, for the acquisition of knowledge or Vidya which is independent of its acquisition. Those who champion the opposite view, in the contexts of Karma (action) and Gnana [Knowledge) no established or fitting illustration has been propounded by them because Karma or sacrifice is conditional depending on the help of others such as priests and other articles and accessories of worship for its performance, knowing them all as begotten of the actions of the body, mind and the senses, whereas Gnana or knowledge blossoms on its own, needing no external medium like components of worship, assistance etc.

Hence, the goals to be achieved in these two cases are productive of divergent results. Sagacious individuals should discern that they do not incur sin or impiety even when they relinquish Karma or actions, for the reason that only ignorant individuals anticipatingly believe they commit sins or are irreligious if they discard any religious 'Karma'. Sacrifice in the form of knowledge is superior to sacrifice performed with material things. The wise, when they have their minds established in self-realisation by knowledge, therefore, remorselessly and gradually, forsake all kinds of religious obligations and rites. For all actions without exception culminate in knowledge. With the acquisition of this superior knowledge there is no more subjection to delusion. The fire of knowledge reduces all action to ashes: there is no purifier like knowledge.

So an aspirant under the tutelage of a divine preceptor who patronizes and educates, should comprehend the heart of or the connotation of the assertion of the vedas such as "Tattwamasi" which signifies - 'I am he', the Supreme God.

The subservient aspirant is now blissful and content, his mind has taken roots in tranquillity similar to mountain Sumeru; he recognised the unitary nature of his soul and God being synonymous with a subtle difference that God is the Almighty Soul and the aspirant with a super imposition of limitations is only a limited individual soul. If it is repudiated accordingly that the differential attributes or capacities which are finite in the individual but infinite and omnipotent in God, then it should be proved inferentially that both of them - the individual and God have the same substratum, which is, pure consciousness. First the word meaning of the sentence which is an oxymoron 'He is Thou' or 'I am it' should be apprehended to accomplish this. Then rescind the undesirable adjectives in 'He' and 'Thou' to ferret out the true and enduring import in them and bring the subject 'He' and the complement 'Thou' and the eternal predicate 'is' for cognizing the authentic symbol of unity of 'he is thou' or 'thou art he'. When the significance of an integral indivisibility innate in 'He is Thou' is cognized with the analytical methods of what should be relinquished and what should be retained, then "He" and "Thou" will be wholly and scrupulously indistinguishable.

The body of an individual being is only a gross composition known as the 'Sthula Sarira'. Therefore it lives, evolves, deteriorates and is renewed perpetually. The body that entertains pleasure, prosperity, poverty, disease imperatively binding him with pain and misery, joy and adversity, are only the sequels of his deeds of previous births. The natural and exteriorized elements such as earth, water, fire, air, ether, which are known as the five gross phenomena or otherwise called 'Panchatattwa' or five natural elements go to constitute the body. The subtle body called 'Sukshma Sarira' an amalgam of thoughts, senses and will with the determinative faculty is another infusion in the soul of the Individual. In other words, the Indriyas, Mind, Buddhi and Ahamkara together with Prana form an amalgam which is called the 'Sukshma Sarira' made up of such fine stuff that they endure for long. long eons. The life elements of the 'Five Pranas', the five external and internal senses and with five undeveloped natural elements or essence of air, earth, fire and water called 'Apanchikrth Mahabut' together with the subtle body reside in the material or gross body with feeling and experience of all sorts of happiness and misery or pain and pleasure. The soul has yet another causal body called 'Karana Sarira', the prime agent or substratum of the two bodies, which has its existence mainly on God's Illusion called

'Anirbachaniya superimposed upon it that is neither real nor unreal. The infinite and perpetual soul, which has no structure or anatomy, is framed by these three bodies - the Sthula Sarira or gross body, the Sukshma Sarira or subtle body and the Karana Sarira or the casual body and is conjectured to be synthesized with them Inorder to cognise the soul, the individual should with meticulous competence and prurience discriminate these bodily dissimulations as the intrinsic soul is distinct from these kaleidoscopic bodies analogous to a pure crystal which is distinct when juxtaposed with assorted colours. In a similar fashion the soul is reflected in the five chambers called 'Pancha Kosha', is ascertained to feign their traits and temperaments, but in reality, the soul is entirely an exclusive entity. free from them. The soul apparently becomes animated in and through the body when the waves of thought called 'Vrittis' of mind rise or move in consonance with the organs, Pranas or life elements in the three stages of wakefulness, dreaming and sound sleep. It is unwise to unduly attribute the waves of thought to the pure absolute spirit called Absolute soul, Siva, as infact they are only fabrications of illusion. As long as the vibrant ebb and flow of the waves of thought persist in the mind which is encased in this destructible fleshy frame constituted with apparently diverse elements, so long will life fraught with recurrent cycles of Births and Deaths prevail.

It is obligatory that a person should by relinquishing all worldly objects and vitiating decrees, should discover his own soul and thereby saturate his mind in its sweet lusciousness corresponding to one who extracts the juice of coconut and discards the external futile cover.

Authentically the soul is the substantial cause of adversity and anguish in an individual, though transcendental knowledge is esoteric bliss eternal to him. Yet there should be no reason for the soul to be miserable or ignorant as it is unborn, immortal, indestructible, everlasting, attributeless, blemishless chaste and perennially blissful, self illumined, omniscient, omnipresent and non pareil. The individual by his delusion misapprehends worldliness to be reality, similar to a person who by misconstruing one thing for another, as the rope is recognised in the case of rope-snake as snake, and, in a similar vein assumes his corporeal body as intrinsic, collaterally, people blinded by nescience misconceive God for the world, because for them worldliness is ascribed to God.

Egotism is born of nescience and misconception upon Brahman. This immaculate Supreme Reality eclipses all Individual souls, and has no illusion and mutation. But for the traits of desire, jealously, greed, happiness and misery, which are the ground work of an individual's unhappiness, dissatisfaction and perplexity. which positively generate endless births and deaths, otherwise, the inherent nature of the individual is peace, bliss and divinity making him always peaceful, blissful and divine. The individual himself, when in the deep sleep state, where mind is devoid of mental impulses and vibrations, is constantly realising his blissful and divine soul.

The spirit or Jiva of an individual is sheer light, reflected on mind or intellect attributable to the kaleidoscopic illusionary sources, and in truth, the way of reflections of his soul or Brahman transcends the sphere of intellect or the determinative propensity of mind When all ignorance evaporates, the ostensible Jiva is, in as much, realized to be none other than the reflection of the eternal conscious spirit and the entity and Jiva too become non-existent. His soul stands as a mere witness of all his activities. Though the soul is the bestower of life, it stands as the mere witness of all his activities, is so limited in the intellect or mind. This animated soul confounds itself with the material body and the material body mistaken for the soul because they apparently commingle with mind akin to heated iron which looks like fire and similar to fire which looks like a round iron-ball Therefore, what obviously appears to be the reality is solely ignorance by which the spirit is reflected on matter and matter on the spirit.

The awakening, as soon as possible, from the sleep of ignorance and taking shelter under the aegis of one's divine teacher, the 'Sathguru', the quality of discrimination can be acquired to cognize the distinction between the soul and the matter, and then, to be capable of repudiating all gross material which are conceived to be real or spiritual.

Raman further enunciates that He is the infinite reality who is self illuminated, so He is unborn, having no beginning or end, absolute, resplendent, ever, extravagantly chaste and divine, luminous, superlative, constant, blissful, liberated, unfathomable, beyond the realm of thought and imagination, imperceivable, imperceptible, boundless without any limitation and Supreme. But, yet, He pronounces emphatically that He is constantly envisaged by savants in their sanctified hearts by virtue of their knowledge of the ultimate purport as on which they profoundly meditate. Just as medicines alleviate a malady, so too all classifications and attachments of nescience shall be absolutely expunged by such lofty visionary reflections acquired by spiritual knowledge. If a discerning aspirant chastens his mind, contemplates incommunicado in a secluded and tranquil locus gaining ascendancy over deceiving activities, emotional fluctuations and impulses of mind and sense organs by which he is held hostage, he can by his inner vision envision the soul abiding in his self. Again, if he envisages

God outside of himself and inside himself and in the entire Universe, thereupon, he shall be transformed into an ever perfect, conscious, immaculate, self-contended and ever blissful person. Through spiritual practices, he can envisage that one infinite God, who, infact, is the only cause of all the mundane objects and phenomena in the interior of his self too. For in his mind, the whole Universe manifests as a mirage, and no other existence appears to him beyond the existence of one God.

The spiritual aspirant before immersing himself into the faraway goal 'Samadhi',-the great peaceful stage of an outstanding experience of identified communion with, and motionless abiding in the untroubled serenity of the pure blissful self-he should astutely cognize that the world is a nonentity, which is an indispensable prerequisite, and it is but the word 'OM' constituting the three letters A.U.M. The letter 'A' indicates the Pursuha or the gross shroud on the soul; 'U' designates the subtle body incorporating the soul and 'M' signifies the causal body encompassing the soul. These operations of cognizance is only the initial step, a prelude, and not the ultimate realization. Therefore savants engage in this so long as Samadhi is not accomplished, but never after Samadhi has been attained. Hence the first step of the spiritual aspirant is to merge his gross body called 'Bishva' into the subtle frame 'Taizas' which should also be synthesized into the third body, the causal body, 'Prajna'. This ongoing process of 'A' into 'U' and 'U' into 'M' and finally the compound word 'OAM' the peerless vibration of the Universe, should be assimilated into the soul the ultimate source, the Universal all, the fundamental cause of all the causes and energies. Thus the call of Truth will awaken the aspirant to the immutable truth of his oneness with Brahman and he realizes that he himself is nothing but Supreme Soul Brahman. Eventually he finds he is unfettered, liberated from all terrestrial bondage and attachments, participating at once in the Light, Power and Bliss of transcendental existence and is the sacred sanctuary of eternal divine knowledge. Thus, abiding in this sublime conception, he is self- content and beatified. Thereafter, losing all connections with this transient, destructible, temporal world he is blissful, composed, free and established on the plane of conscious existence of Infinite peace as the waveless and tranquil boundless ocean. The aspirant by harnessing all the impulses of his sense organs, he is capable of rooting out all his vicious mental reflections with mastery over his six fold traits such as wrath, lust, covetousness, bondage, egotism and jealousy, and in fine, recognizes himself to be one with Raman, that is God.

Temporal materialistic bindings will no longer have their pertinacious sway over the savant who is absorbed in his soul incessantly. Also, he will have saturated his self with Raman's self, if, the impetus of his egoistic vagaries is duly arrested, and he spends his life living artlessly and ingenuously, maintaining life on the meager sustenance's that he procures, providentially.

The individual should abnegate the fruition of vedic rituals that instigates the path of actions and take to the path of only meditation upon his soul, as all other steps are hardly meritorious, which is part and parcel of the Universal soul, while coming to terms with the secular life fraught with misery from the beginning to the end. In the way that milk in milk, space in space and wind in wind are virtually identical, in the same way, there is no distinction between the drop of water of the ocean and the other mass of water of the same ocean. Likewise the individual, when he becomes accustomed to cognize and envision everything (God, Universe, material objects etc.) to be the same as his soul, it follows naturally that he perceives no distinction between his soul and mind too. If at the consummation of his inner evolution the sage adjudicates the world to be deceptive as the two moons to be seen in the sky by defective vision, then he will also be percipient of the connotation of what all these common vedic rituals and karma are, the pursuit of them having the inherent danger, enmeshing the doer in a secular frame work for some reason or other. It is exhorted that the aspirant should devotedly persist in his spiritual practices and worship with love and faith incessantly, so long as he does not conceive the whole world to be nothing but Raman's own form of God, such a sincere devotee, it is espoused, shall forever espy Raman residing in his heart.

Raman, addressing His dear brother Lakshman makes him discern the concentrated essence of all the Vedas which He has replenished him with, and which He Himself has fully realized to be holistically authentic and beneficial. An aspirant who has complete access to them and follows them to the core shall be instantly purged of his accumulated gross sins. Raman solicits Lakshman to abnegate the world which is but illusory. Further, Raman exhorts Lakshman to nullify with sturdy determination. If' any such worldly vision ever crops up in him, and he should fill his heart exhaustively with his immanent presence to make himself eternal, beatific and absolutely free from all sorts of causes, convictions and angst.

Raman proclaims that an aspirant who cherishes a lofty aspiration in the heart extensive enough for the realization of Him, denying all narrow limits, who concentrates his mind one pointedly, incessantly, on His formless Supreme Entity or may even eventuate sometime to worship His incarnated and universal form, He stipulates that such a person is deemed pure and venerable, and even the dust of his feet illumines and glorifies the three worlds analogous to the rays of the sun.

Raman vouchsafes to Lakshman that He Has imparted to him the prevailing purport of the Divine knowledge, more secret than secrecy itself, enshrined in the scriptures. He also expounds that the scriptures are His seasoned and treasured songs of the spiritual facets of the Vedas. Raman asserts that an individual shall, unequivocally, be amalgamated into Him if the individual discerningly assimilates this inspirational scriptural philosophy, with the assistance of his preceptor and adheres to them with devout faith, steadfastness and sincerity.

Chapter - VI

Killing of Lavanan by Sathrughnan and Birth of Lava and Kusha

Sri Raman is visited by the cardinal sage Chyavanan who is accompanied by a retinue of sages. The cause being to advice Raman on the harassment and torture of the repulsive and atrocious demon Lavanan, living on the banks of the Yamuna, of whom they are in terrible fear and in danger of their lives. He champions the cause of the countless sages for whom he is the head, seeking support and succour from Lord Raman to tide over the fear and anxiety gripping their lives, generated by the demon Lavanan.

In the first place, Raman offers them a warm reception and hospitality, and then, as He proclaims to be the loyal servant of devoted Brahmins, He espouses to render all assistance to rescue them from their awful plight.

At the outset, Chyavanan recounts the story of a pious demon named Madhu dating back to the Sathya yuga. At that time, Shivan who was highly satiated with Madhu's qualitative and quantitative pietistic penances and prayerful services had favoured him with the three-piked trident which could incinerate any animated body when wielded. He also says he had heard in the past, that Ravanan's younger sister Kumbhanasa was His wife. Contrary to Madhu's pious nature, the demoniac Lavanan was born to Him. And now, because of Lavanan's intolerable persecution and killings of many sages, they have sought His refuge. Raman assessing the facts, assures the sages He would do away with the demon outright and also requests them all meanwhile to return to their dwellings safely.

Raman summons his brothers and deliberates on the predisposition of the one among them who would volunteer to go for the demon outright and kill him in the bargain. Bharathan meekly requests Raman that he may be permitted to obliterate Lavanan immediately Sathrughnan intervenes soliciting Raman to empower him in accomplishing this feat as both, Bharathan and Lakshman have heretofore, accomplished onerous duties, professing their affinity and affiliation to Him Raman, each according to his station. Bharathan had discharged the arduous responsibility of living in Nandhigram and Lakshman too had accompanied divine Raman into the forests and has achieved success in battles there, and now it is his task of annihilating Lavanan.

Raman is pleased with Sathrughnan's volitional and altruistic spirit. Initially, Raman states His mind to crown Sathrughnan head of the state of Mathura. He authorises him to hasten to Mathura instantly. At the behest of Raman, Lakshman has dexterously arranged the necessary paraphernalia for the coronation of Sathrughnan.

Raman, before Sathrughnan departs for Mathura, negotiates with him the strategic conspiracy for ensnaring Lavanan into death's trap. He commands Sathrughnan to lie in ambush at the gates of the city of Mathura in the early hours of the morning when Lavanan would venture into the forests to hunt for his food. Further, He instructs him to be very vigilant and take advantage of killing Lavanan on his return because, when he goes out at such wee hours he abandons his precious trident which he worships at home, Further Raman vows to despatch thirty thousand soldiers and one thousand elephants and horses soon after his departure Furthermore, Raman counsels him to take the throne after killing Lavanan and dwell there. Thereafter, Sathrughnan takes leave with Raman's benedictions, and He bids him adieu.

Thus, Sathrughnan is denied all difficulty in annihilating Lavanan. After his effortless victory, he takes over the reins of the kingdom and governs Mathura as he has been counselled by Raman. He captures the hearts of the citizens by his good governance and the country thrives prosperously under his benevolent rule.

Now focusing attention on Sita who has been allegedly banished by Raman, there in the hermitage of sage Valmiki, cheerful tidings fills the air, Sita has begotten male twins. The sage christens the elder Kushan and the younger Lava. He undertakes the responsibility of performing their investiture ceremony and also the adornment of the sacred, thread, The fraternal twins are handsome, princely and precociously talented and intelligent that the sage educates them in the vedic principles and initiates them into the various skills and techniques of archery and warfare. Also, he inclucates them with the 'Ramayanam' which he had intricately designed in epic form conforming faithfully and accurately to the eternal facts God

Shivan had already enunciated to Goddess Parvathi.

These lads, Lava and Kusha, live with Valmiki in his hermitage. There in the precipate of the hermitage, spending their time by lingering on and savouring every verse, these silver tongued boys sing very sweetly the mellifluous hymns from the excerpts of the 'Ramayanam', thus, becoming acquainted with the chronicle. Sages and saints from far and near, panegyrize the acumen of the boys, their brilliance and decorum too, and acclaim that such exalted songs and heavenly vocabulary were unheard of on earth so far.

It is imperative for the highly illustrious and noble Raman who decides to perform Ashwamedha yagna to substitute for His consort Sita, living in exile, a statue of her made of gold as the yagna would be incomplete without the married wife by his side Celebrated sages, scholarly Brahmins, saints savants, learned people invited by Raman attend the ceremony, after which Raman proffers huge quantities of gold to them as Dakshina. Valmiki, honoured as the greatest sage is also invited. He attends the ceremony with Lava and Kusha.

The ambience is one of religious piety and fervour, conducive to the lads who thirst for an illumination on spiritualism from their preceptor Valmiki who is absorbed in serenity. Their query is a yearning to know how the individual soul forms a nexus with worldly activities. Kusha desires also to know how the clutches of bondage can be cut asunder to attain salvation. They supplicate the omniscient sage to perceptibly, yet briefly, impart knowledge on these elevated moot points.

The sage highly appreciative of their Inquiry into such transcendental mysteries assures to enlighten them briefly on what bondage and purification are, and also the established procedure for a comprehensive understanding of realising one's soul.

The sage expounds the truth that the soul has no material or immaterial form; it is formless. But when the body encases the soul and it is prevalent in the body, the domineering Mega Ego of the individual is the principal operator like the plenipotentiary of a ruler. Apparently, it is misunderstood that the soul acts in and through the body because it seems heterogeneously fused with its ego. Therefore, truly, the inflated ego is the actor together with the intellect and mind in which it has its tentacles like desires, aspirations, sensation, thoughts etc., rooted, that is appended to familial classifications and secular affairs, which is the doer of all sorts of countless actions and deeds, accordingly. The interplay of such precogitation, attachments and sentiments in the mind of the individual are called 'Sanghalpam' and they are the cause for the activities coloured either by pleasure or pain, prosperity or adversity together with a mixed conglomeration of worldliness. These Sanghalpam or thought patterns are classified as 'Sathwik (quiscent) Rajasic (Materialistic) and Thamasik (Predatory). The thamsik Sanghalpam or predatory thoughts give birth to lower forms of creatures like insects, beasts and other animals. Mediocre individuals who are bom into the life of householder are maneuvered into the labyrinths of worldliness by Rajasic sanghalpam or material thoughts. Noble individuals are guided through life's journey by the Sathwik Sanghalpam or quiescent thoughts. By detaching mind from all such thoughts, the aspirant ever satisfied, content and blissful should maintain an imperturbed mind and saturate it with his soul's consciousness. Though the aspirant may assiduously persevere in his penances for long years, he can never attain emancipation and eternal peace unless he brings all his senses under stringent subordination and extirpate his desires and impulses. The highest exigent endeavour for an individual to attain salvation is to rein in his surging' unbroken exterior and innermost thoughts and to curtail activities of mind called 'Sanghalpam' which translates itself into 'I shall do this, I shall do that', 'I can do everything' and the like.

Concluding his homily, sage Valmiki finally instructs Kusha to he warned of desire, the obscure perpetrator which harasses and animatedly propels an individual to act; desire, the nucleus of actions as well as thoughts should he destroyed permanently. These endless actions being yoked to the thoughts and desires, which by weilding strong weapons; such as pertinacity, dogged perseverance and constant application should be erased from the mind Further, he should cherish and nurture equanimity of mind in the course of his life but without taking recourse to action with interested motives he should perform his nature-born duties and deeds according to the commands of God and only for His sake. Thus he shall disentangle himself from all actions and desires, prosperity, jealousy, wrath, lust greed etc., and accordingly he should saturate his mind into the pure consciousness of his soul. In fine, the sage exhorts him to relinquish all delusive convolutions with the acquisition of Supreme Knowledge, inorder to attain the loftiest ecstasy of transcendence, bliss and infinitude.

Chapter - VII

Raman Retains Lava and Kusha

Sage Valmiki's homily serves as the torch of knowledge and spiritualism to realize exalted truths and dispel dark ignorance and vain misconceptions that has clogged Kusha's mind. From then on, Kusha goes about, outwardly, performing his day-to-day activities and duties dispassionately.

The sage counsels the lads to go into the City of Ayodhya for propagating the highest ideals of spirituality and philosophy by singing hymns of the Ramayanam. He also advises them to go and sing to the executive head of the state, Lord Raman, if He so wishes to hear them sing, but dissuades them against receiving or accepting any kind of reward or prize.

Reports of the melodious recitals of the extracts from the Ramayanam by the lads entirely saturated with the sequels of Lord Raman's own life are brought to the knowledge of Sri Raman Himself. He also learns that sages, saints and the denizens of the kingdom listen to the recitals with a spell bound rhapsody everywhere and in the city of Ayodhya too. Raman, who is also fascinated sends for the boys so that they may sing during the intervals, as recreation. between the sacrificial rites when a mixed congregation of feudal chiefs, philosopher's politicians and citizens too present there are fortunate to hear Everyone who is enthralled by their remarkably euphonic strains are also stupefied at the conspicuously explicit resemblance of the boys to Sri Raman. At the end of the rendition, Raman exhorts Bharathan to guerdon them with thirty thousand gold coins, which they decline to accept, they leave the place.

After their departure, the fact that they are the sons of Sita, widely disseminates The impact propels Raman to beckon Sathrughnan, Hanuman, Vibhishanan, Anghadan, Bharathan and Lakshman to go into the forests and bring Sita back to Ayodhya from the oasis of sage Valmiki's hermitage. He adds that on her return she should by taking an oath in the presence of all the citizens attest to her chastity proclaiming to the whole world her purity and fidelity.

Thereupon they deliver Raman's exhortation to Sage Valmiki at his cottage. The sage asserts that as Sri Raman is her only lord, She, Sita, is virtuously obligated to accede to His predetermined decree, and assures them that Sita would on the following day take the oath in the presence of all as ordained by Raman.

Consequently on the promised day, the multitudinous crowds which congregate for witnessing the oath taking ceremony comprises officers of all ranks and citizens from all walks of life. When sage Valmiki and Sita Devi arrive in the modus as the occasion demands, the multitudes, enthusiastically applauding and praising Sita and the sage, welcome and greet them with due respects.

The sage addressing Raman, announces loudly that since the day He, Raman had abandoned Sita, she had been residing in his cottage in the forest. Initially the sage vows that he, being born as the tenth son of Prajapathi Pracheta, as such, can never utter a lie or act unrighteously. He again declares under oath that he is holistically knowledgeable that Sita is a chaste lady ever faithful to Sri Raman, and upholds the fact that Lava and Kusha are His own twins. He categorically asserts that by this, if, he has unscrupulously prevaricated now, he would unmistakably lose all his sanctity, veneration and piety accumulated over the years by his austere penances.

Raman acknowledges and endorses the statements made by the sage as true and openly apologizes for having deserted Sita whose fidelity to Him, He consciously and scrupulously knows, even when she had entered into the blazing fire to establish her spotless Immaculacy, when He had brought her from Ravanan's Asoka garden in Lanka, is unquestionable and beyond doubt. Moreover He supplicates to be forgiven as the force of circumstances had driven Him to deport Sita for so many years, because the people of His kingdom had sullied His reputation for keeping her with Him. He also ascertains that He is cognizant of the truth that Lava and Kusha are His own twins. So saying He pledges His eternal Love to abide perennially in Sita. The oath taking ordeal is occasioned by the need for the august presence of the Gods Shivan, Brahman, Indhran and others amongst the huge bodied monkeys and the populace at large.

Sita, who is all set to take the oath, exercising a modest grace vocalizes addressing the Goddess Earth; supplicates the respected Mother Earth very honestly and deferentially to grant her a niche in her bosom if she is faithful to none other than Sri Raman. And behold, forthwith much to the amazement of all, a glorious throne of gold appears from out of the depths of the earth and Mother Earth taking Sita very solicitously places her on the divine throne and retreats disappearing miraculously. Flowers rain from the heavens, sweet words and glad cheers hailing Sita are echoed from every direction of the earth and the heavens. This spectacular marvel throws everyone into a state of electrifying astonishment and incredulity that some helplessly look at Raman with awe, some open-mouthed with their sight glued to the spectacle are stupefied while others remain absorbed in a quiet surprise. This marvel lasts only for an Infinitesimal moment to the great wonder of the spectators. Like a mediocre human being, Raman, apparently, is labouring under overpowering sentiments of desolation and hopelessness weeping like an ordinary householder at the cryptic separation of Sita, despite His percipience of the sequels that would follow, and is consoled by the sages and the prudent Brahmins. Raman however culminates His ritual sacrifice in due time distributing jewels, gold and huge sums of moneys to scholarly Brahmins and priests. He brings His sons under His own aegis and from then on lives as a saintly yogi, a recluse.

Mother Kausalya pours out her maternal sentiments about Raman in a garland of praise hailing Raman as supreme God, absolute being, the Paramathman, the immanent entity in every being. She eulogizes Raman as the lord of the universe though He by His play is born as her son now. She acknowledges that it is her robust faith and earnest prayers to Him, conjoined with her past pious deeds, holy penances that she had subjected herself to in her previous births, as formerly indicated by Raman Himself, have materialized in His being born as her son. She yearns for the right knowledge to know and see things in their correct perspective. As she is grappling with the harsh reality of life, senectitude, she ventilates her feelings and concern about her last stage of this human life and consequently supplicates Raman to expound the ways by which one can attain salvation.

Forthright, Raman significantly spells out Bhakthi yoga, Jnana Yoga and Karma yoga as the three paths to the supreme state, salvation. He delineates that to acquire the highest esoteric knowledge the only integral qualifications are renunciation and cultivation of love with single minded devotion to God, by disinterested actions which lead to a pure spiritual life with full contentment and through which liberation is achieved. Further, He classifies Bhakthi yoga as of three kinds - Thamas, Rajas and Sathwik and augments a fourth one, namely, Para Bhakthi the supreme love of God, as superior to the aforesaid three types. The superiority of the mode of Para Bhakthi consists in the superiority of the object of that love that is, God.

Thamasic or low or scanty Bhakthi in a worldly wise devotee is that he cherishes a distinction between himself and other living creatures and without a trace of true inner devotion, apparently pleases God demanding many things of Him in return for a petty sacrifice or a meager offering, bargaining with Him as a barter even at the cost of the interests and the happiness of his fellow beings. Again a worldly wise devotee who engages in external worship without true inner devotion in eagerness for attainment of wealth, prosperity, honour and fame pleases God, but is free from malice towards his fellow beings is Rajasic. The devotee believing it to be his foremost obligation to worship god as he is the ultimate source of all fortunes, virtues and happiness is Sathwik, the highest devotion of the three.

The devotee who with fervent inner devotion based on constant immaculate love and extreme affection as that of a servant to his master, or of a lover to his lady love and has his purified mind yoked to Him similar to a river which only aims at uniting with the ocean, is the most superior to the aforementioned three, for he has nothing else to do than to love Him alone. It is by love alone that the devotee can know Him. It makes it easy for attaining divine communion which is the actual blessed experience of the soul in God fellowship. As his mind is to absorbed in Him all worldly ties and superficialities vanish of themselves. No more of worldly accumulation of secular objects, fame, name etc., except, the thirst, the yearning and the search of Him alone. Hence he is content and blissful with the goal of saturation with him, before Him. The goal of Bhakthi yoga is to know, perceive and gain the Lord in His real form and nature.

To such a true-blue devotee, Raman promises in unequivocal terms, either unification with His universal consciousness or an honoured place to live by His side or be blessed with His own illusive form, or be graced with a life in Raman's own illusive abode or be bestowed with superpowers to become omnipresent, omniscient and omnipotent or abide in His perennial presence as His most beloved devotee.

An aspirant can gradually blossom into a corresponding stout, resolute devotee by initially cherising such a profound and pious aspiration augmented with unalterable, untarnished love, which can be acquired by understanding that the sense of doership should be denied with regard to all activities of mind, the sense and the body, renouncing attachment and the desire for the fruit of all activities. With enlightened faith he should cultivate unquestioning faith in the all-pervading presence of Raman and cherish the noblest conception of His divine personality. He must be always free from malice towards all creatures, nurture universal love for all, steer clear of egoism, be quiet and calm in the midst of pains and pleasure, be full of the noble tendency of forgiveness considering all being as equal because the soul is nothing but God himself in all beings. He should eliminate all hypocrisy and dishonesty. He should cultivate courage, charity, dispassion, endurance, fortitude, humility, piety, scriptural study, self discipline Truth, non-violence and unselfishness. He should evolve into a perfect devotee by listening to the Lord's deeds, chanting His holy names, repeatedly dwelling upon His leelas in the mind, performing service to the feet of God, friendship with Him and finally total surrender of Self to Him. To this must be adjoined the conceptions of perfect goodness and beauty, perfect love and mercy, perfect sympathy and benevolence, perfect justice and righteousness. All these attributes should be acquired by virtue of his practices in the style of a true yogi. The unalloyed mind of the yogi is devoid of earthy materialism and bondage analogous to the scent which leaving its temporary sources of flowers suffuses with its true form of the olfactory sense organ. So long as an spirant fails to realise that Raman transcends the entire universe, that He is all pervasive, is the Self of all individual selves and dwells within the heart of everybody and every object, He takes to the worship of idols due to the malady of nescience, dragging the ideal, supreme reality by the image worship down to the level of the image itself. This kind of worship is a primary necessity for a novice till he is able to transcend the preparatory state of mind regarding worship and not for a mellowed devotee who cognizes-Raman everywhere and in everything for an idol would be superfluous to dissolve his mind in the Universal Conscious, Existence, Knowledge and Bliss.

Raman Placates mother Kausalya's languishing mind by prescribing either Bhakthi yoga or Jnana yoga to disentangle herself from the trammels of bondage and worldliness and her pure maternal love for Him as her son too, as she will tread the highway to attaining salvation and remain ever blissful with the understanding that she envisions Raman immanent everywhere,

Consequently, cocooned by Sri Raman's mellifluous, honeyed verbiage, Queen Kausalya by constant meditation refocuses and anchors her mind and heart in Raman and His philosophical homily finding it beneficial to transcend all the three stages of life for attaining the highest goal. Eventually the queen mothers Kausalya, Kaikeyi and Sumithrai ascend to heaven after their death and unite with their husband king Dasarathar there.

Chapter - VIII

LakshmanTakes Samadhi

Illustrious Bharathan's remarkable abilities, expertise and skill in warfare have been also commissioned and corroborated by his conquering three crores of Gandharvas at Yuddhajit's habitation. Also he has founded two cities, Puskar and Taxila, after which he returns to Ayodhya to acknowledge Raman's magnanimity in gifting the conquered territories to his two sons. Raman issues a decree to Lakshman to sojourn to the western part of India to defeat the despot king there and hand over the conquered territories to his sons, Angad and Chitraketu.

In compliance with Raman's decree, Lakshman vanquishes all the Bhills, constitutes two kingdoms for Angad and Chitraketu and returns to Ayodhya.

Masquerading as a sage, the God of Death, Yaman, reaches Ayodhya in good time and prays for an audience with Raman who responds by hosting a warm reception with the merited homage due to him. The sage, at Raman's request states he has come to communicate to Him very confidential tidings under the seal of secrecy and collects an oath from Raman that He, Raman, would kill any person who dares to eavesdrop on their clandestine tête-à-tête or even espy them dialoguing together. Conceding to the sage's demand, Raman admonishes Lakshman to stand without and on no account he should permit anyone within the room. Thereafter, the sage, acting as the mouthpiece of Brahman, acquaints Raman with the message from Brahman who has intimated Him of the stipulated time frame of His stay on earth drawing to a close and to ascend to heaven where the celestials and gods are avidly desiring and anticipating His arrival there.

Moreover the sage conveys Brahman's resume, acknowledging himself as the master of creation and his eldest son, for he had come into being when Raman had created the wide Universe with His illusion, when He had first created Him and then Seshang, the God of Serpents named

Anandtha who abides since the time of the creation of both animate and inanimate objects in the ocean. He is reminiscent of Raman designing the earth from the flesh and bones of two mighty giants, Madhu and Kaitabh, whom He had slain. He is evocative of the appellation Prajapathi meaning Brahman given by Raman and also investment of the responsibility of creation with him authorized by Raman. He euloglzes Raman for the sustained protection of all His creation from every kind of ruin and turpitude whenever superincumbent. Taking pride in Raman's tour de force of annihilating the implacable demons including Ravanan, Brahman is mindful of his structured time frame of eleven thousand years earmarked for His residence on the earth, which is expiring now. Hence Brahman desires to know whether Raman wishes to negotiate a compromise of either extending His stay on earth or repairing to His abode. Raman articulates that the consummation of His incarnation is near at hand as He has accomplished His mission on earth. And as Raman is desirous of visualising Brahman and all the other Gods, in good time, He articulates His wish of returning to Paradise, which the sage should convey to Brahman.

Incidentally, when Raman, and Yaman, the God of Death, are preoccupied in the clandestine tête-à-tête, sage Durvasa arrives at Raman's door and petitions Lakshman for an interview with Raman. Lakshman mindful of Raman's earlier espousal reluctantly constrains sage Durvasa from meeting Raman for the reason He is intently pursuing some discreet assignment and so he himself volunteers to convey his message to Raman. Instantly Durvasa seethingly blurts out a crude profanity that he would incinerate all of them and even their offsprings to ashes if he does not instantly, communicate the news of his arrival to Raman. Lakshman's altruism surfaces as he resolves to pay the high price of sacrificing His own life, lest Sage Durvasa's categorical assertion threatening to annihilate them all and their progeny materializes and so instantly hastens to Raman and conveys the arrival of sage Durvasa waiting at His doorstep to have an audience with Him.

Raman dismissing the God of Death, interviews Durvasa who supplicates Him to break His fast, which He has been observing for twelve long years, by offering pure siddha food. Raman propitiates the sage by proffering the entreated food stuffs and bids him adieu; but, concurrently, is profoundly afflicted by the promise of having to kill Lakshman which He has to uphold. It does not behove Him to spell out a word about it to Lakshman. Lakshman begs Raman not to renege on His deal but to keep His promise than let him live otherwise, it shall be a dereliction of duty as Head of the State, defaulting His righteousness resulting in obliteration of the whole Universe itself. Again, he pleads with Raman to carry out His promise which if He fails to fulfill, shall make Him disinherit His sanctity and piety. Raman in consultation with His ministers, citizens and His preceptor Vashisthar who all counsel Him to implement His promise, exhorts Lakshman to leave Ayodhya and go wherever he pleases as He conceives banishment tantamount to death punishment. Very dejectedly Lakshman leaves Ayodhya and wends his way to the banks of the river Ganges where he gets into the state of Samadhi, dismantling his fleshy coil. Whereas, no one is aware of the truth that Lakshman had been taken to paradise by Raman Himself.

Chapter - IX

Raman's Departure to Heaven

The moment of sublime perfection has arrived when Raman entrusting the Kingdom of Ayodhya to Bharathan announces His desire to depart to heaven. On the other hand, Bharathan swoons when he hears that Raman alone is to ascend to heaven without him. When Bharathan has recovered from the syncope, he begs Raman to bounteously consign the kingdom to Lava and Kusha, and categorically declares that he cannot abide even for a moment in His absence on this earth, for to him Ayodhya without Raman is a reminder of a wilderness. Besides Bharathan, there is a dramatic escalation of involvement of the citizens too of Ayodhya, who eloquently articulate to follow Raman to heaven as they never want to leave Him.Emissaries are delegated to Sathrughnan who arrives in Ayodhya in no time. He dissipates all the worldly ties by relinquishing his kingdom and entrusting the same to his sons. He too is prepared to enter the door to effulgent glory. Raman therefore sanctions entry to paradise to all the denizens as well as His brothers along with Him.

The promising day of the great passage to the house of God from Ayodhya, the earthly paradise, is determined. All the monkeys demons, bears led by Vibhishanan, Sugrivan and Angadhan arrive in Ayodhya and receive Raman's consent for following Him. Rut Raman promulgates an edict to Vibhishanan and Angadhan to abide on earth for still some more time and rule over their respective kingdoms. To Jambavan, Raman portends a reincarnation of Himself as krishnan in the Dwapara Yuga, when He would have to fight with him for a certain cause and so orders him to wait on earth until such time. Raman bestows on, Hanuman a happy and independent life on earth as long as His name is alive, till the delusion of the Universe when he shall amalgamate with His own self.

The clarion call is sounded for all the people to go with Him. A joyous congregation in mass of jubilation, rents the air. The masses follow Raman in supreme ecstasy which is born in a moment of Spiritual connection with Raman when they experience an inner distancing from mundane pleasures and attachments, becoming oblivious to their earthly treasures, wealth and prosperity and transcending the limitations of worldly existence. The voluminous exodus of people from Ayodhya renders the city completely desolate akin to a desert with not a speck of vegetation or organic life visible anywhere. The entire multitudes of people and creatures reach the banks of the river Sarayu in a state of preparedness to ascend to Heaven. Meanwhile the whole scenario transforms itself into one of celestial glory, bliss and fervour when Brahman, Sivan and other gods and sages, seers and saints manifest themselves in the sky which is over spreadingly packed with their air chariots of different designs, shapes and sizes. The lingering luxuriance of fragrance from gay flowers and blossoms that are being showered on Raman hovers over in the sky. Soulful hymns and heavenly songs in various mellifluous tunes are being sung and melodious music played by the gandharvas, fairies and deities.

Brahman in great reverence with folded hands glorifies Raman as the Supreme God Vishnu, the Master of the Universe Omniscient, Omnipresent, Omnipotent and Eternal. He eulogizes and in the same breath acknowledges with gratitude Raman's victorious tour de force on earth, His propitiating the wishes of all His aspirants and devotees and achieving His own designs.

Brahman offers himself as a humble servant to Raman and pledges his constant worship to Raman's celebrated Lotus Feet. He ennobles Raman's benevolence to His devotees whom He guards and guides with detailed care. He supplicates Lord Raman to transform Himself into His inceptive Vishnu form and ascend His heavenly abode so that His irresistible presence may make the family of Gods and all the celestials all prosperous, happy and blissful. Inevitably, and instantaneously Lakshman mutates into Seshanag, Bharathan and Sathrughnan morph into Vishnu's conch shell and mace respectively; evidently Sita manifests as Goddess Lakshmi.

The blessed and glorious scene is most enchanting and divine as Brahman, the creator, Indhran, the Chief of Gods and all other deities worship, pray and glorify Lord Vishnu and the Gandharvas,Kinnaras, fairies and all the celestials gather round Lord Vishnu and dance and sing His praises in an elevated trance.

Raman ordains the creator Brahman to constitue a separate abode in paradise for the habitation of all His devotees, the God-drunk souls, animals and insects who are pursing Him to heaven. Brahman substantiates his privilege as creator and constitutes the heavenly abode named 'Santanik' where henceforth, all pious devotees of Raman shall also inevitably claim a rightful place in this abode after their death similar to them who are now following Him to heaven. With the exception of Sugrivan who amalgamates with the sun, all the others mount up to Santanik which resembles Raman's abode called Vishnu Lokha or 'Vaigundham' after Raman directly leaves the earth for the eternal abode.

Lord Shivan has acquainted Devi Parvathi with the eternal truths and mysteries about the infinite Lord Raman the Manifest Being commanding eternal devotion, worship and pure love. Thus God shivan has illustrated the latter period of life in the history of Raman in the 'Uthara Kandham' which is held in the highest spiritual and religious regard, and its verse is drenched with the potency to absolve all gross deeds instantly.

It is staunchly promised that those who embark on a recital of or even listen to Raman's saga being read shall be bestowed with prosperity, illustrious posterity during their life time on earth itself, shall be purged of all their stubborn vices and cardinal sins, be sanctified, and they shall claim their rightful place in Elyisium after death.